International Dictionary of Adult and Continuing Education

PETER JARVIS
IN ASSOCIATION WITH A L WILSON

KOGAN PAGE

<u>YOURS TO HAVE AND TO HOLD</u>
BUT NOT TO COPY

First published 1990 by Routledge
This edition published 1999 by Kogan Page

Kogan Page Limited
120 Pentonville Road
London
N1 9JN
UK

Stylus Publishing Inc.
22883 Quicksilver Drive
Sterling
VA 20166-2012
USA

© Peter Jarvis, 1990, 1999

British Library Cataloguing in Publication Data

A CIP record for this book is available from the British Library.

ISBN 0 7494 2671 3

Typeset by Kogan Page Limited
Printed and bound in Great Britain by Biddles Ltd, Guildford and King's Lynn

Preface

Preface to the First Edition

Adult and continuing education is changing at a tremendously rapid rate in this contemporary, urban world. Indeed, by the time this dictionary is published some of the information will already be obsolescent. This is a feature of today's society. It might be wondered, therefore, if this is an opportune time to prepare such a dictionary. Obviously, the cliché that there is never an opportune time is as valid here as it ever is. That some of the information might be less valid because of change only reflects the dynamic nature of society and the manner in which adult and continuing education is adapting to respond to these changes.

However, adult and continuing education is still a complex field to enter and it is hoped that this dictionary will at least act as a guidebook to those who wish to find their way through. Naturally, it reflects one person's understanding of the field and consequently it contains its own limitations. If any colleague is prepared to send me corrections and changes, these will be incorporated in any new edition.

This selection of information must necessarily be my own and, consequently, it reflects on my own understanding of the field. It will be seem, for instance, that there are many references here that could have come from initial education. This is because I understand the field of education to be a single field with many common elements across the different forms, rather than a number of separate fields. It will also be noted that here are terms from a variety of the social science disciplines because I understand education to be a field of study which in its practical form utilizes their knowledge bases.

As the field is international, I have tried to record some information about the wider world of adult and continuing education. This is useful because it enables us to compare what is happening in our own society with that occurring elsewhere. We can learn from this and it may enrich both our own understanding and practice of education. However, spelling presented problems. I have therefore tried to give as much information as I can and consequently I have included the expressions, titles and so on in their first language, wherever this has been possible.

Words that appear in italics can be cross-referenced in the dictionary and so I have not repeated information from different references, unless it seemed appropriate to do so.

I owe a great debt to all scholars in the field whose work I have read and who have influenced my understanding of the field. I have not included a bibliography of works consulted for this dictionary because it could not be complete. I can but express my appreciation for all that I have learned from them, often my friends and colleagues, who have helped me so much. One colleague who has known about this project from its inception, has encouraged me throughout and has done me the great honour of reading some of it, is Alan Chadwick. I have been most grateful to him for his support. For the constant support of my wife, Maureen, and my children, Frazer and Kierra, who are often only aware of my presence at home because they are aware that I am in my study, I can only once again express my love and gratitude.

During the preparation of this volume for publication Emma Waghorn has been diligent in her proof-reading and copy-editing, far beyond the call of duty; but because of her careful work and patience many errors have been avoided. I am most grateful to her for all that she has done throughout this period.

When I started this undertaking, I understood something of its magnitude. On completion of this phase of it, I realize that I underestimated it. The field is very wide and ever-changing. I can only hope that students of adult and continuing education who consult this book will find it useful. While many people have helped me and provided me with information, the mistakes are my own.

Peter Jarvis

Preface

Preface to the Second Edition

In the Preface to the First Edition of this Dictionary, I acknowledged that preparing it was a work of much greater magnitude than I had estimated at the outset. I also realized that since the field was changing so rapidly I might have to produce a further edition. The field has actually changed much more rapidly than I anticipated and many new concepts and terms have gained prevalence.

Because of the changing state of the field, I appreciated that the Dictionary would be out of date before it was published – a view that one of the reviewers also made. Such criticism might certainly be made for this Second Edition also, since the fields of adult, continuing, higher and lifelong education appear to be changing and merging even more rapidly now and the term lifelong learning is certainly becoming more prevalent. Perhaps there is never an opportune time to produce a volume such as this – but perhaps it is also a time when it is most useful to have access to such a reference book.

In preparing this Second Edition, I was conscious of the advice that I was given after the initial publication, both verbally and in the quite generous published reviews. The First Edition was very long – over 5,000 references. This edition has been shortened by about a third, so that I hope that it will be much more accessible. Even so, there are no clearly defined parameters to the fields of education of adults and so the choice of what has been included still broadly reflects my own personal understanding of the trends that are occurring.

Another of the reviewers commented on the fact the original work was only my perspective and that I would have been wiser to have worked with others – advice that I have taken. Dr Arthur Wilson, from North Carolina State University, has been a friend and rigorous critic of my work. He has read all my original definitions, corrected many and made many other suggestions about the Dictionary. His colleagueship and his scholarship have been greatly appreciated and the book is richer for his many interventions, although the errors remain my own.

One of the unforeseen consequences of the First Edition has been the effect that it has had on a number of European projects in which adult education associations in different, often new European countries have prepared their own dictionaries of adult education. Their efforts have been greatly encouraged by the work of Hans Hovenburg who has initiated a multi-lingual project in adult education in and, now I believe beyond, Europe. He did me the honour of using a selection of terms from the First Edition to help form the basis of his own work. When he knew that I was producing a second edition, he generously provided me with a list of all the terms that he had used which had assisted him in his project and which he thought should not be omitted from this edition.

I remain grateful to those family, friends and colleagues who have encouraged me to produce this Second Edition and I can only hope that it will also prove useful guide to this complex field for those who use it.

Peter Jarvis
Guildford
October 1998

Aa

ability Persons are said to have this if they can carry out mental, emotional, or physical tasks with or without instruction. Abilities are learned rather than being innate, although human beings may be born with genetic tendencies to act in certain ways.

Abitur The high school diploma in Germany, necessary in order to enter university. Adults can also sit the Abitur later in life, if they did not gain it whilst at school, by enrolling in an Abendgymnasium.

Aboriginal education In Australia educational programmes have been established for the education of the indigenous peoples.

Aboriginal studies In Australia there is both research and teaching about the culture and history of the indigenous peoples.

abstract 1. A noun, being a synopsis: of a book, of a chapter of a book, or of an academic paper. 2. A concept, or idea, which makes no reference to empirical objects.

abstraction A generalization, an idea, or a concept. Abstract ideas form the basis of theory; they are concepts and generalizations that relate to, or provide explanation of, specific and concrete phenomena but are not the same as them.

academic 1. Relating to a place of learning. 2. One who spends time studying. 3. A member of the teaching or research staff of an educational institution, ie the academic staff as opposed to the support staff. 4. Often contrasted to the practical in the sense of being theoretical.

academic dress The regalia that may be worn by graduates of academic programmes.

academic education Often used to describe an education in the classics and liberal studies in both school and post-compulsory education.

academic failure A person who is generally regarded as having failed in formal education. A great deal of time and effort in education for adults is directed towards supporting those who, having been regarded as failures, seek to return to the educational or training system later in life.

academic freedom 1. Freedom of academic institutions to decide upon the courses that they will teach, the processes that they will employ to teach them, and the areas that they will research without coercion from outside bodies. 2. The individual freedom of the academic to teach and of students to study without coercion or restriction by others. 3. The freedom of the academic to express views and opinions without fear of sanction or reprisal, by virtue of being a tenured member of a university. This latter form of freedom appears to be being eroded as universities are becoming incorporated in a more general higher education system, and educational institutions are assuming a more corporate management function. 4. Sometimes referred to as the autonomy of the professoriat in the United States.

academic standards The criteria determined by an academic body to set the levels of teaching by the academic staff or the levels of achievement by the students following courses run by that institution.

academic year Sometimes referred to as the school year. The period of the school/ university year, usually September through to the beginning of July, but varying from country to country, and even in some cases among institutions in the same country. For example, the Open University academic year in the United Kingdom begins in January rather than in September, and ends in October/November rather than June/July. However, there is a movement in the public schools in United States to year-round schooling.

academy 1. The body of academic scholars. 2. A place where academic pursuits are practised, eg a school, college, or learned society.

accelerated learning A technique designed to enhance the pace by which a person learns.

acceptance 1. A letter of acceptance is usually a letter accepting an offer, usually of a programme of study or a place on a course. 2. An uncensuring attitude towards a person's behaviour and/or attitudes and recognition of that person's worth as a human being, without either condemning or condoning those actions or attitudes.

access 1. The opportunity, through further study, to acquire entrance qualifications, usually for higher education, eg second chance education. 2. The opportunity to acquire qualifications that are regarded as equivalencies to a recognized qualification. 3. The opportunity to study on a particular course which provides an entrance route into an institution of higher education. See *access course*. 4. Open access refers to the fact that some institutions accept students for courses without any

formal educational qualifications as prerequisites. 5. The widening of access is usually taken to indicate a form of democratization of education.

access course Course of study that is specially organized to prepare unqualified adults for higher education, without pursuing the traditional routes. Access courses are often mounted by lower level educational institutions, in liaison with specific universities or higher education institutions. They were originally established in the United Kingdom to prepare unqualified adults for training for the professions, for teaching and social work. They have subsequently developed much more widely.

accommodation 1. The physical premises in which teaching and learning are conducted. 2. The tendency to alter cognition to fit structures and objects that are encountered during the process of living. 3. A learning style, associated with specific learning style inventories, eg Kolb's.

accommodator One who learns by responding to problems in a trial-and-error manner, and learning through dialogue with other people, in such a manner as to indicate that their own views are not fixed and unchangeable.

accreditation 1. The recognition and acceptance of the academic standards of an educational establishment by an outside agency, association or body such as an examination board, a professional and qualifying body, or a more senior educational establishment. 2. The recognition accorded to an educational institution in the United States, through inclusion on a list of accredited or approved institutions issued by some agency or organization (professional, regional, or state). The established standards or requirements that must be complied with in order to secure approval. Membership is voluntary and extra-legal. 3. The system of granting credit, ie placing some recognized standard on a course, so that the ensuing certificate, issued on successful completion, can be used towards a further qualification at a later date in the same or a different educational institution.

Accreditation of Prior Experiential Learning (APEL)   Schemes established by educational institutions to give credit for learning from the experiences of daily living. See *Assessment of Prior Experiential Learning*.

Accreditation of Prior Learning (APL) Schemes established by educational institutions in order to grant formal credit for prior learning, usually other courses in other institutions. This credit usually acts either as an alternative method of satisfying entry requirements, or as a method of being granted remission of part of the course requirements. See *Assessment of Prior Learning*.

accredited correspondence education In some countries, eg the Netherlands, correspondence institutions have to meet certain conditions specified by the Ministry in order to gain accreditation.

acculturation   A socialization process whereby a person or persons learns the culture or subculture of a group or nation.

achievement   Level of performance.

achievement need   The psychological state in which people feel constrained to be successful, to satisfy their drive for success.

achievement orientation   1. Attitude orientation towards individuals depending on what they have achieved in terms of career. 2. An attitude which regards educational qualifications as a mark of success. 3. An approach to studying which is competitive, so that study methods are organized in order to gain success.

achievement test   An examination that seeks to test the extent to which a learner has acquired knowledge or skill, usually as a result of specific teaching. Usually

standardized and scored according to predetermined statistical norms.

action   A state or process of doing. There are many theories of action.

action-centred leadership   Leadership courses developed in the United Kingdom that involve small group work.

action learning   Learning through doing, either through simulation or through the actual situation. It is a learning process involving the learner's reflection upon, or memorizing of, the action experience and/or its results. Learning as an intended and important part of an (real or simulated) action. A form of *experiential learning*.

action research   1. A form of research in which the researcher is a participant in the phenomenon under scrutiny, the actual process of the action is itself the subject of the research, and the research measures the outcomes of the action. 2. A form of research designed to assess the effects of an intervention on a social process. See *collaborative research, participatory research*.

action science   Inquiry into the way in which human beings design and implement action in relation to one another.

active learning   Methods by which learners actively participate in the learning process, eg discussion group, problem-solving, experimentation, etc.

activism   Action in pursuit of a chosen cause, occurring in community action and in some other forms of community education. Some community educators consider that educators should take a stance in social situations about which they teach, but this is not a position that is universally accepted by adult educators.

activity   1. An operation. 2. State or process of doing.

activity method   Teaching and learning methods that are participatory, so that they involve learning by doing. See *action learning*.

activity-oriented learner   One who enrols in educational courses for reasons related to the activity rather than the content of the learning. One of Cyril Houle's three types of learner: see also *goal-oriented learning, learning-oriented learner*.

activity-orientated learning   A form of learning which involves participating in physical activities.

adaptive further training   The term used in Germany to refer to that form of continuing education which prepares members of the workforce to handle new techniques, processes, and organizational forms. It is not regarded as preparation for career advancement, but training so that the present job can be undertaken more efficiently.

adjunct professor   A full-time, or part-time, teacher in a US college or university, whose position is not part of the establishment of posts of the institution, so that the post is not tenure tracked. Sometimes called *visiting professor*.

admissions tutor   The academic member of staff in higher education who is responsible for processing applications and interviewing applicants for specific courses in an academic department.

adolescent   A young adult, someone between the ages of biological and social maturity. Sometimes now referred to as a *young adult*. Similar to the US term *pre-adult*.

adult   1. One who has achieved biological maturity. 2. One who has achieved the legal chronological age, which a society has legislated as adulthood. 3. The age at which a person feels himself or herself to be an adult; to behave in a mature manner. 4. To be adult is to be treated in a mature manner by

their social group. The variety of meanings given to this term is one reason for adult education being a difficult concept to define.

adult armchair education   Informal adult education. Associated with Leon Howard Sullivan in America, who discovered that many adults who were on feeder programmes to the Opportunities Industrialization Centres learned better in informal surroundings and at times convenient to themselves. He started an adult education programme, which became known as the adult armchair programme.

adult basic education (ABE)   Education of adults in the areas of primary knowledge, such as literacy and numeracy, of social and life skills, of understanding of community life, necessary to responsible participation in society. See also *adult elementary education*.

Adult Classroom Environmental Scale   An approach to the study of *classroom ecology*.

adult community education   1. An educational activity that takes place beyond the walls of the educational institution. 2. An adult education activity, in which the community constitutes the subject of study.

adult continuing education   The fusion of two concepts, adult education and continuing education, as in the National Institute of Adult Continuing Education, is an attempt to end the historic division between adult liberal education and vocational education and to illustrate that both are about the education of adults. It should be noted that the two terms are frequently used separately but in the same phrase, ie adult and continuing, eg in the 1989 Handbook of the American Association.

adult counselling   Counselling is a generic term which is used to cover a number of processes, such as interviewing, advising, guiding, and even providing therapy in areas of personal problems. There are different techniques employed by counsellors, such as non-directive counselling.

adult development   1. Sequence of continuous change and growth through the various stages of adulthood. 2. The multidisciplinary study of the physical, psychological, sociological and intellectual changes in people during adulthood.

adult education   1. The social institution offering learning opportunities to adults. 2. Liberal education for adults. 3. Any organized and sustained communication designed to bring about learning in adults, excluding education following directly after initial primary and secondary education, and excluding vocational education. 4. The entire body of organized educational processes, whatever the content, level, or method, whether formal or otherwise, whether they prolong or replace initial education in schools or colleges, and universities as well as in apprenticeship, whereby persons regarded as adults by the society to which they belong develop their abilities, enrich their knowledge, improve their technical or professional qualifications, or turn them in a new direction and bring about changes in their attitudes or behaviour in the twofold perspective of full personal development and participation in balanced, independent, social, economic, and cultural development (UNESCO). 5. The term carries with it overtones of a democratic social movement committed to expand the learning opportunities for adults, as opposed to the education of adults which does not have this history. 6. The educational process conducted in a mature (adult) manner. See also *education of adults*.

Adult Education and Development
The half-yearly journal of the *Institute for International Co-operation of the German Adult Education Association*. The journal started in 1973 and it is published in English.

Adult Education Association of the United States of America   Formed in 1951 and remained independent until it became a constituent member of the *American Association for Adult and Continuing Education* in 1982.

Adult Education Centre   Place where *adult education* courses are provided.

Adult Education Institute   In the United Kingdom, the provision of adult education courses in a specific region might be undertaken by an Institute. See *Educational Centres Association*.

Adult Education Quarterly (AEQ)
The academic journal of the American Association for Adult Continuing Education.

Adult Education Research Conference (AERC)   Established in 1960, an annual research conference of adult educators, mostly North American although it does have an international participation most years.

adult educator   1. One who is involved in the teaching of adults. 2. One who is involved in the organization of the adult education service.

adult elementary education   *Adult basic education.*

adult guidance   Advice given to adults in respect of their choice of adult education. A form of counselling.

adult learner   A participant in a programme of education for adults, or someone pursuing a self-directed learning programme.

Adult Learners' Week   A week devoted to publicizing *adult education*. Was adopted in the 1997 UNESCO Conference as a goal for all countries that are members of UNESCO.

Adult Learning   The practitioner magazine of the American Association of Adult and Continuing Education.

Adult Learning Information Centre Europe (ALICE)   A European database about *non-formal education* in Europe.

adult literacy   1. Adult education to teach adults to read and write. 2. Adult basic education.

Adult Literacy and Basic Skills Unit (ALBSU)   Established in 1980 in the United Kingdom from the *Adult Literacy Unit*, and charged with developing within the general education service a basic education service designed to improve the proficiency of those adults whose second language is English, in *literacy, numeracy* and basic skills. Renamed *Adult Skills Agency*.

Adult Literacy Day   The day each year, 8 September, which UNESCO devotes to the recognition of the need for *adult literacy*.

Adult Literacy Unit (ALU)   Established in 1978 under the auspices of the *National Institute of Adult Education* with a remit for three years to provide adult literacy tuition, excluding English as a second language. See *Adult Literacy and Basic Skills Unit*.

adult pedagogy   An activity that involves the purposeful creation of learning activities for adults. See *pedagogy, social pedagogy, andragogy*.

Adult Performance Level (APL)   Used in the United States in the 1970s in respect to the level of achievement by adults in tests for *life skills* and *functional literacy*.

adult nutrition education   A community education programme offered to poor people in developing countries to teach them about diet.

adult religious education   1. Education about religion for adults. 2. The form of education employed by the churches to teach their members more about their own belief system. Some commentators separate adult religious education from adult Christian education.

adult returner   An adult who returns to formal study later in life. Often it is these potential students who require courses in *study skills* in order to make the most of their return to a learning environment.

adult school   A separately organized school for adults and young people beyond the age of compulsory schooling. The first adult school was established in Britain in 1798, in Nottingham, with the aim of teaching men and women to read the Bible. Gradually the schools offered a wider syllabus.

Adult Skills Agency   See *Adult Literacy and Basic Skills Unit*.

adult training centre   Centre where adults can learn new skills and techniques. Often used for education of the unemployed, but also used for those who have other social disadvantages.

adult vocational education   Education that is designed to provide either training or retraining for adults in order to assist them in gaining employment or advancement in their career.

Adults Learning   The practitioner magazine of the National Institute of Adult Continuing Education in the United Kingdom.

advanced course   1. Courses that follow an introductory or foundation course. 2. Those UK further education courses that are so designated as having advanced status.

advanced diploma   A postgraduate award, usually part of a Masters degree programme.

advanced further education   Higher education, not normally available to those under 18 years of age. It covers certificate, diploma, and degree-level studies.

advanced graduate standing   A recognition that a student has reached a stage in the process of reading for a higher degree in the American university system, usually commencing the dissertation.

Advanced International Certificate of Education (AICE) Introduced in 1986 by the University of Cambridge Local Examinations Syndicate, this is a broad-based certificate for school leavers in which at least five, and maybe more, subjects are studied in which there must be one subject from each of the following: mathematics and science, languages, and the arts and humanities.

advanced organizer A short introduction to prepare readers or listeners for the thesis or argument that is to follow, so that they can adjust themselves mentally in order to comprehend more clearly what follows.

advanced placement test A test designed to appraise whether a student can bypass an initial course in a college and commence at a more advanced level.

advanced standing The status of students who have received credits as part of the course requirements with respect to their prior learning.

advisement 1. An American term for supervision of postgraduate students.
2. A US term for guidance and counselling of undergraduate students, especially in relation to course choice.

advisor 1. In the United Kingdom, the term has been used for a Local Education Authority person who is employed to advise teachers, eg an adult education advisor. The advisor acts as an inspector. 2. In the United States, the term is used to refer to one who advises students about the selection of courses and about the directions of their research.

advisory centre A centre in which educational guidance can be offered to adults.

Advisory Council of Adult and Continuing Education (ACACE)

Established in 1977 in the UK to advise the Secretary of State about adult and continuing education. It functioned until 1983. The Russell Committee actually proposed a Development Council.

advocacy 1. The act of speaking out on behalf of another. Often adult educators need to perform this role or to prepare others to perform it. 2. Advocacy sometimes occurs in human resource development, especially when alternative strategies are being examined.

advocate One who speaks out on behalf of others.

AEDNET An experimental electronic network for adult educators, initiated by the Department of Adult Education at the University of Syracuse.

aesthetics Study of the nature of art forms in society from a variety of perspectives. A sub-discipline of philosophy, and an occasional subject on programmes in adult education.

aetiology Examination of the causes and derivations of psychological and social states.

affective domain The aspect of life that relates to the emotions or affections. Adult educators have concentrated upon this domain more systematically than have those working in initial education.

affective education The education of the emotions, sometimes referred to as *experiential education*, although this is a restrictive use of the concept of experience.

affective learning Aspects of learning that have been gained through emotional experiences rather than intellectualism, whether in a formal educational setting or otherwise.

affirmative action A concern of adult education, it is the process whereby positive action is taken in respect of minority groups and women. In the United States this is a specific legal position to facilitate the admissions opportunities to education, and employment, for historically socially excluded minorities, including women.

after care   Social programme introduced to help those recently released from a total institution (prison, hospital) to be rehabilitated into the community, frequently includes an educative component.

age   1. The period of time a person or animal has lived. 2. An era, a period of time characterized by specific traits.

ageing   The lifelong process of growing old, its study constitutes an important part of gerontology and education of older adults.

agency   1. An organization, usually working in the community. Hence a community education organization might be referred to as agency. 2. In some studies it refers to a person or organization initiating action, as opposed to the social structures that might inhabit it. See also *agent*.

agenda   1. Something to be done. 2. A list of topics to be discussed during a meeting.

agent   1. One who acts. It could refer to one who takes the initiative in social or community activities. 2. In sociological literature it need not be an individual but an organization which takes the initiative. 3. An individual who performs in a consciously meaningful manner.

aggression   A form of behaviour apparently intended to cause harm to self or others, although aggressive behaviour may stop short of actually causing harm.

agogy   The study of teaching and learning. Used in Europe in similar manner to pedagogics.

agology   Theories of community education and development. Term used in Belgium.

agricultural college   An educational institution that provides studies in agriculture. See also *land grant colleges* in the United States.

agricultural development   The improvement of agricultural techniques. This is the main aim of the *Co-operative Extension Service* in the United States.

agricultural extension   Adult education in rural communities, especially for farmers. See *Co-operative Extension Service* with reference to the United States. In the Federal Republic of Germany there is an agricultural extension service – a continuing education for farmers. It is based in offices throughout the country to which farmers are invited to participate in monthly seminars led by staff members of the Service. In Germany this service is free by law and all costs of the service are provided by the State.

agricultural school   A school for the training of agricultural workers. See *home economics school* in Denmark and *agricultural college* in the United Kingdom as nearest equivalents.

aim   1. The broad philosophical goal of a curriculum, or of a specific course. 2. General statement of intention by teachers, or educational organizations. See *objectives*.

alfalit   Term sometimes used to refer to the type of literacy that studies words in isolation from their social context.

alienation   A concept of self-estrangement that was made popular by the writing of Karl Marx, although it was not used first by him. It is a learned state of powerlessness, isolation, and estrangement.

alimiyah   Doctoral degree in higher Islamic culture.

alma mater   An individual's old school, college, or university.

alphabetization   Adult literacy education. See *adult literacy*.

alternative adult education   The form of adult education designed to help the learners question the most fundamental values and purposes of any system and to enable them to recognize the manner by which the social system operates. See also *radical adult education*.

alternative attendance patterns   Patterns of time-tabling at different times each day, week, etc to ensure that students who are prevented from attending some sessions of a course can attend others.

altruism   The practice of putting the needs of others before one's own. This is an important principle in humanistic adult education.

alumnus (plural – alumni, alumnae)   Former student of a school, college, or university. More frequently used in the United States.

American Association for Adult and Continuing Education (AAACE)   Formed in 1982 at the San Antonio Conference as a result of a merger between the Adult Education Association of the United States of America and the National Association for Public Continuing and Adult Education. This has become the national association for adult education in the United States. It is also active in lobbying on behalf of adult education in America.

American Association for Adult Education   Founded in 1926 as a result of a Carnegie Corporation initiative.

Americanization education   Education of immigrants into the American way of life. In 1917 Congress demanded literacy as a requirement of naturalization.

Americanization became almost synonymous with adult education for a period, with the result that evening schools gained more state support.

analysis of variance   Statistical testing to determine whether the variance between the mean of different sets of data is greater than that which could be expected by chance.

analytic marking   A system of marking assignments whereby the assessor checks every aspect of the work, rather than providing an overall impressionistic assessment. Used as a tutoring method in *distance education*. See *global marking*.

andragogee   An adult learner.

andragogical cycle   A programme-planning exercise. A six-stage cycle which includes: the analysis of needs and motives, planning the educational process, programming the educational content, preparing and organizing the process, implementing and evaluation of the process, and the product of the exercise.

andragogics   The study of andragogy.

andragogue   An adult educator who employs andragogic methods in the teaching and learning transaction.

andragogy   1. First employed by a German school teacher, Alexander Knapp, in 1833 and derived from the Greek word for man. Ever since there has been a debate as to whether adults learn differently from children, and whether it differs from pedagogy. 2. In the United States this term has been popularized by the work of M Knowles, who defined it as the art and science of helping adults learn, and who originally maintained that it was a process different from pedagogy. His definition has been disputed by many scholars, but remains quite potent in adult education literature. Eduard Lindeman was the first American theorist to use the term, in 1927. 3. In Holland, it means the overall study of social work, community organization, and adult education. This usage is similar to that in other parts of Europe, especially in Eastern Europe. 4. The field of study of adult education, and regarded as an academic discipline in parts of continental Europe. See, for instance, *penal andragogy*.

andragology The Dutch employ the term for the study or science of andragogy. The term was first used in the Netherlands when Ten Have published an article in the periodical *Volksopvoeding* in 1960. In the same article he also employed the term *social agogy*.

animateur (animator) 1. Community education worker. 2. French term for an individual who is employed to encourage sport and physical recreation in a locality or community. 3. Member of a small teaching or discussion group, whose role is to stimulate discussion and enquiry. Not necessarily a subject expert and may be one of the students. See also *facilitator*.

animation Short for 'animation socio-culturelle'. The stimulation of people to awareness of their own needs as a group, so that they define the nature of the needs, determine the means to satisfy these needs and act to do so. Thus it is neither organization nor teaching, but initiation, catalysis and counselling. This definition constitutes rather a goal to be arrived at than a description of current practice. The term is currently used of functions that have a large element of direction, organization and instruction. It is a form of community education in France.

annotated bibliography A bibliography that contains notes on each item within it.

anomia, anomie 1. A basic concept in sociology denoting a society without generally accepted moral rules, desocialization caused by eg rapid and deep changes in the socio-economic structure.

2. The condition of normlessness, in which one feels out of touch with the surrounding norms and values.

Antigonish Movement A community movement in Nova Scotia, Canada. It was a blending of Christian ethics, social justice and adult education. The aim was to create a self-help co-operative movement for the fishing people in the area. See *Tompkins*.

anti-racism training A form of affective education which seeks to make people aware of racist attitudes and prejudices. See *racism awareness training*.

anxiety 1. Complex emotional experience, often unconscious in origin, with fear or dread as its most notable characteristic. 2. A general state of stress or unease. 3. In learning theory, the term refers to a conditioned drive that functions to motivate avoidance of an unpleasant goal, so that avoidance response is reinforced by the reduction in anxiety.

AONTAS The national adult education body for Ireland.

a posteriori A proposition that can only be known to be true or false by reference to a known actuality.

applied research Research activities designed to investigate specific problems for which immediately applicable findings are required.

appraisal An evaluation of a person's performance, eg on an annual basis and conducted by either a peer or a superior within an employing organization.

appreciation class An adult class organized to help adults learn to appreciate the arts, ie to learn about their qualities.

apprentice A young person serving a period of time, usually attached to a master, in order to learn a trade or occupation.

apprentice library Collections of books that could be borrowed by apprentices, attached to some of the early mechanics schools in the United States.

apprenticeship The period in which a young person is attached to a master, or an organized programme of training, in order to learn a trade or a profession. Hence, the derogatory phrase 'sitting by Nellie', because it was basically, and perhaps wrongly, regarded as just a matter of learning to copy the expert. The term has enjoyed a return to popularity in more recent years, since the increasing emphasis on the place of *practical knowledge* in vocational education.

a priori Knowledge arrived at without reference to experience. The basic premise, or premises, from which deduction begins.

aptitude 1. Skill, or ability, that is conducive to a person's ability to learn and attain a level of attainment in a given field. 2. In mastery learning, the time required to learn a specific task to a given level under ideal conditions. 3. Potential ability.

aptitude test An examination designed to measure a person's potential to learn to perform certain forms of activity.

archives The historical records of an institution.

area co-ordinator An adult educator who co-ordinates the provision an adult education throughout a geographical area, often a section of an area adult education institution.

area college A college of further education in the United Kingdom that offers some advanced work. Some now call themselves colleges of further and higher education.

area principal The principal of an adult education institute that is situated on a number of different sites within a given geographical area in the United Kingdom.

area vocational education school A department of a community college, university or high school in the United States which provides occupational preparation in at least five different occupations, and which acts under the supervision of the State Board.

artificial intelligence The capacity of a computer, or some other machine, to perform functions that are normally associated with human intelligence.

artificial language Specially created language, such as Esperanto.

artist 1. One who is engaged in creative and performing arts. 2. A painter. 3. One who draws.

arts The arts usually refers to drama, film, literature, music, painting, poetry and sculpture – what some sociologists would call high culture. However, there is no general agreement on their constitution, although there is more agreement on the fact that the arts are a social construct.

assertiveness training 1. A technique to help people understand the effects of their socialization upon them and so free them from it so that they are empowered in order to enhance personal relationships and renegotiate social situations. 2. Training to promote self-confidence and well-being. Used in some forms of professional education and in women's groups.

assessment The process of placing a value upon, deciding the degree of excellence of, adjudging standard(s) of, or deciding the correctness of an artefact, piece of academic work, performance, or procedure. The process is largely subjective although the degree of subjectivity depends upon the condition of knowledge underlying the work, procedure, or performance, etc. For instance, the level of correctness of simple mathematical knowledge may be assessed much more objectively than the social skills expertise of a professional practitioner. There have been many attempts to make assessment more objective, eg the use of multiple choice questions and the preparation of assessment criteria, but the extent to which the subjectivity has been removed is debatable.

Assessment of Prior Experiential Learning (APEL)   The measurement of prior learning from life's experiences for which no previous credit had been awarded. See *Accreditation of Prior Experiential Learning*.

Assessment of Prior Learning (APL) The measurement of learning that has been acquired outside of formal educational course for which credit has been sought. See *Accreditation of Prior Learning*.

assessment pack   Often prepared to accompany study packs by distance learning institutions. They consist of a series of computer marked assignments, self-assessment questions, etc.

assignment   A project or task set a student – often it is marked or graded.

assignment sheet   A handout to students containing the assignment(s) specified for the course. They can be used in all types of teaching situations.

assimilation   The tendency to absorb, distort or alter the meaning ascribed to encounters in order to make them fit existing cognitive structures.

assimilator   *A learning style*, in which people prefer to learn from the abstract rather than from people.

assistant professor   The first rank of a university teaching career in the United States, usually untenured.

associate degree   An award for the successful completion of studies, usually requiring two years and is regarded as half of the four year bachelor's degree course in the United States, typically granted by a community college.

associate professor   The second level of a university teaching career, usually tenured.

Association Internationale de l'Université de Troisième Âge (AIUTA)   The international body of the Universities of the Third Age.

Association of Educational Gerontology (AEG)   UK association concerned with education and the elderly.

Association to Promote the Higher Education of Working Men   The original title of the *Workers' Educational Association*.

attention   The ability to concentrate upon one phenomenon and exclude other possible phenomena from the immediate perception.

attention span   The length of time a person can continue to concentrate without interruption.

attitude   1. A predisposition to perceive, feel and behave towards specific objects or certain people in a particular manner. Attitudes are learned from experience, rather than innate characteristics, which suggests that they can be modified. Traits, which are more persistent and general personality characteristics, are thought to be more the product of innate constitution. 2. An orientation towards some phenomenon, having cognitive, affective, evaluative, and conative components. 3. A combination of a perception and a judgement, which may result in an emotive orientation towards a phenomenon. 4. Attitudes often occur as the third dimension of syllabi in professional education curricula, along with knowledge and skills.

attitude scale   Ranking scale designed to measure traits of personality, orientations towards particular phenomena. See *Likert scale*.

attitude survey   The use of survey techniques using attitude scales to measure attitudes. Useful in needs assessment, human resource development.

attitude test   An examination designed to test the attitudes held by an individual, or a group, towards some particular phenomenon.

attribute   The characteristic, or traits, of a person or other subject.

attrition rate   The proportion of students from a cohort who fail to complete their course of study. Drop-out rate.

audience reaction team   A group of persons who are primed to interrupt a speaker in order to assist in clarifying points that might appear obscure.

audio-cassette   A prepared cassette containing learning material which might be included in a study pack prepared for either distance learning or self-directed study.

audio-conferencing   A telephone networking system that enables a group of learners to interact simultaneously with the teacher and with each other. Used in some forms of distance education.

audio-recording   1. The recording of spoken words or other sounds. 2. A research technique that uses a tape recorder to record answers to questions or any other form of audio-data. 3. A teaching technique that employs audio-recordings to stimulate discussion, or to transmit information, etc.

audio-tape   Audio material recorded on a open-reel tape.

audio-typing   The ability to type directly from the spoken word, or from a prepared audio cassette.

audio-visual aid (AVA)   A device to assist in the teaching and learning process using drawings, diagrams, models, or other technical machines.

audio-visual instruction   A form of teaching which employs a variety of media in the presentation, ie the use of audio-visual aids.

aural learner   One who learns best through listening.

author/authoress (female form sometimes used)   One who composes a book, article, paper, or other piece of written work.

authoritarian personality   The authoritarian personality both receives and obeys legitimate authority, but also acts in an authoritarian manner when placed in a position of authority. Associated with the work of T Adorno.

authoritarianism   An ideology or a practice, which emphasizes the place of authority in interaction. The exercise of authority, eg 'teacher knows best'. See *paternalism*.

authority   A form of legitimized power. 1. Power is legitimized by virtue of the position the individual holds, eg teachers' power is legitimized in as much as they are employees of an educational institution; the teacher is in authority. 2. Teachers' power may also be legitimized by their students; they are an authority. 3. Academics' and researchers' power is also legitimized by their peers; they are an authority.

authority figure   A person who is perceived by others to be in, or to have, authority as a result of a dominant presence.

autobiographical method A life history method of research, whereby the researcher seeks to understand the phenomenon under investigation, like learning, through the study of autobiography.

autocratic Action which is authoritarian and allows little opportunity for discussion.

autodidact A person who is self-taught.

autodidaxy Self-teaching.

autonomous learner 1. See *self-directed learner*. Although these terms are not quite the same conceptually, since the word autonomy has distinct connotations, they tend to be used synonymously. 2. One who has the capability to learn independently and to choose the mode of learning best suited for the learning task.

autonomy The philosophical idea that the individual's will and actions are governed only by their own principles and laws rather than by external constraints. This is a philosophical position espoused by humanistic adult educators. See *freedom*.

auto-tutorial devices Aids that can be employed by *autodidacts* or by other learners independently of a teacher.

average The arithmetic mean is the usual measure of average, although both the mode and the median are measures of average.

aversion therapy A form of therapeutic learning which seems to eliminate undesirable behaviour by conditioning a person to associate the behaviour to be changed with unpleasant experiences.

award 1. A student prize. 2. A grant towards fees. 3. Formal recognition, such as a certificate, diploma, etc indicating the successful completion of a course of study.

award unit The amount of credit that is given to a specific course of study, eg a credit hour.

Bb

baccalaureate   1. The French school-leaving examination, taken at the end of secondary school in order to achieve qualification for university entrance. 2. When referring to a degree, it is the first-level degree. It is always used this way in the United States and French-speaking universities, and also in some European universities.

baccalaureate degree   In the United States, a first degree.

bachelors degree   A first level degree awarded by universities.

banking education   1. Professional education of those people who work within banking. 2. Paulo Freire employed this term to refer to that form of education in which information presented by teachers is merely memorised by the learners in an uncritical manner.

bantu education   Term used in South Africa during the apartheid period for education for the blacks.

bar chart   Statistical data presented diagrammatically. A graph composed of bars, either presented horizontally or vertically. Useful for comparative purposes.

barriers to participation   A great deal of research has been undertaken to discover why adults do not participate in adult education activities. This term has been used to refer to the obstacles which appear to prevent adults from joining such activities. It has been recognized that there are three sets of barriers: situational, due to the individuals' position within the social structure; institutional, which refers to the types of procedures of educational institutions, and the time-tabling of educational programmes that inhibit certain groups from participating; dispositional factors, which refer to the negative attitudes of non-participants towards education. Finally, some research suggests that there are informational factors that also inhibit participation. In the United States this is sometimes referred to as *deterrents to learning*.

basic education   Educational programmes devised to provide learners with proficiency in language, number and literacy for everyday life. See *adult basic education*.

basic English   Devised in 1948. An attempt to limit vocabulary to 850 basic words, which has resulted in the development of graded vocabularies.

basic human needs   These are defined in terms of the individual's consumption of food, shelter, and clothes, and in terms of people's access to social services, health care, public transport, and educational and cultural opportunities. In recent years there has been a variety of 'hierarchies of needs' such as Maslow's hierarchy, in which there is a progression from bodily needs to those of the self. In addition, others have suggested similar hierarchies such as – first-order needs (bodily); second-order (self-expression); third-order (luxury). Adopted as one baseline for developmental education.

basic mathematics   There was a growing awareness in the 1970s that *numeracy* was almost as great a problem as *literacy*. Thus there emerged a movement to teach adults basic mathematics, which became incorporated in the adult basic education curriculum.

basic reader   The required text-book on a course.

basic research   Research activities designed to test fundamental theory.

basic skills   The types of social and other skills that are required to function in contemporary society, eg listening, speaking, reading, writing, and mathematics.

basic skills test   Examinations designed to assess the competency of individuals in the use of *basic skills*.

basic test   A basic skills test.

behaviour   1. An observable act. 2. A response to a stimulus.

behaviour modification   1. Change of behaviour. 2. Techniques employed to change behaviour in therapy and some forms of experiential learning, based upon conditioning. See *behaviourism*.

behaviour patterns   1. Similar forms of behaviour performed by different people in similar situations. 2. Short sequences of acts that are repeated in a variety of situations.

behaviour therapy   Forms of therapy that assume that through learning and conditioning, certain forms of disorder may be eliminated or diminished.

behavioural learning model   An approach to learning based on the idea that learning is a change in behaviour as a result of experience or practice. It is a theory that is open to criticism, since learning is much broader than behavioural change.

behavioural objective   This specifies the behavioural changes that will occur as a result of a teaching and learning session. The goal of behavioural change as a result of teaching. Associated with behaviourism in which learning is defined as a change of behaviour that is measurable. See *educational objective, expressive objectives*.

behavioural science   Studies in those subjects that are concerned with human actions, either as individuals or in groups. Psychology and sociology, for instance, are often referred to as behavioural sciences. It is also referred to as human studies.

behaviourism   An experimental and theoretical approach in psychology, associated with J B Watson and B F Skinner, in which experimental psychologists study observable, measurable behaviour.

belief   A principle accepted as true but without sufficient evidence to prove it. This is a form of ideology, often taken as knowledge, but it is not verifiable by the normal means of verifying knowledge.

bell-shaped curve   The shape of a normal distribution diagram in statistics.

bench fee   1. Fee payable, over and above the basic fee, for the use of laboratory space. 2. Fee payable over and above the basic fee of the institution, charged by a department. This is becoming increasingly common as higher education needs to find additional income.

benchmark   To indicate best practice.

bibliography   List of academic papers, books, journal articles etc. consulted by an author (authors), which should appear at the end of every academic piece of writing, whether essay, academic paper, or book.

bilingual education   Teaching and learning in two languages.

bimodal distribution   Statistical distribution in which there are two peaks in the distribution curve, indicating that there is more than one maximum frequency.

biographical method   Research into people and their learning, through the use of *life history*.

bivariate analysis   A form of research in which there are two variables, one dependent and the other independent.

black book   The first major book published in the USA in which adult educators claimed their place as a separate profession. It was entitled *Adult Education as an Emerging Field of University Study* (1964).

black literature   Writings by black authors.

black studies   The study of the society, culture, economy, and language of black people, especially in the United States. This field of study is becoming increasingly common and significant in other countries of the world.

blackboard   Formerly a black slate board on which the teacher could write with chalk so that a class could all see; now frequently green and rarely of slate but serving the same purpose. Adult educators are sometimes critical of the teaching methods that use 'chalk and talk'. See also *chalkboard, whiteboard*.

blind   Educationally, the blind have to rely on hearing and touch as their main means of receiving information and stimuli for learning.

blind marking   The second marking of a student assignment, when the second marker does not see the first marker's comments or grade.

block release   A system whereby employees are released from their work for a period of time in order to follow a course of study.

block release course   An educational course taking place during work time, but for which the participants have been released from work for a continuous period of time, which may vary from several days to several months, in order to undertake the study.

Bloom's Taxonomy of Educational Objectives   These are the objectives in the cognitive domain that Benjamin Bloom, and his research group, considered were the elements that should be tested in an examination. They suggested a six-level hierarchy of knowledge: knowledge, understanding, application, analysis, synthesis, and evaluation. While this has not gone uncriticized, it has provided stimulus for a considerable amount of subsequent research. Sometimes linked to *behavioural objectives*.

blue-collar worker   A manual worker. See *white-collar worker*.

board   A committee convened for a specific purpose, eg Board of Examiners.

body   The physical aspect of the person, much neglected by educational researchers although more recent research in biology is causing educators to place more emphasis on the physical body.

body concept   Physical elements of the *self-concept*.

body language   Non-verbal communication by means of physical posture and bodily movement.

body of knowledge   1. The amount of knowledge or information which it is intended to impart to students in a particular course or subject. 2. The sum total of the accepted knowledge about any field of study. 3. The knowledge base considered essential for an occupation or a profession, so that the body of knowledge became one of the characteristics of an occupation having achieved professional status.

book box   A small library of recommended reading brought to adult classes, especially traditional extra-mural classes, often by the tutor and usually in a box.

book club   A group of people contributing to a common fund to purchase books for mutual benefit.

book list   A list of recommended reading for a course.

bookmobile   Travelling library. See *mobile library*.

brainstorming   A problem-solving technique in which members of a group suggest solutions to a problem without interruption or criticism. Having gathered a number of suggestions, the group analyses them and seeks solutions to the problems.

brain train   Groups of people studying distance education courses meeting in a commuter train each day. There have been instances where railway companies have reserved compartments in the train for those wishing to pursue their studies during their journey. See *education train*.

brainwashing   Literally, to wash the brain clear so that it can be reprogrammed according to the ideological viewpoints of those who are controlling the process. See *indoctrination*.

branch programme   A route, following a specialization, through a modular course of study.

brand   More common in business and industry, but it is beginning to occur in education – where a high status organization allows its name to be used on approved products. See *franchise*.

bridging course   A course designed to assist a student transfer from one course to another at a much higher level. See *feeder course, gateway course*.

British Aerospace Virtual University
The first corporate university in the UK, due to offer its first full programme of courses in 1999.

British Institute of Adult Education
Established in 1921 by Mansbridge and Haldame. In 1949 it became a constituent member of the *National Institute of Adult Education*.

brochure   A publication containing the list of courses being offered by an educational institution over a specified period. See *also catalogue, prospectus*.

brokering   Educational brokering is a system of putting potential teachers in contact with potential learners, and vice versa. It has been done through the use of newspaper advertisements etc. There is a sense in which some voluntary organizations which claim that 'anyone can teach, any one can learn' (such as the *University of the Third Age*) is an educational brokering service on a membership basis.

buddy system   A slang term for apprenticeship. See also *mentor, Sitting by Nellie*.

bureaucracy   The system of organization and administration associated with most large organizations, including educational institutions.

burnout   A cluster of exhaustion reactions that occur in people who are working under great stress. It appears to be occurring among teachers and educators.

bursary   A financial scholarship or a grant made to a student.

business education   Studies in commercial and management subjects.

business game A game designed to simulate actual business conditions, often used in business education.

business studies Studies in commercial and management subjects.

buy-in The process of employing personnel on a part-time basis when there is insufficient time or expertise among the full-time staff for the work to be conducted to a satisfactory standard.

buzz group A teaching and learning technique in which members of a class or seminar briefly break off in small groups to discuss a point that has been raised during the session.

Cc

cable television   Local television system delivered by cable, ie narrow casting, rather than broadcasting.

calendar   Diary of events, often the forthcoming year's events of an educational institution.

calisthenics   Rhythmical method of physical education, without using apparatus.

calligraphy   The art of beautiful handwriting using special pens; a popular adult education course.

Campaign for Learning   A national campaign about *lifelong learning* organized by the Royal Society of Arts in the United Kingdom.

campus   The site of a school, college or university, usually self-contained and distinctly separate from the outside community. In the United States it also refers to training sites for business centres.

candidate   A graduate student in the United States who has passed the qualifying examinations and has been granted permission to commence dissertation study.

capitation fee   The amount of money that an educational institution may have to pay to a central body per student fee.

career   1. A path through life, or through an organization, eg through a period of academic study, or one's occupational history. Sometimes referred to as a career path.

2. The occupation or profession chosen to be one's lifetime vocation.

career education   1. A process designed to relate the curriculum to the work demands of society. 2. The form of education and training during which individuals are prepared for their chosen occupation or profession.

career guidance   The process of offering advice and guidance to people about their career.

career path   An individual's occupational history. See *career*.

careers officer   An employee of an educational institution or authority responsible for providing information and guidance about careers to students.

careers service   This service was commenced to assist school-leavers and now students leaving higher education with advice about future work opportunities, but the service throughout the United Kingdom has expanded its work and frequently offers a service to adults as well.

caretaker   Person employed to clean and maintain the educational premises.

Carnegie unit   See *credit unit*.

case analysis   Discussion of either an actual or a prepared case study which helps participants understand more deeply the problems and issues of professional practice.

case book method   An approach to instruction based upon the idea of constructing a number of case studies and recording them in a single book. Frequently used in legal education.

case history   An educational aid consisting of a written description of an event, incident, or situation used as a basis for discussion and problem-solving. See also *case study*.

case study   1. The type of project often employed in professional education in which the learner selects (or has selected) an actual situation in professional practice and has to prepare a report upon it for discussion and assessment. 2. In educational research, the concept is more confused since the case study is both the process of learning about a case and the product of the learning.

case study method   A research process to study, analyse and report findings from an empirical investigation of a case study.

catalogue   An information booklet, usually published by institutions to publicise their list of courses. See also *brochure, prospectus*.

catechism   Instruction through a series of questions and answers, especially of a religious text, based upon correct answers being given to the text which has been learned.

catechist   One who has the designated role of teaching the catechism.

catechize   1. To teach or examine through a series of questions and answers. 2. To give oral instruction in Christianity. 3. To put questions to someone.

category   1. A logical grouping based upon specified criteria. 2. A specific product or finding resulting from qualitative research.

causality   The theories that seek to explain the relationship between cause and effect.

ceiling and floor   The top and bottom marks or grades in a test may be referred to in this manner.

centralization   The process of concentrating authority and decision-making in the centre, or at the top of the hierarchy, of an organization.

central tendency   A statistical concept referring to the fact that most frequency distributions appear to be around a mid-point score.

certificat en andragogie (Canada)   An undergraduate-level award of the University of Montreal since 1969, when it was the first French-speaking university in Canada to recognize andragogy as a field of academic study.

certificate   1. A legal document which specifies that a person or agency may perform stipulated services. 2. An award from an educational institution indicating that an individual has successfully completed a prescribed course or programme. 3. A university award of a certificate is usually regarded in the United Kingdom as equivalent to one year's full-time undergraduate study. 4. A postgraduate certificate awarded by some British universities is regarded as one-third of a Master's degree, equivalent to one year of part-time study.

certificate of attendance   A document certifying attendance of the bearer at a course, but having no academic validity.

certificate of competency   A document specifying that the bearer has reached a certain specified standard and has demonstrated it by test or examination.

certificate of completion   A document issued specifying that the bearer has completed a part or whole of a course. It does not have to specify that the bearer has been tested for competency.

Certificate of Education (Cert. Ed.)
1. The academic award for a one-year full-time or a two-year part-time course in further or higher education. 2. It was the award that school teachers gained on qualification in the United Kingdom, before school teaching became a graduate profession.

Certificate of High School Equivalency
A formal document issued by individual State Departments of Education in the United States certifying that the bearer has met the requirements for high school graduation on the General Educational Development tests. It is an official document accepted by some, but not all, colleges, universities, and employers. Often called GED.

Certificate of prevocational education
Introduced into the United Kingdom in 1986. A one year course for a wide ability range of young people of 16 years of age and older who do not intend to progress to the General Schools certificates.

certificate renewal The re-issue of a certificate at a given time when the previous one has expired. The bearer has to demonstrate that the conditions for renewal have been met.

certification The process whereby an awarding agency grants a credential to a person.

chain In learning theory, the series of responses and stimuli arising from an initial stimulus.

chain learning See *chain*.

chain of response model (COR)
A theoretical model of participation in organized education developed by Patricia Cross (see her book *Adults as Learners*), incorporating a number of factors that stem from other research. It is a theoretical model designed to identify relevant variables and to hypothesize their interrelationship.

chair 1. A teaching or research professorship, often endowed. 2. The head of a department in an American college or university.

chalk and talk A rather derogatory term to refer to the teaching method whereby teachers use their own speech and writing on a chalkboard or whiteboard as the only teaching aids accompanying their input, having little or no student participation.

chalkboard A board on which a teacher/tutor can write with chalk, eg blackboard, greenboard, etc.

chancellor The highest office in an institution of higher education. In many instances in the United Kingdom, this is an honorary position.

change agent An individual who introduces, or is a catalyst in, organizational change, ie changes in culture, procedures, structures, etc. Change agents might be human resource developers, managers, consultants, leaders, or merely experts, etc.

channels of communication 1. A term that is used to refer to the fact that people receive their sense experiences through a number of different senses, or channels, so that there can be a compensation if one of the senses is in any way defective. 2. In organizational terms, this refers to those routes through which messages are expected to go to reach the different people, although there are informal routes which are often more effective.

chaplain A representative of a church or churches attached to an educational institution to serve the religious needs of staff and students.

characteristic A trait, often used in personality theory to depict a pattern of behaviour.

charisma   1. Personal quality or gift that enables a person to inspire and influence others. See also *personality*. 2. A sociological term that is used to describe a person or leader who has the characteristic of inspiring others to follow. It is not necessarily a personal characteristic, shared by each person, since the actual authority of charisma ultimately resides in the followers and they can both give or withdraw their allegiance.

charitable foundation   An organization established to administer a fund which is subject to the laws of charities.

Chartists   A movement of working people in the early part of the nineteenth century, mostly in the midlands and north of England, in which adult education was widely used as a means of propagating their ideas. This was especially used with the Christian Chartist groups.

Chautauqua   Established in 1874 on the shore of Chautauqua Lake in the United States as a summer school programme for Sunday School teachers by Dr John Vincent and Lewis Miller but this soon expanded beyond Sunday School teachers. By 1878, a general adult education programme was offered on a national scale through the newly established *Chautauqua Literary and Scientific Circle* (CLSC).

Chautauqua Literary and Scientific Circle   Established in 1879, it was established as an arm of *Chautauqua*, and it initiated its first correspondence education, which became very successful. Although not now so prominent, CLSC provides its members with significant non-fiction books so that they can continue their education.

Chautauquan   The magazine of the *Chautauqua Literacy and Scientific Circle*.

checklist   A pre-specified list of topics to be covered or areas researched. Useful planning tool.

chi square   A statistical test of association, used to see if association occurs by chance.

Christian Socialism   A nineteenth-century Christian movement that was responsible for many of the early adult education developments. See *social gospel*.

chunking   1. The number of chunks of information that individuals can retain in their short-term memory. 2. A pedagogical practice of organizing information for short-term and long-term mental storage.

circulating library   Libraries that were transported from area to area. It was claimed that they issued fiction whereas the *subscription libraries* were of a more serious disposition.

circulating schools   A system of schools started in Wales in the nineteenth century, which endeavoured to have a school for children and adults in each parish by employing itinerant teachers.

Citizens' Advice Bureau (CAB)   An advice, information and counselling service offered to adults in the United Kingdom.

Citizens' Forum   Adult study and action groups established by the Canadian Adult Education Association in 1943, using radio broadcasts as study material. The expressed objectives of this were to influence policy and produce a more democratic Canada at the end of the Second World War. See *Education for Reconstruction Conference*.

Citizens' League   Started in America in 1952 and developed during the following thirty years, stressing citizen research and debate using community issues as the agenda. A form of community education, and also a form of *participatory research*.

citizenship education   1. Education to make individuals aware of their rights and duties as a citizen. Associated with immigration into a country, although many argue that this should form part of the compulsory education curriculum. 2. Education designed to inculcate social behaviour considered desirable in a particular society or community. 3. An element in Dewey's *progressivism* that taught children and adults critical thinking skills.

City and Guilds of the London Institute Established in Britain in 1879, with the express purpose of making grants at the same rate as the *Science and Art Department* for successes in non-engineering subjects. The Institute became a leading early exponent of the training of adult educators, as well in the training of adults in many vocational subjects.

city college A community college in the United States.

civic education A form of education designed to make persons aware of their rights and duties as citizens, and capable of exercising them effectively and responsibly. See *citizenship education*.

civic university A provincial university created in the United Kingdom during the nineteenth and twentieth centuries.

civilization 1. The culture of a particular country. 2. Culture generally, which distinguishes humankind from the animal kingdom.

clarify To make clear or easy to understand.

class 1. A group of people who meet with a teacher in order to study a specific subject for a predetermined length of time. 2. The way that people are identified in society according to specific characteristics, such as occupation, wealth, etc. See *social class*.

class meeting A Methodist Church institution in which groups of church members meet to engage in study. During the nineteenth century it was closely associated with self-help. See also *study circle*.

class size The number of students in the group being taught.

classical conditioning The process of behaviour modification whereby the person learns to associate the presentation of a reward with the stimulus which appears fractionally prior to it, so that behaviour is adjusted to the stimulus in anticipation of the reward. This is associated with the work of Ivan Pavlov.

classical curriculum A curriculum which reflected the idea of a single culture in a society and that its culture contained the truth so that its aim is to communicate the worthwhile knowledge from one generation to the next. See *romantic curriculum*.

classics 1. Study of the traditional languages of Western civilization, eg Latin and Greek. 2. Something that becomes established and highly respected.

classroom A room in a school or college in which the class meets to be taught.

classroom climate The atmosphere or *ethos* established in the class, usually as a result of techniques and teaching style of the teacher. This climate can be related to the teacher-student relationship, interrelationships between students, group motivation, etc.

classroom ecology A branch of educational research which has not been widely developed in adult education in which the classroom is itself the centre of research, eg interactions within it. See also *Adult Classroom Environmental Scale, ecology*.

classroom interaction The study of interaction within the classroom.

classroom observation 1. Initial practical placement for student teachers, during which they watch experienced teachers teach. 2. A form of research in the classroom, not so well developed in adult education as in initial education.

clearinghouse   A centralized agency for the collection and distribution of information and materials, commonly used within US education, eg ERIC Clearinghouse on Adult, Career and Vocational Education.

client   1. A customer. 2. One who pays the fees and as education is becoming more of a business, so fee paying is becoming more significant. 3. A patient in a therapeutic, or social work, relationship.

client-centred therapy   A form of therapy pioneered by such psychologists as Carl Rogers, which concentrates upon the client's own perceptions. Has influenced adult education method.

clinic   1. A place for treatment. 2. An extended series of meetings that involves diagnosis, analysis and treatment of conditions or problems. This term is occasionally used in adult education with this meaning.

clinical experience   A practical placement for trainees in the medical and health professions.

clinical psychology   A branch of psychology concerned with the recognition and treatment of mental disorder.

closed circuit television (CCTV)   A closed circuit of video recorder and screens that allows events to be recorded and viewed at a later date. This is a method frequently used in teaching adults, so that participants can learn from viewing the event. Frequently used in tutor training.

closed communication structure   A structure of communication within an organization in which members may interact only with specific personnel, often only a named central person, about the functioning of the organization. It is bureaucratic in nature.

closed further education   A term employed in Germany relating to certain forms of further education which are offered to specific clientele, such as the trade unions, etc. See also *open further education.*

closed question   A question that is set that restrict the respondents' answers because it asks for specific information. Used in examinations, questionnaires.

closed test   The type of test that may be used only by those personnel especially trained to administer it, such as some of the psychological tests that are available.

closure   1. To bring to an end. 2. To bring to an end in such a manner as to leave no unanswered question. 3. A term used in Gestalt psychology to indicate that people have a tendency to perceive complete figures rather than open ones, or complete situations rather than incomplete ones.

cluster   Refers to a group of scores that fall close together in a correlation matrix in statistical analysis.

cluster analysis   A statistical technique in factor analysis examining interrelations in a correlation matrix.

cluster sampling   An approach to sampling in which sub-groups within the whole population are randomly selected.

Clusternet   The network within the National University Teleconferencing Network in the United States, which has the ability to link up its productions with the orbiting satellite network so that live and interactive programmes can be transmitted.

coach   1. To train or give instruction, usually employed with reference to physical exercise and sports performance. 2. To prepare students for examinations. 3. One who trains, or coaches.

coach and student method   A teaching method in which a pair of students teach each other a procedure or a skill.

Coalition for Literacy   An alliance in the United States of many organizations concerned with adult literacy.

Coalition of Adult Education Organizations   Established in 1973, a loose coalition of adult education organizations in the United States. See *Galaxy Conference of Adult Education Organizations.*

code   1. A list of procedures or rules. 2. The accepted form of behaviour within a social group. 3. A style of language, eg vocabulary and speech patterns. 4. Symbols for the conversion and analysis of quantitative data.

code of ethics   A profession's statement of the standards of behaviour and occupational performance that it expects of its members, often regarded as an essential prerequisite for professional status.

codified knowledge   Systematic knowledge that can be written down or stored electronically.

coding   A system of applying symbols to quantitative data to prepare them for manipulation and analysis by computer. See *decoding.*

coding frame   A system that is constructed in quantitative research to enable data to be translated into the symbolic form in which it can be analysed.

coding schedule   The document containing the *coding frame.*

co-educational   The education of males and females together.

coefficient of contingency   The degree of association between two variables, when each is expressed in several categories or qualities.

coefficient of correlation   This provides a measure of the degree of linear association between two variables.

cognition   Thought, as distinct from emotions or skills.

cognitive development   Stages of growth through which individuals pass as they mature; most of this research concentrates upon children although some research has taken this research into adulthood.

cognitive dissonance   This refers to the discomfort experienced by individuals when they hold logically inconsistent thoughts about an object or an event.

cognitive domain   The mode of thinking, rather than doing or being emotionally orientated.

cognitive learning   The acquisition of knowledge, principles, beliefs, etc.

cognitive learning theorists   Theorists who seek to explain learning only in cognitive terms.

cognitive map   Schemes constructed by individuals about phenomena, as a result of their own learning experiences.

cognitive mode   The process of human functioning through thought, as opposed to doing or feeling.

cognitive skills   What a person knows, perceives, and understands and the manner in which these are used in subsequent learning and problem-solving.

cognitive strategy   Method by which a person uses knowledge and skills in future learning. See *cognitive skills.*

cognitive structure   The general framework of thinking, similar to ideology, world-view. Something that might alter with experience.

cognitive style   The characteristic manner by which a learner approaches the task of learning, perceiving, gathering, and processing information. A variety of different styles have been identified, usually in terms of opposites, eg convergent/divergent. See also *learning style* which is sometimes used synonymously.

cohort   Term used to refer to a complete group, eg a year entry, a group being studied in educational research, etc.

co-leader   One whose responsibilities are to share in the leadership of a group or organization.

collaborative assessment   A form of assessment that is a negotiation between teacher and learner about assessment method, criteria, grades, etc.

collaborative learning   Learning situations where learners work together to assist each other in the learning process. See *peer learning.*

collaborative research   1. A form of research in which the researcher and the researched work together in the project. 2. Research in which a number of researchers work together on a project.

collaborative teaching   The teaching and learning process in which the teachers and learners collaborate, a democratic approach to teaching, commonly used in adult education. See *peer teaching, team teaching.*

collage   A display, often on the wall of a classroom, using a variety of different materials.

collection   1. An accumulation of resources, books, etc. 2. A number of papers gathered together in a book. 3. An archive.

college   An educational establishment, usually referring to an institution of post-compulsory education.

college boards   Examinations prepared by the *College Level Examination Board* in the United States.

College diploma   An award made by a college itself, rather than one accredited by an accrediting institution or a university.

College Level Examination Board   A non-profit agency with a membership of over 2,500 educational institutions involved in helping all forms of education. It has an *Office of Adult Learning Services.*

College Level Examination Program (CLEP)   Administered by the *College Level Examination Board*, this programme seeks to measure knowledge acquired outside the formal educational system. Test scores can sometimes be used to gain remission from certain required courses for college students (usually adults).

college of advanced education   A tertiary level educational institution established in Australia in the 1960s. Both vocational and general educational programmes are offered in these colleges. Adult education programmes are run in some of them, including the training of teachers of adults.

college of advanced technology (CAT)   A college of higher technical education in the United Kingdom. These institutions were granted university status in the United Kingdom in the 1960s.

college of education   1. A school teacher training college in the United Kingdom, prior to the 1970s when it became educational policy for school teacher education to be integrated with the *higher education* system. 2. A college in an American university in which all forms of education are studied, including *adult education*, but it is historically related to school teacher training and this is still its major function.

college of further education   Located in the United Kingdom, they provide courses for post school-leaving students, often part-time. These institutions have a vocational bias although this is not always the case. Some students use this type of college as a route to higher education, but the colleges themselves have expanded their role from working mainly with 16–19 year olds to colleges with a lifelong education orientation, especially in relation to continuing vocational education. See *community college* for the US equivalent.

college of further and higher education   As some of the *colleges of further education* have sought to expand their role into higher education they have changed their titles to colleges of further and higher education.

college of higher education   The title adopted by some of the colleges of education which diversified in the 1970s in the United Kingdom.

college of technology   A college of further education, in which technology is regarded as central to its curriculum.

College of the Sea   Established in 1938 in the United Kingdom, by Albert Mansbridge, as a part of the adult education service which he wished to offer seamen.

College Work-Study Program
Commenced in 1984 to assist college students to be involved in local projects. At its height, 3,400 colleges were receiving funds from the *Secretary's Initiative on Adult Literacy* and were expected to participate in *adult literacy* work.

colloquium   1. An informal gathering for discussion. 2. An academic seminar.

colloquy   1. A formal conversation or conference. 2. A modification of the panel

approach to teaching and learning in that a group of six to eight persons are selected, some to represent the experts and some to represent the audience. The latter ask questions of the former in the presence of an actual audience.

Comenius Award   An annual award made by the *European Society for Voluntary Association* to an outstanding *adult educator*.

Commission of Professors of Adult Education   Established in mid-1950s in the United States, this organization has become a professional association of university professors in adult education and its meeting usually precedes the annual meeting of the American Association for Adult and Continuing Education.

committee   A small group of people appointed, or elected, to perform a task that cannot be performed as efficiently by the whole organization.

Committee for Study and Research in Comparative (International) Adult Education   Established in 1987 by the *International Council for Adult Education* and the *International Congress of University Adult Education* to examine international adult education.

common foundation course   Where a modular course is introduced for a number of different specialist groups, eg the various branches of nursing, there is often a basic foundation course which they all follow. See *core course*.

common knowledge   The mutual understanding that makes communication possible.

common skills   These are the basic *life skills* and fall into the following categories: self-development; working with others; problem solving; decision-making and investigating information; quantitative and numerical; practical skills. See also *coping skills*.

Commonwealth Association for the Education and Training of Adults
Inaugurated in 1987 and sponsored by the Commonwealth Foundation; concerned with the professional development of adult educators in the Commonwealth.

Commonwealth of Learning
Established in 1988 by the Commonwealth governments to promote co-operation in *distance education*, in order to promote human resource development within the Commonwealth.

Commonwealth Relations Trust
Formerly the Imperial Relations Trust, this Trust offers an annual bursary to an experienced *adult educator*, between the ages of 28 and 50 years of age, to study adult education in some part of the Commonwealth.

communication   1. The production and reception of messages, sharing and exchanging information, feelings and meanings through a variety of media. 2. A dynamic process between two or more persons.

communication channel   A pathway for communication; it may be covert rather than overt.

communication pattern   A systematic arrangement that defines the origin, direction, and structure of communication within a group.

communication system   Means of exchanging information.

communication technology   The medium through which communication occurs.

communications   The subject matter, or the study, of communication.

communicative action   The thesis at the heart of the work of Jürgen Habermas that is based upon the idea that those in communication with each other reach an understanding about the situation, and then their plans of action are co-ordinated and agreed.

communicative competence   The ability to communicate ideas to people, irrespective of the grammatical correctness of the language used.

community   There are said to be over 90 different definitions of this word in sociology. However, in adult education the word seems to have four different basic meanings: 1. A group of people who either live, or work, together. 2. A geographical area where people live and interact. 3. An educational activity beyond the walls of the educational institutions. 4. An ideal arrangement of people living and working in harmony. This last is the picture that was presented in the 1960s and 1970s of life in the past in areas where people lived, worked, and interacted in close relationship. See *community education*.

community action   Action undertaken by residents in a locality, who organize and take action on some matters of local or national concern. Regarded as the radical element in *community education*. See also *direct action*.

community activator   One who alerts people in the community to all forms of community possibilities, including adult educational opportunities.

community activist   One who takes direct action in the community to achieve desired ends. There is a debate within some areas of community education as to whether or not the community educator should also be an activist.

community animateur   One who intervenes in the community in order to assist groups or organizations to achieve their desired goals, usually on behalf of the whole community.

community arts   The activity of artists in a variety of different art forms working in local communities, often in an educative manner and involving the members of that community in creative art. See also *community theatre*.

community association   A voluntary private association, geographically based, in which the members participate in its organization and its activities. The purpose of such an association is to improve this sense of identity and interest in the community and to improve its social, cultural and material life.

community-based organization   An organization that is representative of and controlled by members of a local community, involved in a variety of social activities and concerns.

community care   A system whereby people who need support and who might normally reside in an institution live in the community and are cared for by health, social welfare and educational organizations.

community centre   A local centre, often organized by people who live in the community, having community purposes, often of a social welfare and educational nature.

community college   1. In the United Kingdom, it is an educational institution providing both secondary and adult education. 2. In the United States it is a college providing a wider education service for a region, often vocationally based, and they also run a two-year degree programme in higher education for people. These lead to an associate degree which is a prelude to a full four-year degree programme and students can then transfer to a four-year college. See *college of further and higher education*.

community development   The process of enriching the social, cultural, political, economic and educational life of a specific geographic area.

community development officer
A community worker whose task is to work in a local community seeking to enrich its life, often the role is performed by a community educator.

community education   1. The idea that education should originate in and be designed to meet the interests of the community, be directed to improving its quality of life and that the community should exercise responsibility for its provision. 2. Body of social, recreational, cultural and educational activities, organized outside the formal school system for people of all ages, intended to improve the quality of life of a community, but often using the local school as a basis for the activities. 3. The form of adult education adopted in Scotland. 4. Education devoted to *community development*. See *community action*.

community educator   One who is involved in teaching and learning with people outside the formal educational system, in order to achieve desired educational goals within a local community.

community learning   Learning related to the exercise of civic responsibility in the public interest through community political structure. See *community action*.

community of scholars   1. In the past, this was literally a group of scholars residing in an academic or religious institution in order to pursue scholarship. 2. The term now refers to the scholars who share similar academic interests.

community problem-solving project   A form of *community education* in which the residents of a local area are helped to solve a particular problem by engaging in relevant learning activities and then putting their learning into practice.

community reading centre   Part of the non-formal education programme in some developing countries is to provide reading rooms in communities where people will be able to read newspapers, periodicals and books. It is planned that these rooms should become distributive centres of knowledge.

community school   1. A contemporary of the village college in the United Kingdom, the community school seeks to provide education, recreation, and cultural activities for the whole of the locality it exists within. The school may also be a base for community development, or even some forms of community action. In addition, it may be managed by the main groups who use its facilities. See also *community education*. 2. A normal school in the United Kingdom which assumes certain adult education functions might be granted the status of a community school.

community service   1. Academics in the land grant universities in America are often expected to provide adult education services to the local community. 2. Work, usually of a voluntary nature, carried out to assist in *community development*.

community studies   The study of the way that communities function and develop. Frequently used in *community education*.

community survey   A survey, often conducted by learners, of a geographical location, obtaining data about the area, opinions of its residents about the area and its resources, problems, etc. See also *community studies*.

community television   Television programmes made about the local community, and often made by local residents. See *community education*.

community theatre   The use of drama in an educative manner in the local community, often used in *community action, community education*, etc.

community tutor   A member of staff in an educational institution having responsibility for education in the community, usually involved in adult education: a *community educator*.

commuter study clubs   Started in the United Kingdom in 1977 by De Pamela Le Pelly, with the support of British Rail. Courses are organized on commuter railway trains, provided the journey is longer than 30 minutes. See *brain train*.

comparative adult education   See *comparative education*. Comparative adult education is less well advanced than comparative initial education because adult education rarely constitutes a single system in a country. It should be noted that this is not necessarily international or even between countries.

comparative education   1. The study of educational systems, comparing the factors that lead to the development of the different systems, both within a country and between countries. It is an empirical study. 2. An academic journal devoted to comparative education.

comparative need   1. Used in adult education to illustrate the degree of educational need one person or community has in relation to another. 2. The gap that exists between the services received by individuals of similar characteristics. Term more frequently used in the welfare services than in education but has become more prevalent in adult education when it has been seen to be fulfilling a welfare-type service.

compensation   1. The process of emphasizing the strengths of learners to make up for the weaknesses. Hence in examinations good scores may be used to compensate for poor ones. 2. Used in psychology, the term is used to explain how individuals make up for certain deficiencies in their character.

compensatory education   The opportunity for adults to remedy the deficiencies in the initial education later in life.

competence   1. The level of skill and knowledge (and sometimes attitude is also specified) necessary to perform work efficiently, according to the standards accepted by a profession or occupation at a given time. 2. The ability to perform at an agreed level of proficiency, consisting of knowledge, skill, attitudes and professional values. 3. Some definitions of competence omit knowledge and regard it as only being skill-based.

competency-based education   Education based on the acquisition of competence in specified *knowledge* or *skills* (usually of an occupational nature. As this form of education is normally modular and self-paced it does allow for the course of study to be completed in varying lengths of time).

competence-based learning   Approaches to learning which explicitly specify the outcomes in terms of competencies that are to be taught and assessed.

competency   An ability or capability demanded in the successful performance of a specific act or behaviour. It is regarded as being a measurable skill.

competency-based vocational education That form of competency-based education in which the occupational task is sub-divided into a number of competencies and each comprises a module in the vocational preparation. See also *training*.

competency test   A test or examination designed to assess whether a certain skill has been achieved to a satisfactory standard.

competition   Rivalry that leads to participants endeavouring to achieve the highest or first place. This is sometimes encouraged in initial education as a mean of

motivation, but is less encouraged in adult education where co-operation between students is favoured as a more idealistic and realistic approach to classroom and other group dynamics.

complementary studies   The minor subject of a course of study.

complete learning method   An experimental procedure whereby a student works through specified learning material until one complete errorless set of answers has been achieved.

completion question   The type of question where the learners are required to finish an incomplete statement.

completion test   Any test in which students are given parts of items and are expected to complete them, eg fill in the blank space, etc.

complex   In psychoanalytical theory it is a descriptive device to convey a psychological state, but the term also has pathological implications, eg inferiority complex.

component behaviour   In learning a skill, the skill is often sub-divided into elements, or components, so that each can be learned separately.

composition   1. A completed piece of work. 2. An *essay*.

comprehend   To understand.

comprehension   1. A process of understanding a phenomenon. Psychologists suggest that there are two aspects to this – interpretation and utilization of the phenomenon under consideration. 2. A form of test to assess whether learners have understood – used in language teaching.

comprehension orientation   An approach to studying in which the learner seeks to relate the ideas being learned to the wider society and actual life experience.

comprehension test   A test which has been designed to assess the extent to which learners have the meaning of what they have read, what they have learned.

comprehensive high school   A secondary school in the United States having both academic and vocational programmes.

Comprehensive Manpower Service Program   A US programme to create and develop job opportunities and education and training that will help individuals obtain and retain employment.

compressed video   Two-way audio-visual linkup using electronic communication systems. This can be done using personal computers.

compulsory continuing education   The practice whereby professionals and other practitioners are compelled to attend additional education courses in order to retain their licence to practice. See *mandatory continuing education*.

compulsory education   Education that has to be undertaken according to the law of the country or state. Usually refers to the education of children, but some vocational education might be classified as compulsory, especially in *continuing vocational education*. See *mandatory continuing education*.

computer assisted learning (CAL)   An approach to distance teaching using a computer to assist in the presentation of teaching materials or to assist learners to work through an already prepared learning programme. There are advantages in allowing learners to pace their own learning and to do so without a teacher being present. See *computer-mediated instruction*.

computer-based training   This is an approach to training that uses a computer

program to simulate the main functions of an industrial process so that it enables trainees to work through most of the likely situations that occur in the workplace.

computer literacy   The level of knowledge and skill necessary to understand and use a computer program. However, at present no real agreement exists about a more precise definition.

computer-managed learning system   This is a computer system which is programmed to undertake the whole administration and management of a learning system, eg budget, time-tabling, etc.

computer marked assignment   Assignment which is marked by a central computer using a prepared program; it is usually in the form of multiple choice questions. Used by distance teaching institutions, such as the British Open University.

computer-mediated instruction   A teaching programme presented to the learner through the use of a computer.

computer software   Programs that are written in a special language to instruct the computer.

conation   The aspect of mental processes relating to volition. Not frequently used.

concentration   1. The ability to become absorbed in a task. 2. In analyses of distribution, the number of times a few scores occur in relation to the total number of occurrences.

concentration span   The length of time an individual can remain absorbed in a task.

concentric method   An approach to teaching where subjects are revisited at different stages at greater depth. See *spiral curriculum*.

concept 1. An abstract idea, or thought. 2. A term used to contain a family of phenomena having similar characteristics, eg *education* is used in this manner without reference to any of the specific types or forms of education.

concept formation The process of developing concepts. Piaget introduced a developmental sequence in concept formation but his research did not examine this process in adulthood.

concept learning One of the later stages in Gagné's hierarchy of learning. A concept has been learned when individuals respond to a wide variety of stimuli that belong to the same category.

concept map Diagrams seeking to represent meaningful relations between concepts in the forms of propositions.

conceptual style See *cognitive style*.

concrete experience 1. First stage in some *learning cycles* eg Kolb's. 2. Specific primary experience, which often results in *concrete operational thought* in the early stages of thought but which can lead to reflection.

concrete operational thought 1. One of the earliest of Piaget's stages of conceptual development which is concerned solely with thinking about specific objects or phenomena. 2. It is also essential in understanding some of the theoretical ideas of experiential learning since these start with the idea of concrete experience and the thought processes that are associated with it.

concurrent sessions When two or more sessions are mounted at the same time. This is a common occurrence in conferences whereby participants have a choice of presentations to attend.

condition To alter the response of a person (or animal) to a particular stimulus or situation.

conditioned reflex A response to a stimulus that is not normally associated with it but which occurs without thought or volition. See the work of Pavlov.

conditioned response See *conditioned reflex*.

conditioning The process of behavioural modification that occurs as a result of external force and without the intelligent, or critically aware, consideration of behaviour being changed. There are two types: *classical* and *operant*.

conductive education A form of education which teaches mastery of the disordered movements of the disabled body to a degree that enables independent functioning. Developed at the Peto Institute in Budapest.

conductor One who practises conductive education.

conference 1. A formal meeting in which two or more people confer, consult, and/or exchange opinions. 2. A meeting of an academic or professional association, often annually.

conference call Telecommunication between more than two persons (either audio or visual) that enables group discussion to occur. Used in some distance education provision.

conference centre A large, often residential, centre especially equipped to mount conferences.

confidence level A statistical measure used to determine whether the differences between two findings might have occurred by chance.

Confintea V The fifth UNESCO world conference on adult education, held in

Hamburg in July 1997.

conflict 1. In psychology, conflict refers to opposition between human drives. 2. In sociology, it refers to the type of analysis of society in which change is regarded as occurring as a result of social forces opposing each other.

conformity Compliance with accepted knowledge, values, standards of behaviour or performance, skills.

congregation An academic assembly.

connectionism Thorndike regarded the mind as the sum total of the connections between perceptions and memories of situations. Learning was for him, the creation of a connection between a response and a stimulus. See E L Thorndike's work.

conscience The sense of right and wrong that governs a person's actions. See *superego*.

conscientization Term introduced to the educational vocabulary by Paolo Freire to indicate that oppressed individuals would become conscious of the social forces that causes their social condition through the learning process. He suggested that he did not use it in the later years of his life.

consensus An agreement among a group of people.

construct A construct is created when a relationship is established between several objects or phenomena. See also *concept, personal construct*.

constructivism The process whereby perceptual experience is constructed from, rather than being a direct response to, the stimulus.

consultant One who is brought in to provide advice.

consulting The study of the art and

science of consulting is in its early phases, but it is developing rapidly as result of the tremendous expansion in Management Consulting.

consumer education Education in intelligent and effective methods of buying and using goods and services and recognizing the consumers' rights, competent money management, and relationship of the consumer to the economic system. It is a form of education espoused by the Co-operative Movement and other groups. Recently it has been included in more community education programmes.

consumer society A society based upon the assumption that human beings wish to acquire goods and commodities, and whose economy is based upon such a premise. As education is increasingly being regarded as a commodity, so the ideas of consumption are entering the educational vocabulary.

Contact The journal of the International Association of Universities of the Third Age.

contact hour A measure of time in which the teacher and the learners interact formally in a teaching and learning situation. The duration is actually often only 50 minutes.

contact time The amount of time that teachers are expected to spend teaching their students in classes, often measured in hours per week.

content 1. Usually refers to the knowledge, skills, and attitudes that learners are expected to explore or acquire during a lesson, course, etc. 2. The data contained within a document. 3. It is an intrinsic element of a curriculum.

content analysis 1. The analysis of data contained in documentation, often undertaken in a quantitative manner. 2. A research technique, is occasionally employed in adult education research.

content mastery Being proficient in all aspects of the specified content of the course or curriculum.

context The necessary framework within which to set an event, or a piece of writing, to enable a full understanding of the event, or the meaning of the words, to occur.

context dependent question The type of question that often occurs in a professional examination when the field of practice, eg a case study, forms the basis of the question which elicits either a response relating to the theoretical, the practical, or a combination of both.

context studies Those studies that are undertaken, often of a minor nature, which help put the main studies in perspective.

continuation school Mainly for young people in Denmark who have left school (folkeskole) but are too young to attend the folk high school. These are private, independent, and residential and function as an alternative to grades 8–10.

continuing education Those learning opportunities which are taken up after the end of full-time initial education. See *adult education, extended education.*

continuing education for women (CEW) Part of an American educational programme for women, initially concentrating on women returners but it has more recently been involved in outreach programmes. See also *New Opportunities for Women, Wider Opportunities for Women* for similar initiatives in the United Kingdom.

Continuing Education in New Zealand The journal of the National Council of Adult Education in New Zealand, established in 1968.

continuing education record card Some professional groups issue their members with record cards in which they are required to keep a record of all their continuing education activities. See *portfolio.*

continuing education unit (CEU) Ten hours of formal continuing education constitutes one continuing education unit – widely used in the United States.

Continuing Higher Education Review The journal of the National University Continuing Education Association in America.

Continuing Library Education Network and Exchange (CLENE) An American association concerned with the use of libraries in *distance education.*

continuing professional development The development of the professional practitioner, after initial training, through staff development plans, advice and guidance, career counselling, etc. See *mandatory continuing education.*

continuing professional education (CPE) All vocational and professional learning opportunities that are taken up after the completion of initial professional preparation. See *mandatory continuing education.*

continuing vocational education (CVE) All vocational learning opportunities that are taken up after the completion of initial vocational training.

continuous assessment The process of assessing students throughout the whole of their course rather than at the end of the course only. It is often claimed that this is a less stressful form of assessment but evidence is mixed about this. Continuous assessment is often confused with course work assessment. See also *formative assessment.*

contract learning A teaching and learning situation where both partners (teacher and learner) enter an agreement about how the learning is to be undertaken, eg the learners will be self-directed, consult the tutor at specified times and complete the project by an agreed date. Often the contracts are informal, but some practitioners prefer formal written contracts.

contract research   Research carried out under contract between the researcher(s) and the contracting agency, often the contract is agreed as a result of invitations to tender for the research in a normal competitive tendering arrangement.

control group   A group of individuals in a research project who match closely the subjects being researched, but who are not themselves being researched. Data about the control group form the baseline against which the changes in the research group are measured.

controlled experiment   A research project in which the majority of independent variables are held constant, whilst only one or two are altered at each stage of the research.

convention   1. A tradition. 2. An assembly of members, delegates, or representatives from the local branches of an organization. See *conference*.

Convergence   The journal of the *International Council for Adult Education*.

convergent thinking   The process of thinking characterised by synthesising ideas, knowledge, information in order to solve a problem. See *divergent thinking*.

conversations   1. A method of engaging people in public debate about contemporary issues, first employed in America by Margaret Fuller Ossoli in the early nineteenth century who charged an admission fee for the series. 2. An organized discussion group led by one person. See *study circle*.

conversion course   A course which is offered to prepare people for an occupational position, or entry into another

level of education, when the previous education has only partially equipped them to enter the next phase.

convocation   An assembly of graduates of a university.

Co-operative Assessment of Experiential Learning   Started in 1974 as a project of the *Educational Testing Service* in the United States, but changed its name in 1977 to *Council for Advancement of Experiential Learning* when it became independent.

Co-operative College of Canada   See *Western Co-operative College*.

co-operative education   A form of education in which the school and the occupational field co-operate in order to provide a joint educational programme with alternate attendance in both school and work. A concept used in US education.

co-operative extension   The extramural programme offered by land grant universities in America to the agricultural communities. Among the largest adult education programmes in the world. See *Co-operative Extension Service*.

co-operative extension agent   An educational organizer who works for the *Co-operative Extension Service*, the first ones were appointed in 1906.

Co-operative Extension Service   The extra-mural programme of the land grant universities, established in 1914 in the Smith-Lever Act. The term 'co-operative' stems from the fact that the service is funded by a co-operative arrangement of federal, state and county funds.

co-operative learning   Small group of students working together to achieve a common goal.

co-operative programme   US equivalent of the sandwich course in the United

Kingdom, where a student spends blocks of time in an educational institution and blocks in the workplace. Courses of this nature are usually either at professional qualification or undergraduate level.

Co-operative Society   Founded in Rochdale in 1844, it has traditionally devoted as much as 2.5 per cent of its funds to educational purposes, especially education for the under-privileged.

co-operative teaching   See *team teaching*.

Co-operative Women's Guilds Established in 1883 to help women take their place in the Co-operative movement, involved very early in *consumer education*.

coping skills   The skills necessary for people to deal successfully with personal, social, and work-related problems. See *life skills*.

core course   A basic course which acts as a foundation for a number of different branches of study. See *common foundation course, core curriculum*.

core curriculum   1. Generally regarded as that part of the curriculum, which is essential studying for every student. See also *option units*. 2. It is also the basic programme to which other credits can be added. See also *required course*.

core skills   1. Those skills that well rounded workers require in order to perform their present occupation. 2. Skills required to be able to acquire more sophisticated skills when necessary. 3. Skills that are crucial to the performance of any activity.

corporate classroom   Large industrial and commercial companies are now organizing a great deal of their own continuing professional education. This term reflects their involvement in education.

corporate culture   The values and beliefs that are shared by members of an

organization that help to shape management style and the employees' behaviour.

corporate university   Large industrial and commercial organizations are now starting their own highly sophisticated education and training systems and establishing their own universities. This is the next phase in the development of the university: in history, the church established universities, the state did the same, and now the large corporations have commenced the same process in the knowledge society.

correction   The process of assessing students' work and highlighting the faults. In adult education it is usually suggested that this process should be undertaken in a positive manner so that the self-concept of the adult learner is not threatened but positively enhanced as a result of the feedback.

correctional education   US term for education that takes place within penal institutions. See also *penal andragogy, prison education*.

correspondence college   1. When *correspondence education* was widely used a number of private schools, or colleges, were established which prepared *correspondence courses* for students who could then sit public examinations. 2. In the United States, a large number of such colleges were established following the success of *Chautauqua*.

correspondence course   See *correspondence education*.

correspondence education   Education conducted by the postal services without face-to-face contact between teacher and learner. Teaching is undertaken by written or tape-recorded material sent to the learner, whose progress is monitored through written or taped exercises sent to the teacher, who corrects them and returns them to the learner with criticism and advice. Started in the United Kingdom as early as 1840 when Pitman started teaching shorthand through correspondence, and in America it really began with *Chautauqua* in 1879 which was institutionalized in the University of Chicago in the 1890s.

correspondence school See *correspondence college*.

correspondence tuition A form of *correspondence education* where the actual tuition process, eg how and what to learn, rather than the content of the course is central. Many *correspondence courses* merely provided the teaching material didactically.

cost-benefit analysis A method for finding the maximum value for a given expenditure.

Council for Adult and Experiential Learning (CAEL) Formerly Co-operative Assessment of Experiential Learning, this is a non-profit-making organization devoted to the recognition that learning occurs in all types of situations; it has pioneered *accreditation of prior experiential learning schemes* in the United States and elsewhere.

Council for Advancement of Experiential Learning (CAEL) Formed in 1977 from *Co-operative Assessment of Experiential Learning* was renamed *Council for Adult and Experiential Learning* in 1985.

Council for Non-Collegiate Continuing Education An American association concerned about continuing education outside of the educational system.

Council for the Education of Adults in Latin America This organization represents more than sixty different national adult education groups in Latin America; it is an associated organization of the *International Council for Adult Education*.

Council of National Organizations Established in 1952 to co-ordinate the work of national adult education associations in the United States.

Council of National Organizations for Adult Education A co-ordinating body for adult education organizations in America; formed in 1959 from the *Council of National Organizations*.

Council on the Continuing Education Unit US council established to propose the principles for the use of the *continuing education unit*.

counselling A generic term which is used to cover a number of processes, such as interviewing, advising, guiding, and even providing therapy in areas of personal problems. There are different techniques, such as non-directive counselling.

country extension agent An adult educator working in the *Co-operative Extension Service*.

course 1. A specified number of lessons and assignments to be studied. 2. The content to be studied during a specified number of lessons.

course board The committee responsible for the management of a course, often includes student members. See *course meeting*.

course manager Some larger courses employ an administrator to manage the daily organization of a course.

course meeting A gathering of academic and administrative staff to manage the course, often includes student representative. See *course board*.

course pack Selected additional readings for use within a programme of study. See *study pack*.

course paper   An academic assignment submitted at the end of a course of study. See also *term paper*.

course requirement   The obligations and demands imposed upon the student before the award of a certificate to signify satisfactory completion of an academic course of study.

course team   A team of academics, and other professionals such as educational broadcasters and designers if involved in distance education, who prepare an educational course.

course tutor   1. A teacher for a course of study. 2. In the British Open University, a course tutor is a part-time member of the academic staff responsible for offering tutorial support and grading assignments. In 1997, the title was changed to assistant lecturer.

course work   The academic work that students are expected to undertake during a course of study.

course work assessment   The process of marking students' assignments. In some instances course work grades are used as part of the final assessment, but this need not be the case. See *continuous assessment*.

county agent   An agent working for the *Co-operative Extension Service*.

cow college   It is a pejorative and slang term for *land grant college*.

craft education   1. Teaching and learning the traditional and modern crafts – it has become a major area of adult liberal education. 2. Some forms of vocational education are referred to as craft education.

creative learning   Learning through synthesising and reflecting, so that new ideas and meanings are created in the learning process. See *creativity*.

creative writing   1. The art of writing in an imaginative manner. 2. The title that is sometimes given for a course in the art of writing for publication.

creativity   The process of bringing something new into existence. A much valued concept among adult educators, especially those who adopt a more humanistic perspective. Some psychologists regard it as one of the outcomes of divergent or lateral thinking. Some adult educators might regard it as a learning outcome of critical or reflective thinking of which everyone is capable. It should include elements of transformation, innovation, novelty, etc and should include the development of the learner's own self, as well as the product of the learning.

credentialing   The process of being licensed, or gaining the necessary qualifications, to be able to practise at the relevant level.

credit   The unit of value awarded for the successful completion of a course of study. In the United Kingdom a single credit is usually regarded as the equivalent of ten hours of learning time. In the United States credit is usually awarded under a different system. See *Carnegie unit, credit hour*.

Credit Accumulation and Transfer Scheme (CATS)   Launched in the United Kingdom in 1986 and administered by the Council for National Academic Awards. It is a scheme which accredits courses and modules run by education and educational departments in industry and commerce. Having common credits allows students to transfer the value of their completed courses between educational institutions.

credit by examination   Credit earned by the successful completion of a test designed to indicate that the candidate has mastered content that would be taught on a course of study.

credit course   A course of study that is recognized for specific credit by an award-giving educational agency, such as a university.

credit hour   Unit of academic time used in American universities, eg a course may be worth three hours, which is usually equivalent to 30 hours of classroom time, not the time required to complete the course.

credit transfer   The ability to transfer credit gained in one educational context to another. One university will accept as creditworthy the courses followed in another, similar institution.

credit unit   The unit of value that is awarded for the successful completion of a course or part-course, eg a credit hour, a Carnegie unit.

crisis education   Community learning when a local crisis, such as a workers' strike, provides opportunity for study and discussion. Frequently utilized in study circles in Scandinavia.

criterion   Recognized standard or level of performance against which individual achievement might be compared.

criterion-referenced testing   An approach to assessment that is based upon judging phenomena against pre-selected standards or criteria, rather than against the performance of others. See *norm-referenced testing*.

critical consciousness   The process of becoming aware of the social processes that operate within society and acquiring distance from one's own thought processes to reflect upon them.

critical incident technique   1. A technique used in human resource development in which a collection of reports about action or behaviour relating to a specific incident that is crucial to the functioning of an organization are gathered and analysed.

2. An approach to teaching which uses critical points in professional practice as bases for analyses and further learning about that practice.

critical pedagogy   An approach to teaching that encourages the learners to use their own reality as a basis for understanding and analysis. See *emancipatory education, radical adult education*.

critical point   A critical point in practice is where the practitioner is not able to act in an unthinking manner and, consequently, is forced to think about practice and learn from the situation. See *critical incident technique*.

critical theory   A sociological approach to analysing society that owes its origin to the Frankfurt School, especially more recently to the work of Jürgen Habermas. Critical theory finds its roots in Marxism and Freudian psychology, but more recently it has become more philosophical and linguistic. It does not accept the positivist value-free approach of certain forms of social science but asserts that no interpretation of social fact is value free. Hence, it is possible to analyse the values that underlie social action and the methods through which interpretation is socially constructed. This process, claim the critical theorists, is emancipatory.

critical thinking   1. The ability to analyse propositions and to assess the extent of their validity. A thought form very much valued by adult education, but it is not intrinsically linked to *critical theory*. See also *reflection*. 2. Specific processes of problem solving. 3. Process of coming to think critically about how assumptions and experiences shape our understanding of the world.

critical value   The value in a statistical test which determines acceptance or rejection of a null hypothesis in quantitative research.

criticism   The process of analysis and assessment – it does not have to be negative.

critique   A critical analysis of an argument, case, position, etc.

cross-cultural study   An empirical study conducted in more than one culture, designed to compare and contrast variables and phenomena.

cross-sectional study   A research process that studies different groups or categories at the same point in time. See *longitudinal study*.

crystallized intelligence   That form of intelligence that develops throughout life as a result of experience.

cultural action   Popular action by the people to improve their social and economic conditions. Often associated with *community education* and also with *radical adult education*.

cultural activity   Performing, visual and literary arts are often referred to as cultural activities.

cultural animation   Facilitating the involvement of people in cultural development and politics. Associated with *community education*.

cultural capital   The amount and type of culture individuals have acquired as a result of their socialization and upbringing.

cultural centre   1. Local community centres providing cultural activities, including adult education. See *Maison de la Culture*. 2. In some countries, eg the Netherlands, some of these are residential.

cultural circle   An informal method of teaching and learning by establishing groups to discuss relevant social topics, such as nationalism, development, etc. A method of teaching and learning utilized widely in some parts of the Third World. See *study circle*.

cultural development   The process of enriching the cultural context within which an activity occurs.

cultural disadvantage   The disadvantage people suffer as a result of their backgrounds or socialization when compared with the cultural norm of the group or society.

cultural enrichment   The development of cognitive, perceptual and verbal skills.

cultural heritage   1. Inheritance by one generation of the mores, folkways, institutions, beliefs and values of previous generations including their art, literature, music. 2. The culture of one generation that it seeks to preserve and pass on to the succeeding generation. This has been seen by some scholars as the basis of the curriculum for much compulsory education.

cultural house   Cultural centre in Hungary.

cultural imperialism   The dominance of one culture, or sub-culture, over another.

cultural invasion   An aspect of imperialism whereby one society and its culture dominates that of another society, often to the extent of quashing it.

cultural reproduction   The process of recreating cultural patterns across generations. Education is regarded as one of the most powerful forces of cultural reproduction. See also *social reproduction*.

cultural transmission   The transmission of aspects of an established culture to those who have not already acquired it. It is regarded critically by some sociological analysts (see *critical theory, radical adult education*) but seen by others as essential for the survival of society by those with a more functionalist perspective.

culturally disadvantaged group
Culturally disadvantaged persons whose

backgrounds or socialization differ from the norm of a social group to such an extent as to disadvantage them culturally within it.

culture   1. A sociological concept with a number of different meanings, but when used within the framework of adult education it usually refers to the sum total of knowledge, beliefs, attitudes, values, etc of a social group. 2. In common speech, however, it usually refers to the established arts, such as classical music, art, etc. This is sometimes known as the elite theory of culture.

culture of silence   A social situation in which oppressed peoples are unable to exert any control in the decision-making processes affecting themselves and their own society. A concept popularized in adult education by the work of Paulo Freire.

culture shock   The trauma experienced by a person entering a new culture or sub-culture.

cumulative frequency   The sum of occurrences of a phenomenon in a sample or a population.

cumulative frequency curve   The sum of the frequencies of a distribution forming an S-shaped curve.

curiosity   The attraction to novel phenomena – seen by Bruner as one of the bases of learning in childhood.

curriculum   1. Organised course of study undertaken by a student in or under the aegis of an institute of learning, or the course of study required to be followed by new recruits to an occupation or profession. 2. More commonly, the set of studies organized for a particular group of students (eg one age group) by a school, college, etc. 3. All the

educational events offered by an educational institution, and this is more appropriate for adult education. See *programme* in the United States.

curriculum design   The formal process by which educators develop, design and implement a curriculum to embodying specific principles, eg as a response to needs analysis.

curriculum development   The implementation of the curriculum design.

curriculum planning   See *curriculum design*.

curriculum theory   The study of curriculum. There tended to be at least five components in curriculum: aims, objectives, content, method and evaluation – although there are many other approaches to it, eg feminist, post-structuralist.

curriculum vitae   Statement of the biographical details of an individual, used frequently in applications for courses of study or jobs. See *résumé*.

customized instruction   Teaching designed to meet individual needs or requirements. See also *individualized instruction*.

cut-off point   The number or score that is used to distinguish one category or grade from another.

cybernetics   A branch of science concerned with control systems through feedback and subsequent systems modification in electrical or mechanical devices and the relationship between these and communications in constructed and biological systems.

Dd

Danish Council for Adult Education
Founded in 1941, co-ordinating body for all
voluntary adult education in Denmark.

data (datum, singular) General term for
raw research material or information.

database Collection of data, usually on
computer.

database system Mechanism for
organizing and managing the *database*.

day folk high school (Daghøjskoler)
Recently started in Denmark as daytime adult
education institutions with full-time staff,
rather than being run on the lines of the
evening school.

day release The allowance of a day, or a
part of a day, each week release from work to
follow a course of study.

day training centre Established in 1972 in
the United Kingdom as a result of a Criminal
Justice Act, which can enforce young
offenders to attend a training centre on a
probation order.

deaf Persons whose ability to hear has
been impaired so that it affects their learning
performance even with the aid of
amplification. They have to use other senses
to receive information and stimuli.

deaf-blind People who have both visual
and hearing impediments so that they are
unable to learn under normal circumstances
and require special educational provisions.

dean An academic office in an educational
institution, usually head of the Faculty in a
United Kingdom university and head of a
College in an American educational
institution – responsible for both academic
and administrative affairs.

death education Consists of two elements
preparing members of the caring professions
to cope with death and dying; and helping
individuals to come to terms with their own
feelings about their own transience. This
form of education is becoming a more
established part of adult education
programmes. See also *gerontology*.

death instinct Term used in Freudian
psychology to refer to the urge to destroy.

debate 1. The formal academic defence of,
and opposition to, a proposition. 2. A
method of teaching and learning, in which a
proposition is defended and opposed by
small teams of students.

decay Term used in research into memory
relating to the fact that recall becomes less
efficient over time.

decile Statistical term for one-tenth of the
population under consideration.

decoding A system of rules and
regulations that have to be understood
before an activity can be interpreted and
given meaning. This can often be regarded as
a form of problem-solving learning. See
coding.

deconstruction   Form of post-structuralist linguistic analysis in which the signified is examined for the 'play' of meanings in regard to the signifier's intentions.

decoy   An incorrect but feasible response to a multiple-choice question.

deculturation   A term used in anthropology and ethnography to describe the loss of a culture, often because of the influence of a more dominant one.

deduction   An argument that commences from general principles, and proceeds logically to specific conclusions. See *induction*.

deductive method   A teaching method that follows the techniques of deduction, that is by starting with the general and moving to the specific.

deductive thought   Thought processes which start from general principles and moves to specific conclusions.

deep processor   A learning style that refers to the process of acquiring knowledge at a deep level, that is seeking meaning and relevance rather than just the facts. See *surface processor*.

deep reading   Reading for meaning of the whole, rather than seeking to understand individual words and phrases.

defence mechanism   Mechanism to protect the ego against painful experiences.

deference   Term used when one person defers to another, relevant in some peer assessment studies where people of lower status accord higher achievement to those of higher status.

deferred gratification   Ability to postpone immediate benefits for long-term gain.

deficiency model   An approach to the analysis of learning needs in adult education which begins with the assumption that the potential learner comes below a norm in some aspect of learning, or has a deficiency which may be remedied through education, eg *adult basic education*. See also *need*.

define   To specify a precise meaning, sometimes confused with describe.

deformalize   Since education may be seen as both formal and informal and it is recognized that it is relatively easy for the latter to evolve into the former, the question has been asked whether the process can be reversed.

degree   An award conferred by a college or university as an official recognition of the successful completion of a programme of academic studies.

degree mill   Derogatory term used to imply that higher education is an institution geared to the production of graduates. See also *diploma mill*.

degrees of freedom   Statistical concept to indicate the number of changes that can be made to a group of figures whilst still satisfying the external requirements. This number relates to the number of unrestricted variables within the total score.

delegacy   A body responsible for administering an aspect of the work of a university or a college. In the United States, this might be referred to as a *committee*.

deliberate discussion   A technique to ensure that groups pay careful attention to statements made during discussions. It involves having a group deliberate, discuss, and decide what to say next in response to another statement made by a previous group. When the group decides on its best statement it is tape-recorded and played back to the previous group so that it might respond. This is continued until some agreement is reached. See *Delphi technique*.

delivery system   The process whereby learning materials are made available to the learner, eg it could be face-to-face teaching, or through distance education, etc. See *mode of delivery*.

Delphi technique   Developed in the early 1950s, this is a technique designed to obtain group opinions, especially expert opinion on future developments. The experts might be drawn from a number of different disciplines. There are usually three or four rounds of questionnaires to each respondent, with feedback from each round so that the respondents can reconsider their opinions in the light of the feedback. It has been used in adult education research.

demand   1. Economic term, frequently confused with the concept of *need*. In a market model of adult education, provision is made in response to market pressures rather than educational needs. Demand is the willingness to enrol in educational courses at the fee charged. 2. It refers to the requests made for courses to be provided in specific subject areas.

democracy   Literally, it means the power of the people, so that supreme power is ultimately vested in the people and exercised by their representatives. In fact, it is a political arrangement in government whereby the people's wishes may be heard.

democratic leadership   A form of leadership in which the leader takes into consideration the views and opinions of those who are being led. Important technique used in the use of group methods in adult education.

democratic methods   Teaching methods which encourage learners to participate in the planning of the teaching and learning process.

demography   The study of population statistics.

demonstration   A teaching method in which an expert shows precisely how she/he believes procedure should be carried out. In the United States, this method is frequently associated with the co-operative extension service.

demonstrator   One who demonstrates; often employed to give demonstrations in education, but not to teach.

Denman College   The college of the *National Federation of Women's Institutes* in the United Kingdom.

de-ontological ethics   The Kantian position that claims that the basis of moral good is universal laws that are always correct irrespective of consequences, eg one must always do one's duty. See *teleological ethics*.

dependency   1. The condition in which one needs to rely on another person or something else, eg drugs, in order to satisfy wants or needs. 2. A condition of being causally linked with another phenomenon.

dependent variable   A variable whose value is subject to change as the result of changes in the independent variable.

depository library   A library that houses the complete documentation of a government body.

deprivation   A state of being deprived – the basis for some adult educators for *second chance adult education*. See also *deficiency model*.

Des Moines Forum   Community-wide forum offered a new approach to adult education through the discussion of community issues in Des Moines, Iowa, USA, started in 1935. See *National Issues Forum*.

deschooling movement   A movement popularized by Ivan Illich in the 1960s, emphasizing that education might be best conducted in less formal settings than the school, since formal organizations are themselves barriers to participation for some people.

descriptive research   Research seeking to gather data that enable the researcher to provide an overall picture of the phenomenon being researched, as opposed to analytical research. Sometimes claimed to be atheoretical.

descriptor   A term used to characterize a subject area.

desk training   Work-based learning.

deskilling   The process of introducing new methods of production which requires lower levels of skill performance. This has occurred a great deal with the introduction of automation that has affected craft and vocational education. See also *reskilling*.

deterrence   Form of punishment aimed at preventing unacceptable behaviour reoccurring – used in conditioning.

deterrents to learning   See *barriers to participation*.

development   1. A general enhancement and growth in an individual's knowledge, skills and abilities through conscious and unconscious learning. 2. The process through which a country modernizes. See *development education*.

development education   Term that gained currency in the 1960s for education which is aimed at increasing awareness in the plight of people in the Third World; and helping people in the Third World to understand the reasons for underdevelopment and, subsequently, to develop their own societies. There is disagreement as to whether development should be regarded in economic terms, which some regard as modernization, as opposed to the development of the country without specific reference to Western capitalism.

development method   A teaching method whereby learners are taken through each stage at a time in ascending order of difficulty.

deviation   Statistical term used to show how an item's mean score differs from the mean of the total group or population. See *standard deviation*.

Dewey decimal classification system   A library system for classifying books, devised by Melvin Dewey towards the end of the nineteenth century. Subjects are classified into ten main areas and then further sub-divided by tenths as necessary.

Dewey, John (1859–1952)   American pragmatic philosopher and educationalist – influenced many of the early thinkers in adult education.

diagnosis of needs   In learner-centred adult education it is generally maintained that the needs of the learner should be determined by the teacher at the outset of the teaching and learning transaction. See also *needs assessment, program planning*.

diagnostic ability   The skill of a teacher in analysing the strengths and weaknesses of students. See *diagnostic teaching*.

diagnostic appraisal   The initial process of diagnosis which is essential in preparing teaching to respond to learning needs. See *diagnosis of needs, formative evaluation*.

diagnostic teaching   Teaching which is designed to reveal learner needs.

diagnostic test   Tests designed to reveal the nature of an educational need or a mental disorder.

Dial Our Learning Listening Library (DOLLY)   Twenty-four-hour library accessed by telephone in which people can have audio-tapes played to them over the telephone. Operated by Central Piedmont Community College in North Carolina, USA.

dialect   Form of speech spoken in regions of a country.

dialect studies   Study of regional dialects.

dialectic(s)   1. A general term for the study of logical argument. 2. A logical argument or theory by discussion and logical disputation. 3. The art of assessing the truth of a proposition.

dialectical materialism   The basis of Marxist thought, in which it is held that materialism is fundamental, so that socio-economic conditions determine human consciousness.

dialectical thought   The ability to think logically and critically in order to assess and evaluate propositions.

dialogical education   An approach to education in which the teacher enters genuine discussion with the learners in order to understand how they perceive reality, so that the teacher and learners can grow together in the teaching and learning process. This is a process in which the learner becomes teacher and the teacher has to learn to listen to the learners. It is a concept that has been introduced by Paulo Freire, although the method is not unique to him.

diary   1. Written records of events, made during field visits etc. 2. Increasingly used in teaching in order to help students reflect upon their learning process. See also *journal, learning log.*

didactic teaching   A form of teaching in which the teacher presents information, as the authority. The word didactic comes from the Greek word 'didace' meaning 'teaching' or 'doctrine'.

didactics   The art and science of teaching.

dietetics   Science of diet and food.

differential diagnosis   Based on the idea that people are different and that teachers have to respond to each according to their psychological disposition, so that teachers have to be authoritarian when students need it or permissive when students need that approach. Not widely used in adult education.

differential psychology   Branch of psychology concerned with differences.

differential sampling   A form of sampling in which the sample is deliberately biased in a specific direction.

difficulty index   Proportion of individuals in a group who respond correctly to a particular test.

difficulty score   Score that records the highest level of difficulty on a given variable.

diffusion   The process of extending awareness, eg the diffusion of knowledge.

diorama   A static display that combines a three-dimensional foreground with a two-dimensional background.

diploma   1. A formal document certifying successful completion of a recognized course of study. 2. Often the second stage in a three stage degree programme, eg certificate, diploma, degree.

diploma disease   A derogatory term used to indicate that more and more people were studying only to gain the diploma. See *qualification inflation.*

diploma mill   A derogatory term referring to the fact that some institutions are so orientated to getting students through their examinations that other aspects of their education are not emphasized. See also *degree mill.*

direct action   A form of community action that seeks to deal directly with the problem.

direct costs   Costs that increase directly with increases in the scale of operation. See also *fixed costs*.

direct method   Used in the teaching of foreign languages, when the teacher only addresses the students in the language that they are to learn. This approach is frequently used in teaching English as a second language. See *learning by immersion*.

directed observation   Students are guided to study precise elements of events or phenomena.

directed private study   See *directed study*.

directed reading   A course of reading prescribed for a student.

directed study   1. A form of study whereby a student undertakes a project or study having a supervisor who directs the undertaking, although is not actually a teacher. 2. A teaching method whereby the learner seeks to develop skills or acquire knowledge in direct relationship with a resource person who may or may not actually undertake teaching.

directed teaching   A form of teaching, which is teacher-directed; not always acceptable within the education of adults. See *didactic teaching*.

director   The individual in charge of a course, unit, department, etc.

disabled persons   People who because of ill health, physical incapacity, or mental illness, are unable to function effectively in one or more spheres of everyday life.

disadvantaged   Refers to persons who, by reason of physical or social handicap, have not had equality of opportunity to achieve their potential through educational means. See *educational disadvantage, social exclusion*.

discipline   1. The classification of knowledge into specific subjects, or disciplines, based upon the conceptual structure and the methods and approaches necessary to understand and research that branch of knowledge. 2. A field of study. 3. Scholars in some parts of the world tend not to regard adult education as a separate discipline, but to see it as a field of study and an area of practical knowledge that can be studied from the perspectives of some of the academic disciplines, whereas in parts of continental Europe adult education is regarded as a discipline. See *andragogy, field of study, subject*. 4. To control or punish someone. 5. To be rigorous in one's approach to study or to skill performance.

discourse   1. An academic treatise. 2. The language of academic statements. 3. An ideological statement reflecting the way that individuals view the world. 4. Foucault uses the term to refer to the meaning system that people have by which they define their world.

discourse analysis   1. A form of analysing and categorizing the structure of talk, often carried out in the teaching and learning situation. 2. Analysis of structures of cultural, social and ideological meaning. 3. In Foucault's work, it refers more specifically to the structures of power embedded in formal language. More frequently used in initial education research than in research in adult education.

discourse ethics   A theoretical formulation of ethics by Habermas in which he suggests that once an ethical position has been agreed by argumentation as being correct, then it should be put into operation if the act is to be morally good.

discovery learning   1. A facilitative approach to teaching and learning, often cognitive, in which the content to be learned is not given by the teacher but discovered. The teacher plans the activities and the students discover the outcomes. The term is more frequently used in initial education, although the practice is common in adult education. See *facilitative teaching*. 2. At the same time, this form of learning occurs in everyday life, without the aid of the teacher. See *self-directed learning*.

discovery methods   Teaching methods used in the practice of *discovery learning*.

discrepancy evaluation model   An evaluation model used in human resource development to evaluate the difference between what should occur and what actually occurs. See *needs assessment*.

discrete variable   A variable in which the magnitude differs in precise and distinct steps.

discretionary grant   There have been two forms of grant to assist students: mandatory and discretionary. This latter form is one in which educational/employing authorities may choose whether to use their funds to support students following specified courses but do not have to do so by law or company policy.

discrimination   The ability to identify differences between phenomena, arguments.

discrimination learning   A stage in Gagné's hierarchy of learning skills.

discussant   The respondent to a formal presentation, often to a speaker at a conference.

discussion group   A teaching method whereby the students are sub-divided into smaller groups and encouraged to explore their own understanding of a subject or a situation. See also *group process, group dynamics*.

discussion group leader   A participant in the group whose main role is to help the group work together towards the achievement of its goals. The group leader may be a task-oriented leader or an expressive leader.

discussion pack   A pack of material prepared for use by discussion groups. Often used in distance learning. Such packs contain information, suggestions as to how the group might use the material, and cover a number of different topics.

disengagement theory   In the study of the elderly, it refers to the point when some ageing people begin withdrawing from social life.

disjuncture   The mental gap between a person's biographical knowledge and skills and their construction of their current experience, it is the point from which individuals can learn so that they can close that gap and presume upon their next experience. See *disorientating dilemma*.

disordered behaviour   Behaviour of people who are not socially adjusted.

disorientating dilemma   When a person cannot take a situation for granted and is forced to learn from it. See *disjuncture*.

dispersion   A statistical concept that refers to the spread or concentration of values around a given point.

displaced person   The term usually refers to people who have lost their home or place in society. A great deal of adult education has been directed towards them.

displaced homemakers centers   First was established on the campus at Mills College, Oakland, California in May 1976, to assist women who are divorced, separated, or no longer eligible for aid for dependent children. They provide counselling, job training, assistance in finding employment, etc.

displacement   Psychological concept referring to the displacement of a real cause of anxiety by a substitute one.

disposition   A potential state of readiness to perform in a certain manner.

disputation   A form of teaching in which students are expected to defend their argument or thesis.

dissertation   A written thesis, often required for a higher degree. In the United States, the dissertation usually refers to the written thesis for a doctorate.

dissonance   A mental disturbance caused in an individual by two conflicting and irreconcilable positions.

distance education   Any form of education in which the teacher and the learner are separated in either time or space. It was called *home study*, and then *correspondence education*.

distance learning   A term that is being used to replace distance education, as the social phenomenon of institutionalized *education* is being seen as only one mode of delivering learning.

distance teaching universities Universities whose main teaching methods are by distance. The first university to engage in distance teaching, offering degree programmes, was the University of Queensland, Australia, in 1911. In a sense, the Open University in the United Kingdom acted as a catalyst in the formation of distance teaching universities in the 1970s and 1980s throughout the world.

distant student   One who is taught at a distance.

distinguished professor   A term used in the United States, and occasionally elsewhere, for a high-ranking professor.

distractor   An incorrect but apparently possible response to a multiple-choice question.

distribution   A statistical term to refer to the frequency of occurrence of a variable in a population.

distributive education programme   A programme of occupational instruction in areas of marketing and distributive trades designed to prepare individuals for work in these trades.

district agriculturalist   The Canadian term for *country extension agent*.

divergent thinking   The thought process characterized by lateral thought. See *convergent thinking*.

documentation centre   A resources centre that stores and makes available documents for academic study. See *clearinghouse*.

dogma   1. A belief or opinion regarded as authoritative, but not legitimized by the normal criteria of knowledge verification. 2. A religious belief supported by the church.

dogmatic   Characterized by making authoritarian assertions. Often the inability to consider another's viewpoint.

dominance   1. In psychology, it refers to the preferred use of one or the other side of the brain. 2. In sociology, it is the outcome of the successful exercise of power.

dominant culture   The culture of the most powerful group or social class in a society, so that their culture is regarded as the culture of the society. This is evidenced in the formation of the *classical curriculum*.

dominant gene   The gene that always expresses the hereditary characteristics.

dominant ideology   The ideology of the dominant group that appears to represent the group as a whole.

double loop learning   A concept introduced by C Argyris and D Schön. Learning through problematising the situation in which a problem occurs rather than just seeking to solve the problem. See *single loop learning*.

double session Two periods of teaching and learning on the same subject that run consecutively.

Down with Illiteracy The title of a journal started in Russia in 1920 at the start of its literacy campaign.

downsizing The process whereby employing organizations reduce the size of their workforce. See *manpower planning*.

downward mobility Social mobility in a downward direction, eg from middle class to working class. See *upward mobility*.

drawing rights A concept proposed by some exponents of recurrent education who argue that everybody should have the right to a specific amount of post-compulsory education and that they should be able to draw upon it throughout their lifetime. See *individual entitlement*.

dream analysis Method used in psychoanalysis to obtain information about the subconscious and the emotions of a person.

drill Repetitious training.

drive 1. In Freudian psychology it is often referred to as an instinct, an inner-force that when aroused leads to action. 2. It can refer to a motivation state, which is produced by deprivation of a needed substance or a noxious stimulus. There are similarities here with the way in which the term need is used in adult education.

drop-in centre A centre for educational guidance is often referred to as a drop-in centre.

drop-out 1. One who fails to complete schooling, or fails to complete any other course of study. 2. One who is unable to take their place in the social system. See *failure*.

drug addiction A state of physiological or psychological dependence upon drugs.

dualism A philosophical theory that sees everything in terms of two opposites, eg mental and material, good and evil, etc.

dualist A learning style which is similar to surface processing in that it seeks to acquire facts and, in addition, sees everything in terms of correctness or incorrectness, right or wrong.

dyad A pair.

dyslexia Any of the various reading disorders, which are a function of a neurological inability to interpret spatial relationships, or integrate auditory and visual information.

dysphasia Defective symbol behaviour. A dysphasic may have difficulty in dealing with speech, reading, writing, gestures, pictures, numbers etc. Some dysphasics become students in *adult basic education*.

Ee

each one teach one   The phrase which describes the Laubach literacy method. (Frank Laubach 1884–1970, US missionary and educator).

early adolescence   Stage of human development, usually from about 12 to 16 years of age.

early adulthood   Stage in human development, usually from about 22 to 40 years of age, when people learn to choose, create and maintain their own life structure.

early adult transition   A period of transition to adulthood, often from about 17 to 22 years of age.

earned degree   Term used in the United States to refer to a degree awarded by a college or university as a result of successful completion of an accepted programme of study

earth sciences   The sciences that deal with the study of the earth's crust.

ecology   The study of the relationships between living organisms and their environment. Also used with human ecology, which is the study of the relationship between groups of human beings and their environment. Hence, *social ecology*. See also *classroom ecology*.

economic history   Historical studies from economic perspective.

economics   The study of the production and consumption of services. There are few good economic studies of education for adults.

EdD   The doctorate in education, it is a practitioner degree as opposed to the *PhD* which is a research degree, although there has been a tendency in the USA for the type of award to depend upon the awarding university rather than upon the distinction drawn here.

EdM   The Masters degree in education; more commonly MEd.

educable   One who is capable of being educated. Usually used in relation to those who are mentally retarded.

educand   One being educated, a student.

education   1. UNESCO definition is 'the organized and sustained instruction designed to communicate a combination of knowledge, skills and understanding valuable for all the activities of life'. This definition relates to the concept of lifelong education which UNESCO espoused. The definition, however, is flawed because it omits attitudes and the idea of 'communication' may suggest that it is always teacher-directed. 2. The social organization of learning activities. 3. Any planned series of incidents, having a humanistic basis, directed towards the participants' learning and understanding. 4. The study of teaching and learning. 5. The subject matter concerned with the study of teaching and learning. 6. The organized way of learning from the experience of others. 7. Some scholars, such as Richard Peters, consider that it is too complex a term to define and would rather seek to give it a number of characteristics, but by so doing there is an implicit definition.

Education Act   Legislation about education.

Education and Aging   A free bi-monthly bulletin published by Hunter College, New York.

Education and Criminal Justice Programme   A programme sponsored by the *International Council for Adult Education* with five main thrusts: 1. To introduce, develop and gain acceptance for an educational approach in the field of criminal justice; 2. To persuade educational authorities to assume a role in this area; 3. To persuade national governments to adopt a policy recognizing the humanity of prisoners; 4. To persuade university departments to undertake research in this area of education; 5. To persuade governments to amend the United Nations Resolution on minimum roles for prisoners in accordance with the International Council resolution.

education by doing   An expression used to refer to a form of experiential education in which the learners are expected to undertake the designated task and learn from it. See *experiential learning*.

Education et Société   The journal of the Institut National de Formation et de Recherche en Education Permanente in France.

Education for All   An aim of UNESCO's middle-term plan, 1984–89, in which adult education, was specified as one of the concerns. Amongst the others were education and work; education and citizenship; education in leisure and culture; education in later life; women's education;

education and rural development. There was a UNESCO conference held in Thailand at the end of this plan.

Education for Kagisano   1977 Education Act in Botswana; 'kagisano' means social harmony. It is concerned with all aspects of education, including education for adults and social and cultural programmes.

education for liberation   An approach to education that regards learning as freeing the learners from the constraints of their socio-cultural environment. This approach often takes a political perspective (see especially the writings of Paulo Freire), and it is also an element in critical theory.

Education for Reconstruction Conference   Held in Quebec in 1943, when the Canadian Adult Education Association led the way in arguing for a better society after the end of the Second World War, in opposition to the then government of the country. It resulted in the formation of *Citizens' Forum*.

education for self-management   An educational programme in the former Yugoslavia to prepare people to undertake self-management in all aspects of daily living and working.

education from above   An approach to education that assumes that either, or both, the curriculum and the form of teaching are imposed upon the learners in an authoritative manner. See *banking education*.

education index   A library index of educational publications, authors and classifications.

education of adults   This wide term tends to be used to refer to all education of adults rather than the more restricted term, *adult education*. Hence its meaning relates to the conceptual understanding of both education and adult.

education of equals An egalitarian approach to education, espoused by many in adult education.

education officer In some professions there are professional officers responsible for overseeing and advising on the educational processes in professional preparation and continuing professional education. They are also called directors of education.

education para-professional A teaching aide, usually to assist in the classroom. Term is used in the United States.

education permanente The French term for lifelong education, also used to translate the term *adult education*.

Education Permanente 1. A journal published quarterly in France, since 1969, by the organization, Education Permanente about all forms of adult education. 2. A Swiss quarterly, published by the Swiss Federation of Adult Education about all aspects of *adult education.*

education-related military experiences Those military experiences that have subsequent significance in relation to a person's learning. Recognized in the United States as a form of prior learning, where a booklet has been published indicating the credit-worthiness of specific experiences.

education shop A number of experiments have been tried in the United Kingdom in attempting to reach more people with advice and guidance about their future learning needs, and among these have been some using small shops or having a counter in a large store.

education train A commuter train in which a compartment has been put aside for commuters to study. See *brain train.*

education week A week devoted to publicizing adult education. See *Adult Learners' Week.*

Education with Production Established in 1981, the twice yearly journal of the *Foundation for Education with Production.*

educational accountability Responsibility for achieving specific results in the *teaching* and *learning* process.

educational advisory services A service that offers help, support and guidance to adults seeking advice concerning their own learning needs. See *educational guidance service for adults.*

educational aid See *audio-visual aid.*

educational anthropology The utilization of anthropological techniques in the study of education and of anthropological theories in the theorization of education. As yet there has been no distinction drawn between educational anthropology and anthropology of education.

educational association 1. Any organization having an educational aim. 2. In Sweden 11 national educational associations are recognized by the government as organizers of *study circles.*

educational broadcasting In the United Kingdom, this term refers to broadcasts through radio and television with specific educational aims. In the United States the term refers to non-commercial broadcasting in which educational and community organizations have participated.

Educational Broadcasting Corporation An American public television station distributing educational programmes to non-commercial television stations throughout America.

educational brokering A system of advertising educational courses and prospective teachers to intending learners and vice versa.

educational brokering agency   American organizations which offer counselling and guidance to clients and they then direct them towards that educational activity that they consider best suits their clients' learning needs. They appear in different forms, some are independent and others are attached to larger educational organizations; the independent ones have teachers and courses registered with them.

educational centre   A place where educational courses are provided, often adult education centre.

Educational Centres Association
Formerly Educational Settlements Association. This United Kingdom association is an association of *adult education teachers, students* and administrators. It has a national secretary and holds a national conference.

educational clearinghouse   A documentation centre for educational material. See *Educational Resources Information Center*.

educational climate   The social and contextual qualities of an educational institution, as perceived by the participants. It is often considered to have four components culture, ecology, milieu and social system. Considerable research has been undertaken in this in school education, but less in *adult education*.

educational consortium   A grouping of two or more educational institutions combining either to offer teaching or other services, or to conduct joint research.

Educational Counselling and Credit Transfer Information Service (ECTIS)
This was a national computer-based service which endeavoured to record all courses which offered a qualification in the UK in further and higher education with the level of qualification so that a credit transfer service could be effected.

educational disadvantage   People who, because of their physical or social handicaps do not have an equal opportunity in the educational system. See educational *deficiency model*.

educational drama   The use of drama as a teaching technique – sometimes used when learners need to experience the emotions of performing a specific role. See *role play*.

Educational Exchange of Greater Boston   The first known *educational brokering agency*, established in 1923 in Boston, USA.

Educational Film Library Association
American society of associations involved in film and other visual aids in an educational context. It was one of the five associations involved in creating the *Joint Committee for the Study of Adult Education Policies, Principles and Practices* in 1946.

educational games   Methods employed to facilitate learning. See also *gaming*.

educational gerontology   The study of education for older adults. See also *gerontology, gerontology education*.

Educational Gerontology   The name of an academic journal published in the United States on the study of the education of older adults.

educational guidance   A service of advice and counselling about educational and learning matters provided to adults. However, such advice is not always provided within a formal service, HRD specialists, teachers of adults, etc might all provide educational guidance to staff and students at different times.

educational guidance service for adults
A variety of services are provided throughout the United Kingdom offering educational advice and guidance to adults, some through paid workers and others

through volunteers. See *National Association of Educational Guidance Services for Adults.*

educational ideology   The term 'ideology' has so many different connotations that it is difficult to define the concept precisely. However, it broadly refers to a system of beliefs that gives a general direction to the educational policies and practices of educators and those who make policy for education. It works at a presumptive rather than articulative level.

educational institution   A place where education takes place. See *adult education institution.*

educational laboratory   A research laboratory in which empirical research into education can occur, such as a research classroom which has one-way mirrors so that classes can be observed without the researchers interfering with the actual dynamics of the *teaching* and *learning* process.

educational management   The theory and practice of managing the educational services. This area of educational practice is becoming increasingly significant in contemporary society and more preparation for educational managers is being offered.

educational need   1. Term frequently used synonymously with learning need, but more correctly it refers to either the necessity for additional education or to a deficiency which can be rectified by education. 2. The term is also used in connection with overall national educational requirements. See also *need.*

educational objective   The short-term desired learning outcomes of the teaching and learning process. See *objective, behavioural objective, expressive objectives.*

educational planning   1. A management exercise during which plans are drawn up for future educational provision. 2. Planning for a course or teaching session. See also *curriculum planning, program planning.*

educational policy   Strategies about the way that educational provision should be implemented, or the functions that it should serve. It can be formulated at either national or local level.

educational process   A planned and institutionalized process of learning, often under the guidance of a teacher.

educational psychologist   1. A professional psychologist who works with maladjusted or educationally disadvantaged persons, usually children, to diagnose and provide educational guidance. 2. An expert in the psychology of education.

educational psychology   1. The study of the psychological processes that occur within education. 2. The study of behaviour within an educational setting. 3. Psychological practice in an educational setting. *Adult education* research has been dominated by psychological studies, especially in the field of *adult development*, but also in the field of *learning theory* where some psychologists have wrongly claimed learning it exclusively as a field of psychological study.

educational research   Research into any aspect of the theory and practice of education.

Educational Resources Information Center (ERIC)   An information system which has been in operation since 1966, sponsored by the Office of Educational Research and Improvement, US Department of Education. It provides users with access to English language literature dealing with education. There is a central unit in Washington and 16 *clearinghouses* situated throughout America, each focusing on a different aspect of education. The one for *adult* and *vocational education* is located at Ohio State University.

educational science   In parts of Europe, education is regarded as an academic discipline and sometimes referred to as educational science.

educational settlements   These were university missions to working-class areas of England, mostly London, in the Victorian period, which were viewed as *university extension*. Young men and women went to live and work in these areas. Later there were also some non-residential settlements formed. See *university settlement movement*.

Educational Settlements Association
Association of educational settlements. Later it became the *Educational Centres Association*, founded to promote *adult education*.

educational sociology   An aspect of the study of education using sociological theory to elucidate the educational processes.

educational technology   Originally this referred to audio-visual aids and similar hardware but more recently it has come to mean the software as well. Therefore it now also relates to the design and implementation of systems of teaching and learning and the field of study associated with it.

educational telephone network   A telephone-based instructional system in which the telephone is the means of communication between tutors and students, and students and students. The system has been used in the State of Wisconsin in group *continuing education*.

educational television   The transmission of teaching material by television. For instance, there are schools programmes and in the United Kingdom there is now the Learning Zone – adult education programmes broadcast by BBC each night.

Educational Testing Service   An American research and testing organization that provides established tests and assessment services to educational institutions.

educational theory   The body of accepted knowledge about education.

educational thought   See *philosophy of education*.

educational trust   A charitable foundation established to support educational activities.

educational voucher   A document that guarantees that the fee, or part, of the fee, for an educational course will be paid for by some other person or organization. In some schemes, employers will offer vouchers as a contribution towards their employees' non vocational education. See also *individual learning account*.

Educational Writers Association
American association founded in 1947 for everybody who writes about education.

Educazione delgi Adulti Nell'Area Mediterranea   Mediterranean Association of Adult Education – formed in October 1981.

'edutainment'   Literally, the combination of education and entertainment – the process of making learning fun through providing education through leisure time means, such as educational travel.

Effect, Law of   This states that satisfaction serves as a re-inforcer of the *Stimulus-Response* – it was proposed by Edward Thorndike.

effective student hour   A method of funding introduced into grant-aided adult education in the United Kingdom in the 1980s. This measures actual hours of course contact rather than enrolment numbers. It is an approach to cost-effective adult education.

egalitarianism   A philosophy that maintains the equality of people. Important humanistic philosophy underlying many theories in adult education. See *equalitarianism*.

ego   1. From the Latin for 'I' or 'self'.
2. Part of Freud's three elements of the person, the reality principle which mediates

between the drives of the id and the constraints of the *superego*.

ego consciousness   A form of self-awareness.

ego development   The emerging awareness of the personhood of the individual. See also *self development*.

ego ideal   Slightly different from the *superego* in as much as it refers to the idea of what a person would like to be.

ego integrity   Refers to Erikson's final stages of human development, an early study of development and important in educational gerontology. It is the state of acceptance of old age and death.

ego needs   In occupational psychology, this term relates to the needs of the person in the performance of a job and, where fulfilled, will result in job satisfaction. See *need*.

ego trip   Any pattern of behaviour engaged in by a person for the purpose of boosting his/her sense of self-importance. Teaching can often be perceived in this way.

egocentric   Preoccupation with the self, being self-centred.

egoism   Being motivated by self-interest.

eidetic   1. Images in the mind that are imagined and unreal but which are so vivid that they are mistaken for reality. 2. The vivid recall of visual imagery.

elaborated code   The speech form that Basil Bernstein discovered which is used mostly by the middle classes. His work was undertaken with children although his findings relate to adult speech also. It is the type of speech which is abstract and complex, and uses long sentences. Those who employ elaborated speech codes are also able to understand and use *restricted codes*, although the reverse is not true.

eldergogy   A term that has been used to imply the need for a systematic approach to teaching older people. See *educational gerontology*.

Elderhostel   A residential educational provision for elder citizens in the United States to study on university campuses in vacation time. It began in 1975 and was pioneered in New Hampshire; it has more recently become an international network. Based on the belief that retirement should not mean withdrawal from the world, but should provide an opportunity to discover new avenues of involvement and sources of satisfaction through travel and learning.

Elderhostel Institute Network   In 1988, the network of *Institutes for Learning in Retirement* merged with Elderhostel and formed a voluntary association. Since then Elderhostel have sponsored the movement, which has continued to expand. In addition to providing educational opportunities for elders, the institutes provide volunteer services for their sponsoring organizations, usually universities, and to the community at large.

Elderstudy   A precursor to the formation of the *University of the Third Age* in the United Kingdom. Age Concern established a working group in 1979 to investigate the possibility of an Elderhostel type of provision.

elective   An optional module, programme of study, chosen by the learner during a course of study.

electronic university   A private educational institution which conducts its *teaching* and *learning* by electronic means. Offers both credit and non-credit courses.

elementary education   The first school for young children.

elite   The select few, used in Marxist theory to refer to those who hold power.

elitism   1. A theory that holds that the exercise of power by the few is essential to the maintenance of group cohesion. 2. A theory that holds that the most able will always rise in the ranks of the hierarchy of a social group.

Elsinore Conference   The first UNESCO world conference on adult education, held in Elsinore in Denmark in June 1949.

e-mail   Electronically transmitted messages using the Internet.

emancipatory education   It refers to an educational process which results in learners becoming critically aware of the social forces that shape their lives, makes them what they are and locates them in the position that they occupy in the social structure. The idea is present in the writings of Freire and Habermas, among others. However, it was also prevalent in adult education as early as Robert Owen (1771–1858). See *liberation education*.

emancipatory literacy   Adult literacy programmes founded upon a revolutionary ideology which claims that oppressed people can participate in the building and transformation of their own society in a democratic manner. See *Freire*.

embedded knowledge   Knowledge that cannot move easily across organizational boundaries.

embourgeoisement   The theory that as the working classes become affluent they assume middle-class lifestyles and values.

emotion   The emotional domain, or affective domain, is the one of feelings. It is essentially the feeling predispositions a person has towards another person or phenomenon. It is rarely discussed in traditional educational theory but it is one upon which a lot of *professional education* focuses, especially through *small group teaching*. See *affective domain, encounter group*.

emotional intelligence   In recent years there has been movement away from viewing intelligence as something that lies in the cognitive domain, so that it is now viewed as more personal. Emotional intelligence is sometimes regarded as having five domains: knowing one's own emotions; managing emotions; motivation; sensitivity to other's emotions; handling relationships.

emotive imagery   Imagery that provokes emotional response.

emotive learning   Learning through the emotions.

emotivism   The ethical theory stemming from linguistic theory, in which it is argued that the word 'good' has no empirical meaning and so all that it does is to communicate positive emotive sentiments.

empathy   A state of identification with the attitudes and feelings of other people.

empirical   Derived from experience rather than *a priori* premises.

empiricism   The theory that all knowledge of facts is based upon experience.

empowerment   A concept used in different ways, but generally regarded as an outcome of the educational process. 1. Radical adult educators use the term in relation to providing a social class, eg the working classes, with the awareness and knowledge to act in and upon the social structures so that people can restructure society in a more egalitarian manner. 2. More conservative and progressive adult educators use the term to refer to equipping and raising the confidence of individuals so that they can be more successful in the world.

enabling objective   A statement of what a learner should be able to perform in order to achieve a desired training objective.

encoding   The process of putting meanings into words.

encounter group   A small group engaged in intensive personal interaction. Frequently used in some aspects of affective education, emphasizing the emotions and the present rather than the cognitive and the intellectual. See also *T-group*.

endorsement   Additional qualification(s) added to an initial one.

endowment   A cash grant made to an institution for some specific purpose, eg an endowed chair means that a grant has been provided to establish a professorship in a specific subject and the professorship will usually be known by the name of the person who makes the endowment.

engineering   This is both an academic subject and incorporates a wide variety of occupations; it was one of the first occupations to create its own international council for continuing education.

English as a foreign language (EFL) EFL is organized for those non-native English-speakers who wish to come as live in an English-speaking country, or for those who have to use English because of the nature of their work.

English as a second language (ESL) This began in the mid-1960s in the United Kingdom due to the increase in immigration, although other countries, such as the United States, started it earlier. ESL is the teaching of English to or the study of English by persons whose native language is not English. This is regarded as an element in *adult basic education*. As there is more mobility in the world, an increasing number of countries are receiving immigrants and are having to introduce *second language teaching*.

English Heritage Education Service Provides educational information about a range of historic sites that it administers.

English Language Proficiency Survey Commissioned in the United States, by the Department of Education, and conducted by the Bureau of Census in the Fall of 1982. Written tests were conducted of 3,400 individuals over 20 years of age in private homes and it was estimated as a result that about 13 per cent of the population were illiterate.

enquiry-based learning   See *discovery learning, inquiry-based learning*.

enrichment programme   A course or mixed programme designed to compensate those who have been culturally or socially deprived.

enrol   The act of registering, or joining, an educational class.

enrolment week   Many educational institutions, especially *adult education* institutions have one week at the start of the academic year when they try to enrol the majority of their students for the new classes.

Ente Nazionale Acli Istruzione Professionale (ENAIP)   Italian *adult education* in the United Kingdom.

entitlement   The belief that people are entitled to a fixed number of years of education, after their compulsory schooling. See *recurrent education*.

entry requirements   The level of academic competency expected before one can be considered as a suitable candidate for another course of study.

environmental education   Education directed towards making people more aware of the need to protect the environment.

episodic memory   Memory which is stored within the context of the situation in which it was acquired, eg something that was learned at a specific event. See also *semantic memory*.

epistemology   The theory of *knowledge*; a branch of philosophy.

Epsilon Sigma Phi Fraternity   A professional association in the United States for extension agents of more ten or more years of experience.

equal opportunities   In recent years a number of organizations have recognized the need to introduce equal opportunities, not only between sexes and races but also between age groups, health groups, etc. A number of codes of good practice about equal opportunities have now been accepted in adult education.

equalitarianism   A movement in England in the nineteenth century seeking to make higher education less exclusive. See *egalitarianism*.

eradication of ignorance campaign Campaign conducted in Israel in the 1960s, using female soldiers as one-to-one teachers, to help immigrants from Moslem countries to improve their educational attainments. The campaign lasted several years.

ergonomics   The study of a person's physical and mental relationship with the environment, especially at work and with the use of occupational equipment. See also *human engineering*.

ERIC   See *Educational Resources Information Center*. There are a number of clearinghouses for this centralized agency that collects and distributes information and materials about relevant forms of education. See *clearinghouse*.

Erikson, E   Psychologist concerned about the development of the person. His work has been important in understanding *adult development*.

escapism   The desire to evade the present reality and escape, perhaps, into an imaginary world.

Esperanto   An artificial language created to try to overcome the problems of international communication. Its components come from several different European languages.

espoused theory   A concept used by Argyris and Schön to refer to a theory of action to which a respondent gives allegiance and which, upon request, they communicate to others. This may differ from the theory of action that is detected in their actions, to which they refer as *theory in use*.

essay   An extended form of prose composition.

essentialism   1. A philosophical position emanating from Plato which suggests that behind all physical objects is a perfect abstraction. 2. A philosophical position espoused by Aristotle, that all phenomena have certain essences without which they could not exist. Hence in education, there are certain activities, *teaching* and *learning* for instance, that form the very nature of education.

ethics   1. The study of moral philosophy. 2. A code of personal behaviour. 3. A statement of professional standards, usually referred to as a code of ethics.

ethnic studies   The study of distinct cultural and racial groups.

ethnocentrism   The tendency to assess social behaviour and values against those of one's own group. This often results in certain forms of prejudice occurring in people who are ethnocentric.

ethnography   The branch of anthropology that deals with the description and comprehension of individual human societies. Its methods of research involve participant observation and interviewing. These methods have been employed in *qualitative research* into *educational institutions* and *educational climates*.

ethnology The comparative study of human cultures.

ethnomethodology The sociological study of the way in which ordinary people understand and produce co-ordinated social interaction. As a research technique, it has been more frequently used in the study of children's education than it has been in *adult education*.

ethology The study of animals in their normal environment.

ethos Customs, sentiments and rituals of a group. See *educational climate, classroom climate*.

eugenics The study of generic inheritance.

Europe Institute Situated in Munsbach Castle in Luxembourg, this is a folk high school, similar to the International People's College in Denmark, with which it co-operates.

European Association for Research into Learning and Instruction (EARLI) An association of educators, originally school based and with a psychological orientation, although it has an interest group in *adult education*. It holds an annual conference and has its own newsletter.

European Association of Education for Adults (EAEA) Formed from the *European Bureau of Adult Education* in the early 1990s. It has regional offices in Barcelona and Helsinki.

European Association of Management Training Centres Established in 1959 with a view to improving management education.

European Baccalaureate (EB) Awarded by schools which have been established in various states in the European Union. It is regarded as being similar to other school-leaving examinations and provides entry to higher education.

European Bureau of Adult Education A non-governmental organization of national adult education associations of Europe, established in 1953, providing a network of co-operation and exchange across Europe. It has been superseded by the *European Association of Education for Adults*.

European Centre for Catholic Adult Education A Catholic network for adult education, having its offices in the Netherlands.

European Centre for Education (Centro Europeo Dell'Educazione CEDE) Established in Italian law in 1974, but not fully staffed until 1982 to collect European educational documentation and it has developed an extensive array of services in areas of *adult education* since then.

European Centre for Leisure and Education Established in 1968. It was very active in the 1970s producing series of books about adult education in various member countries, but ceased to be active later, especially after the break-up of Czechoslovakia.

European Centre for the Development of Vocational Training (CEDEFOP) Established in 1975 by a decision of the Council of European Communities as an autonomous organization. It works closely with the European Union developing and promoting *vocational training* and *continuing education* at European level.

European Community Action Programme A programme dealing with the transition of young people from school education to work and adult life.

European Folk High School Established in 1976, it was the first *adult education* institution that devoted itself entirely to European issues. It is situated in DK-4780 Stege, Mon, Denmark.

European Materials for the Training of Adult Educators (EURAD) The Council of Europe established this project in 1980 as a *training/retraining* project for part-time adult educators.

European Society for Research in the Education of Adults (ESREA) Established in the early 1990s as an association of *adult education* specialists to promote a network of scholars. It has established networks of specialists in different areas, each holding its own conference or seminar and also there are broader academic conferences.

European Symposium on Voluntary Associations Formed in 1984 from Dutch-Hungarian co-operation. A network for voluntary associations involved in the education of adults in civil society.

European Universities Continuing Education Network Established in 1991 in order to provide a network of universities in order to exchange good practice and innovation in continuing education in universities throughout Europe.

evaluation The process of assessing the merit of an intervention, or a lesson, course, or curriculum. There are basically three forms of evaluation: summative, formative and impact. The first two are concerned with evaluating all the aspects of the course itself while the third is concerned with evaluating the impact of the course on the work/work place of the learners.

Evangelische Arbeitsgemeinschaft für Erwachsenenbildung in Europa The Protestant association for adult education in Europe. It is a European association that seeks to promote adult religious education, to exchange experience and ideas, to promote joint research projects and to co-operate throughout Europe.

evangelization Christian churches employ this term to refer to preaching to convert people to their way of thinking. It is a form of instruction which seeks to achieve a predetermined end-product.

evening class The term often used in the United Kingdom to refer to *adult education* because many of the classes were held in the evenings. However, adult education classes are now held throughout the day in most adult education institutions. The first evening classes appear to have started in the 1750s in Newcastle, and many of the early ones were in mathematics and the sciences for craftsmen.

evening college These are colleges in the United States, attached to universities, which offer part-time adult students the opportunity to read for degrees.

evening high school (Abendgymnasium) Established in Germany after the First World War, it offers a traditional secondary school-type curriculum on a part-time evening basis to people in full-time employment, and has allowed many working-class people to gain access to higher education by successfully gaining the *Abitur*. This is known as the second route (*Zweiter Bildungsweg*) and it consists of two and a half years of evening study, some 20 hours a week, followed by one and a half years study full-time, in order to complete the normal four-year Abitur. During the part-time period fees are minimal and the students work but during the full-time period students are supported by the state.

evening institute A place where part-time *adult education* courses are offered; they used only to provide evening classes.

evening school 1. A term for adult education. 2. Schools for working people, held in the evening after the end of the working day. There were very early examples of this, eg the Danish Education Act of 1814 imposed a responsibility upon the government to arrange evening education for people who had left school and there were private evening folk schools in Philadelphia as early as 1766. 3. **Abendschule**. German evening school sponsored by either industry or local government to provide general and vocational education. See also *night school*.

Everyman's University   The Israeli equivalent of the British Open University, established in 1974 and admitted students from 1976. It is located in Tel-Aviv.

evidence-based practice   1. Professional practice based upon the results of previous research. 2. Professional practice based upon known outcomes.

examination   A formalized method of assessment that occurs at fixed points in some courses.

exclusion   The term used to refer to the process by which people, or categories of people, are prevented from being part of the mainstream. See *social exclusion*.

Exeter Papers   The papers of the first international conference on *comparative adult education* held at Exeter, New Hampshire, USA, in June 1966.

exhibit   An item or a collection of items displayed to assist in understanding the situation or event being described or depicted.

exhibitionist   A person whose actions are frequently designed in order to display their attributes.

existentialism   A philosophical theory, first formulated by Kierkegaard, in which being is of fundamental importance. Each person is aware of their own self and able to act in the world on the basis of experience and the situation. It assumes a number of different forms and it is a theory espoused by a number of educational theorists, such as Carl Rogers, and has consequently been very influential in adult education theory. In more recent times it has gained wider prominence in educational theory.

experience   1. The process of creating an understanding or perception of a situation, which often appears to be a direct participation in an event. 2. The accumulation of previous experiences, both conscious and unconscious, and stored in the mind. In this sense it is the individual biography, which Malcolm Knowles refers to as a rich resource for learning. This is only true if the previous experiences have not inhibited future learning potential.

experiential education   Education that uses the whole of the learners' experiences, including the affective domain. See also *education by doing*.

experiential learning   Learning that begins with experience and transforms it into knowledge, skill, attitude, emotions, values, beliefs, senses.

experiential learning cycle   This is a diagrammatic representation of the learning process through a cyclical diagram – Kolb's cycle is the most well known and this moves from experience to reflection to generalization to experimentation – he has always claimed that it is possible to start elsewhere in the cycle. Some scholars regard this as a useful but rather over-simple representation of the actual processes.

experiment   A research process in which the researcher sets up a situation and controls the variables so that specific hypotheses may be tested.

experimental research   An approach to research which, through the control of variables, seeks to predict future interrelations between them. This approach tends to be quantitative and adopts a *positivist* perspective.

Experimental World Literacy Programme (EWLP)   Launched in 1967 as a result of the UNESCO international conference in Montreal in 1960, as an experimental programme funded by UNESCO, seeking to eradicate *illiteracy*. The programme was terminated in 1973.

expert   A person whose knowledge or skills is acknowledged by their peers to be outstanding.

expert mission   A mission to a developing country composed of internationally regarded experts.

expert witness   This has a number of non-educational meanings, but in education expert witnesses are sometimes used in specific teaching methods, such as a panel or as visiting speakers.

exposition   A systematic statement, often written, about a certain subject.

expositor   One who expounds. See *expository teaching*.

expository teaching   Teaching that is orientated to explanation.

expressed need   The concept of *need* is common but conceptually contentious in adult education. However, some scholars suggest that expressed needs are those which people experience and make known. Underlying all needs type theories in education lies the idea that education is some form of welfare provision, but this belief has been severely strained with the development of a market orientation in education. See also *felt needs*.

expressive arts   Subjects such as music, art, dance, and drama through which people can express their emotions through performance and/or experience emotional satisfaction, and so on.

expressive leader   A leading figure in a group simply because they endeavour to ensure that every member of the group is accommodated. One whose purpose is to ensure that the group's dynamics function smoothly. Often second in command. See *task-orientated leader*.

expressive objectives   These are process objectives rather than product ones, such as behavioural objectives. They do not, therefore, focus upon the end-product of learning but upon the learning opportunities. Many adult educators feel that expressive objectives are much more appropriate for the education of fellow adults. See also *educational objectives*.

expressive writing   Writing that is creative and expresses the emotions of the writers.

extended education   Education that is post-compulsory. See also *continuing education*, *further education*.

extension   This is university outreach to the community. In India it is regarded as the third dimension, being of equal importance to teaching and research. See *field outreach*.

extension agent   An organizer of extension education, especially in relation to the work of agricultural extension in the land grant colleges in the USA. See *county extension agent*.

extension college   During the later part of the nineteenth century a number of extension colleges were founded in Britain, as a result of the *university extension* education of Oxford and Cambridge. These later enrolled full-time students and eventually became the civic universities in the United Kingdom.

extension education   1. Forms of education that extend beyond the boundaries of the educational activity of a normal educational provider, eg *university extension*. 2. Forms of education provided by the *Co-operative Extension Service* in the United States.

extension education centre   A centre established by an American *land grant college* to provide extension education.

extension studies   Education conducted by a college or university extramurally in *adult education*.

external course   A course of study that is organized as an *extra-mural course*.

external degree   The degree awarded to external students who have successfully completed the requirements of that institution. The external degree of the University of London was, for many years, one of the only available ones to adults in the United Kingdom and elsewhere in the world.

external examination   An examination set by an educational institution for students other than its own. This was one of the early ways in which adults were able to gain degrees through the London University external examination system.

external examiner   Colleges and universities appoint one or more external examiners to a course to ensure that its standard is comparable to that of similar courses elsewhere. It is a part of the system of self-regulation of these colleges and universities.

external student   1. Traditionally a mature student who sits an examination, eg University of London degree, although the designated course has not been followed within the constituent colleges of the institution. 2. In the General Certificate of Secondary Education examination, an external student is one who has followed the syllabus prescribed for external students, which does not meet the national criteria, and who has less than 15 hours of timetable study time per week in term time.

external study   Studies organized by an educational institution for external students.

external validity   The consistency of a research instrument with other research on the same phenomena. It is now being argued that this is no longer a valid element of

research into unique and transitory phenomena.

extra-curricular activities   Activities organized by an educational institution that occur outside the confines of its normal curriculum.

extra-mural course   An adult education course offered by an *extra-mural department* of a university.

extra-mural department (EMD)   Some universities have traditionally had departments of adult education which have offered university-type courses to the general public within a specified locality 'beyond the walls of the university'. More generally, an EMD is an educational department offering courses of study which are outside the educational organization's usual curriculum to the general public. See also *Responsible Body*.

extraneous variable   Additional variable in quantitative research that may influence the relationship between the dependent and independent variable.

extroversion   A personality theory in which people direct their attention outwards, away from themselves, and gain satisfaction and pleasure from social interaction and physical fulfilment. See *introversion*.

extrovert   One who has the characteristics of *extroversion*.

eye contact   Making contact visually; necessary for small group work in teaching adults.

Eysenck Personality Inventory   A psychological test, devised by Eysenck, seeking to determine certain personality characteristics, such as *extroversion*, *introversion*, neuroticism and psychoticism.

Ff

Fabian Society   Founded in 1884 in the United Kingdom, this left-wing society had a considerable influence on academic thought in the United Kingdom and the United States through the publication of pamphlets and books.

face-to-face groups   Groups in which there is a direct social relationship.

facilitative teaching   An experiential teaching method whereby the teacher provides experiences that result in learning. The teacher is, in this role, a facilitator rather than a provider of information and the students learn as a result of either problem-solving or reflecting upon their experiences. See also *discovery learning*.

facilitator   A teacher who assists in the learning process without being the provider of information or the demonstrator of skills; one who creates the opportunity to learn.

facility   1. The equipment that exists within an organization or a location that facilitates teaching and learning. 2. In the United States, this refers to the building rather than the equipment.

factor   A hypothetical construct that is assumed to influence some outcome or phenomenon under investigation.

factor analysis   Statistical technique through which a number of significant variables are isolated and correlated with each other.

factory college   Work-based colleges in China; students attend these colleges full-time whilst they are still paid their factory wage. See *work-based learning, corporate university*.

faculty   1. In universities in the United Kingdom and elsewhere in Europe, faculty refers to those groupings of academic departments with similar knowledge bases that form a unit of the university administrative structure, eg the social science faculty. 2. In the United States, faculty refers to members of the academic staff who are employed by the university or other educational institution.

faculty advisor or counsellor   Member of the faculty in a US college or university who is the student counsellor.

faculty exchange programme   A programme in which two or more colleges or universities arrange for the exchange and interchange of academic staff.

faculty load   The teaching load of an academic member of staff, ie the number of teaching hours per week or the number of students supervised, etc.

faculty rank   The occupational status of a member of faculty in an American college or university, that is assistant, associate and full professor.

fading   Gradual removal of supporting cues and prompts in order to assist the learning process.

failure   1. The inability to complete an assignment, course, or examination to the required standard. 2. Term occasionally used to refer to the fact that a learner has not performed at the level anticipated.

failure rate   The proportion of students failing an examination or course.

Fall semester   The semester starting in late summer or early autumn in an American college or university, the first semester in the academic year.

false consciousness   The claim that some people, often from working-class backgrounds, do not know what is in their best *interest* because they have been socialized into accepting the hegemonic, but in-built biases of culture which favour the social elite.

family improvement education   A form of education practised in developing countries designed to improve the quality of family life, eg health education, home care, nutrition, child care.

family life education   US form of education designed to enrich family life or to prepare young adults for adult family life; *extension education* has focused upon this area for a great deal of its work.

family literacy   A wide variety of educational programmes are offered that promote the involvement of parents and children together in literacy enhancing practices.

farm agent   An *extension agent*.

farm institute   An agricultural college.

Farm Radio Forum   Listening groups using radio broadcasts for adult education. Occurred in Canada in the 1930s. See *National Farm Radio Forum*.

Farmers' College on Wheels   See *Farmers' Co-operative Demonstration*.

Farmers' Co-operative Demonstration
An extension education enterprise in which demonstration wagons were taken out to farms throughout the southern part of the United States in order to teach the farmers about seed selection and other aspects of farming. Started by Booker T Washington at the Tuskegee Institute. See also *moveable school*.

Farmers' Institute   An early venture in agricultural education in America, commenced in Connecticut in 1860.

faults analysis   The process of analysing the faults that occur in a process or procedure and specifying the symptoms, causes and remedies. See *evaluation*.

Faure Report   The UNESCO International Commission on the Development of Education produced this report in 1972, entitled Learning to Be.

feasibility study   An initial study in order to examine the practicality of a project.

Federal Extension Service   See *Co-operative Extension Service*.

fee   The cost to a student, or the student's sponsoring organization, of a course of study. ·

Feed the Minds Campaign   A campaign conducted by the Christian Churches to provide inexpensive Christian literature to newly literate people; it was started in the 1960s as part of the world-wide literacy drive.

feedback   Communication about an experience.

feeder course   A course that leads into another programme of study. See *bridging course*.

fellow   Member of a research or teaching staff of a college or university.

fellowship   Position held by a fellow. Often these are endowed posts but others are funded through grant aid for specific projects and are of limited duration.

felt need   A subjective experience of *need*, which may be related to *wants*, but at concept used frequently within adult education literature. The distinction between want and need is blurred and certainly impossible to demarcate empirically. As education has become more market orientated this has also been related to demands. See also *expressed needs*.

feltboard   A board covered with felt upon which visual displays can be stuck; the advantage of this type of display is that the display objects are moveable.

Fern Universität   The German Open University, although it does not have an entirely open admissions policy. See *guest student*.

field   1. An area of study or an academic discipline. 2. An area of professional practice. 3. Place, physical location, where the actual event(s) takes place.

field agent   1. One who works in the field, is associated with the college or university, and is involved in teaching, organizing, or researching in the field. 2. A *co-operative extension* agent.

field centre   A place where some activity or study occurs, situated away from the main site of the educational establishment.

field course   An educational programme conducted in the place where the phenomenon being studied occurs.

field dependency   A *cognitive style* in which the learner is seen as being affected by the whole arena in which the learning occurs rather than just the phenomenon being learned. It is a global form of learning. Field dependents are usually people who are gregarious, affectionate, tactful and considerate. See also *field independency*.

field experience   1. Experience gained by having undertaken a course of study or research in the place where the phenomenon/activity actually occurs. 2. Experience gained from having worked in a situation being studied.

field independency   A cognitive style in which the learner concentrates upon the phenomenon to be learned rather than the whole field; an analytical approach to learning. Field independents are socially independent and have a highly developed sense of their own self-identity. See also *field dependency*.

field notes   Records kept during *field work*.

field of study   An area of scholarship based either upon a field of practice or on a sub-division of knowledge.

field officer   A person appointed to work in the field, away from the main administrative centre.

field outreach   A term used in Indian adult education to refer to the extension work of a university into the community, where the university departments are expected to work in a specific area or community.

field research   An approach to research which is open-ended and qualitative, which does not have single method of data collection but seeks to incorporate a number as the researcher endeavours to study a normal situation rather than in an experimental situation.

field trials   The testing of products before they are marketed – including learning materials.

field trip   An educational visit to learn about a phenomenon or an object away from the educational organization.

field visit   See *field trip*.

field work   Usually refers to research undertaken as part of a research project. See also *field research*.

field work teacher   1. A teacher who trains new recruits to work in the practical situation. 2. In health visiting, in the United Kingdom, the field work teacher trains new recruits during their practical placements during initial preparation.

field worker   One who is employed to work in the place in which the activity under study occurs.

film forum   The use of a film, followed by discussion groups, in order to create awareness of issues.

film society   A local society established both to view and to discuss films.

final examination   The last examination in a course, before the award of the qualification to successful candidates.

Final Report of the Adult Education Committee of the Ministry of Reconstruction, 1919   The 1919 report on adult education published by the British government just after the First World War. See *1919 Report*.

Fircroft College   Established in 1909 having Quaker origins, the second oldest adult education college in England. It is now a residential college in Birmingham for both men and women.

Firmstart   Training provided over a 16-week period for people who have successfully started their own business – initiated by the *Manpower Services Commission* in the 1980s in the United Kingdom.

first degree   A bachelors degree – it is the level of the degree that is significant here. See *higher degree*.

fishbowl   A teaching and learning technique in which group discussion is employed in two ways. Initially a small group of participants sits in a circle, within the larger circles of the remainder of the class. The first group starts to discuss the topic under consideration while the larger group listens – but any member of the larger group can replace any member of the smaller group and join in the discussion, with the replaced person sitting in the outside circle. At the end of the session, the whole class can discuss both the process and the content of the discussion.

fixation   1. The process whereby an attitude or a cognition becomes inflexible. 2. In Freudian theory, the process whereby one becomes attached to a stage of development, or to a person or object, so that it inhibits further development.

fixed costs   The expenses that have to be met by an educational institution independently of the number of students who enrol or who pay fees.

fixed interval   A schedule of reinforcement.

flashcard   Card used for teaching reading, especially word recognition. More frequently used in children's education but sometimes used in literacy teaching.

flexibility   The ability to adapt prearranged and prepared procedures to the circumstances.

flexible learning   A wide range of learning opportunities offered to students; this allows for a degree of student autonomy.

flexi-study   An approach to teaching and learning using a variety of modes, such as the provision of prepared teaching and learning material with tutorial support. A useful approach for the busy, mature student which has been introduced by a number of different educational institutions, especially in further education in the United Kingdom.

flipchart   Large sheets of paper hung from an easel, so that they can be flipped backwards and forwards. Useful for recording small group reports.

Floodlight   The magazine recording all the *adult education* courses that are available throughout London.

flow chart   Diagram depicting the interrelationships between the parts of a more complex whole.

fluency activity   In language classes, time is devoted to free speech in order to improve the learners' fluency in the language.

fluid intelligence   That form of intelligence that is innate and biologically determined. See also *crystallized intelligence*.

focus group   Discussion group examining specific subjects, which have been prepared and pre-tested, having a moderator who keeps the group to the subject under consideration.

focus of attention   The phenomenon to which concentration is directed.

focusing process   The process of adjusting topics or goals in such a manner as to make them more explicit.

folk culture   The culture of the ordinary people: traditions of art, drama, story, etc. of small regional groups of people within a larger society. This tradition is often neglected by educationalists who present high culture or dominant culture as the form of culture to be appreciated.

folk education   Term used in Scandinavia to refer to *adult education*, although there are linguistic differences that reflect the differing perspectives between Scandinavia and many other countries towards life-long education for all.

folk high schools   *Adult education* institutions that began in Denmark in 1844 but which have now spread throughout the world. Many are residential, although in some parts of the world this is no longer the case.

folk university   These are adult education institutions that usually provide *adult education* on a part-time basis. In some countries they are closely connected to the local university, but in others they are more independent.

followership   The ability to be a team member, as opposed to leadership. Followership skills are now taught in workshops.

Food and Agricultural Organization   A UNESCO organization concentrating in the improvement of farming in developing countries; many extension agents and adult educators from agricultural backgrounds are employed in its work.

Ford Foundation   Established in 1936 as a charitable foundation that has supported education, including adult education in America. See also *Fund for Adult Education*.

forgetting   1. The loss of ability to recall, recognize, or reproduce what had previously been learned. 2. In some forms of psychoanalytical theory, forgetting is regarded as a form of repression.

formal education   The hierarchical structured educational system introduced by most states extending from primary schools to graduate programmes in universities. See *non-formal education*.

formal operational thought   The final stage in Piaget's approach to cognitive development, which he considered begins at about the age of twelve years. However, he never researched adults, so that this is not necessarily the final stage of cognitive development. More recently, Piaget's research has been questioned by theorists.

formal organization   A standardized way of organizing people to perform certain functions; a bureaucratic organization.

formal training   A structured programme of work-related *training* by specialist staff.

formalism   An educational philosophy and practice that maintained formal relationships in the classroom; it was this practice that Dewey discouraged through his *progressivism*.

formateur d'adultes   The French term for a *trainer* of adults.

formation   The French term for *training*.

formative assessment   The process of assessing students at the start or in the preliminary stages of a course in order to assess their learning needs, through which a teacher can plan, or help plan, a teaching and learning programme. It is unusual for such an assessment to be used in a summative assessment of the students.

formative evaluation   The process of undertaking a preliminary evaluation exercise, usually during the process of the course, in order to improve the ongoing teaching and learning process. See *evaluation*.

formative profiling   This is the initial *profile* prepared by the students in conjunction with their tutors, to help guide the students through their course, spotlighting both achievements and needs. See also *summative profile*.

forum   1. Panel discussion. 2. A period of open discussion for a fixed period of time carried on between a learning group and one or more persons bringing special knowledge of the subject under discussion. 3. Sometimes called open forum, in which participants question and discuss a total presentation as a group.

Forum for Access Studies (FAST)   A national body established to promote *access* to higher education for mature students in the United Kingdom.

Forum on the Rights of Elderly People to Education (FREE)   Established in 1981, a forum that has campaigned for the rights of elderly people to education.

foundation course   1. In American university study of adult education, the foundation course tends to include the philosophical, sociological, and historical approaches to the study. This differs totally from the United Kingdom, where each of these courses provides a major focus in itself. 2. In the United Kingdom a foundation course is usually the first year of a total course, usually of a bachelor's degree. 3. In the study of art, the foundation course is a course in its own right; thereafter students specialize in their own areas.

foundation education   An early term for adult basic education, first used by UNESCO. It was always recognized that foundation education was wider than just literacy.

Foundation for Domestic Education in Rural Areas   Established in 1935 in the Netherlands to provide domestic education for groups in the rural population that were in the most need.

Foundation for Education with Production   Established in 1982 in Botswana by Patrick van Rensburg as a non-governmental organization, seeking to integrate the educational curriculum with the world of work.

Foundation for Woodbrokers in the Netherlands   Quaker foundation in the Netherlands which runs adult residential schools.

foundation university   Term used to describe some universities founded in the United States from the colonial period until the late nineteenth century.

foundation year An initial year of studies, laying the foundations for further studies.

FORVUX Swedish outreach programme in *adult education* seeking to recruit learners from the work place and from housing estates; it was state funded.

4-H Clubs Young people's clubs that have formed the backbone of the *co-operative extension* movement in the United States. The four Hs are: head, heart, hands and health. It provides a major forum for *adult education* in the United States.

four-year college An American college offering a full undergraduate programme.

fragmentary understanding A partial understanding, superficiality of knowledge.

franchise In commerce, franchising is the process of a manufacturer or producer granting the rights of distribution of the product to another agent – in education, it has assumed a similar meaning, with a higher status educational institution allowing another organization, usually of a lower status, to run its courses.

Frandson Award Literature award in the field of continuing professional education, administered by the *National University Continuing Education Association* in the United States.

Franklin Institute Established in 1824 in Philadelphia for the advancement of science and for the education of the public in science and industry.

Franks Report A report on business education, published in the United Kingdom in 1963.

free association A Freudian technique of the association of ideas under the guidance of a trained analyst.

free educational association In Denmark, an association which offers general liberal education, with the liberal political movement.

free university 1. Learning networks established throughout different cities in the United States providing adult learning through networking. They are organizations which offer non-traditional, non-credit education to the general public, in which anybody can teach and anybody can learn. They began in the 1960s on college campuses but by the 1970s were established widely throughout America. Some are entrepreneurial concerns whilst others are free and based at libraries, etc. 2. In the Free University of Berlin, where 'free' refers to a political phenomenon. See *university without walls*.

freedom 1. Personal liberty. 2. The state of being free. 3. The ability to order one's own actions. 4. A philosophical doctrine of being unrestrained by physical determinants. See *autonomy*.

freelance teacher A teacher who is prepared to be employed wherever there is a need or a requirement.

freewheeling 1. When somebody is letting another do their work. 2. Operating without constraint. See also *brainstorming*.

Freire, Paulo (1921–1997) Brazilian adult educator who became leader of Brazil's literacy movement in the 1950s. Became more well known after he was forced to leave Brazil – an original thinker and famous writer. See *critical pedagogy, banking education, emancipatory education*.

frequency The number of occurrences of the same score in a sample or a population.

frequency distribution The spread of scores in a sample or distribution; they are often recorded in tabular form.

Fresh Horizons Courses started in the United Kingdom in 1966 to provide mature adults with a new perspective on life. The courses originally attracted only women but in their latter years they attracted both genders.

fresh start The term frequently used for courses especially designed for adults who left school at the minimum school-leaving age with few or no qualifications to help them return to study.

fresher One who is just commencing a course of study.

Friends First-Day School Association, (FFDSA) Many of the early adult schools in England were started by the Society of Friends (Quakers). This association became the co-ordinating association for these schools.

Friends of the International Council for Adult Education Although ICAE does not have an individual membership, it does have a network of friends who subscribe to its work.

front-end model of education Term used to convey that education was something that was offered in the early years of life and that, by implication, there was no education beyond it.

Frontier College Started in Canada in 1899 as the *Reading Camps Association* for all labourers who needed *basic education*. Frontier colleges were established in forestry and railway camps seeking to reach all the workers but as the frontiers have been pushed back so the work of the college has changed.

Fryer Report The report *Learning for the Twenty-First Century* which was made to the UK government in 1997, sometimes called after the committee chairman.

full-time equivalent A formula for funding whereby a number of part-time equivalents are assessed as being equivalent to a full-time student, or teacher, as the case may be.

full-time part-time adult educator An adult educator who works as a *part-time adult educator* in a number of different adult education institutions doing what is effectively a full-time job.

functional illiteracy In the United States a term used for those with less than 6 years full-time schooling, although this figure is not fixed.

functional literacy 1. The ability to read, write and calculate so that individuals may engage in all those activities in which literacy is required for effective functioning of their group and community and also enabling them to continue to use reading, writing and calculation for their own and the community's development. It should be noted that the Spanish alfabetización funcional and the French alphabétisation fonctionnelle signify the process of acquiring or of teaching the skill, rather than the state of possessing it. 2. UNESCO has defined this as having acquired the knowledge and skills in reading and writing which enable a person to engage effectively in all those activities in which literacy is normally assumed in their culture or group. See also *semi-literate*.

Fund for Adult Education Established in 1951 in the United States by the Ford Foundation to assist all men and women to continue their education. The Foundation was closed in 1961. Grants from the Fund had four objectives: to increase knowledge and skill; to recruit and train those who could lead *liberal adult education* programmes; to strength university adult education programmes; to assist the use of liberal adult education in training.

further education 1. In the United Kingdom, this refers to part-time and full-time education at the post-compulsory school age, usually regarded as of lower standard than higher education (advanced further education) in the United Kingdom. Traditionally this referred to the 16–19-year-old young adult but now it is much broader. Liberal adult education is also regarded administratively as a sector of further education and many colleges of further education have departments of adult education. 2. The term has become almost synonymous with continuing education. 3. In the Federal Republic of Germany, this term covers adult education, continuing education, and vocational retraining and is defined as 'all forms of continuation or resumption of studies after completion of the first educational phase of varying duration and as a rule after taking up full-time employment'. It is for adults of all age groups and educational qualifications, and may be vocational or general.

further education college   Initially a college that offered education to the 16–19 year olds in the United Kingdom, although these colleges have now extended their work. Similar to the community college in the United States. See also *further education*.

Further Education Staff College   UK college involved in curriculum development, management and *staff development* in *further education*.

Gg

Galaxy Conference of Adult Education Organizations Conference held in Washington, DC in 1969, when twenty adult education organizations held their annual conferences simultaneously. They planned a joint declaration that led to the formation of the *Coalition of Adult Education Organizations* in 1973.

gaming An educational method in which the students participate in games in order to explore issues of social concern, personal growth, and development. Gaming is one method of motivating reluctant participants in the learning process.

Gandhi Shikshan Bhavan An educational institute established in the centenary year of Gandhi (1969) by a body of educationalists concerned with the study of *basic education*. It is now an affiliated college of the University of Mumbai (Bombay).

Gandhigram Rural Institute A rural institute in India devoted to the holistic service of a community: hospital, orphanage, basic school, village planning committee, youth clubs, teaching and research, and adult and continuing education.

Ganga Established in 1969, a Nigerian adult education magazine for the Moslem areas of the country.

gatekeeper One whose approval is needed in order to be accepted.

gateway club Club for mentally handicapped young people providing leisure, recreation, and continuing education for young people with special needs.

gateway course An introductory course to a subject. See *bridging course.*

Gaussian curve Normal curve of distribution.

GED tests See *General Education Development Tests.*

gender The cultural and social construction of sexual differences.

gene The carrier of hereditary characteristics in the chromosome.

general ability It was postulated by Spearman that intelligence could be divided into a general, or overall, ability and a special ability, and that both could be measured.

General Act of Adult Education Passed in the Netherlands in 1985, aimed at producing a coherent national and local support system for *adult education* throughout the country. Its implementation was delayed.

general adult education The alternative educational tradition in Denmark and has its roots in the social movement of the country. It might be summarized as enlightenment about the cultural traditions of the people, and as such it receives a great deal of state support.

General Certificate of Education (GCE) School examinations taken in the United

Kingdom: Ordinary level at about 16 years of age and Advanced level at 18 years of age. The latter is used as a university entrance measure and the former has been replaced by *General Certificate of Secondary Education*.

General Certificate of Secondary Education   Introduced in 1988 to replace the *General Certificate of Education (Ordinary level)* as a single system of examinations for schools in the UK. There are special syllabi for adults.

general degree   A bachelors degree in which the student has not specialized; it may be obtained at either pass or honours level.

general education   1. The term used to refer to all forms of education that are not specifically vocational. This was an attempt to break away from the vocational/non-vocational distinction in a more meaningful manner. See also *non-vocational education*. 2. Education which, in its choice of subject matter, does not envisage any kind of specialization with a view to preparing students for work in a particular sector.

General Education Development Tests (GED)   Tests taken by adults in the United States to gain a *high school equivalency diploma* or certificate. The tests consist of writing skills, reading skills, social studies, mathematics and science. Each state has its own procedures and policies for their administration, although the tests themselves are standardized across the United States.

general impression marking   See *impression marking*.

general industrial class   *Vocational education* classes in US high schools.

general knowledge   The wide variety of knowledge and information gained by individuals in the course of their lives.

General National Vocational Qualifications (GNVQ)   Qualifications

awarded for more general studies within the *National Vocational Qualifications* framework; an attempt to bridge the gap between 'academic' and vocational studies.

general studies   This is a form of *non-vocational education*. See *general education*.

generalist   Person whose interest or occupation involves the spanning of a number of specialities.

generalization   The process of drawing general principles from specific instances. It is also regarded by some theorists as a significant factor in learning, since learning begins with specific experiences, some of which may be generalizable, although the principles of generalization are being questioned at the present time as a result of rapid social change.

generation gap   The period of time between generations in which socio-cultural changes have occurred, thus making the behaviour and values of different generations diverse and sometimes antagonistic towards each other.

generic social worker   A generalist in the area of social work.

generic training   A common curriculum between similar specialities in some forms of professional training.

genetic factor   Inherited characteristics, not learned from experience.

genetic principle   A principle that is intrinsic to a phenomenon. For instance, it has been claimed that there are certain fundamentals that constitute *adult education*.

geriatrics   Branch of medical science concerned with the diagnosis and treatment of illness in the elderly.

German Protestant Workshop for Adult Education   The federal association in the evangelical church in Germany concerned with *adult education*.

German Trades Union Co-operative Institute for Education   Involved in all forms of *adult education*, with special reference to the interests and needs of the workers.

German Trades Union Institute for Vocational Training   This institute is involved in *vocational education* orientated towards improving the working and living conditions of the workers, the democratization of the society and helping them become more aware of the issues in technological society.

gerontogogy   The term used in the former Yugoslavia for *educational gerontology*.

gerontology   The study of ageing. See *educational gerontology*.

gerontology education   Education about ageing and about older people in general.

Gestalt psychology   A school of researchers who maintained that phenomena could only be understood if they were viewed as structural wholes; they had a great influence on early learning theory.

Gestalt therapy   A form of therapy which is usually conducted in groups and seeks to broaden people's awareness of themselves by recalling past experiences, emotional states, and bodily sensations. Used in *affective education* within the humanistic movement in adult education.

gesture   All forms of communication, both verbal and non-verbal.

G.I. Bill of Rights   See *Servicemen's Readjustment Act*.

Gilde projects   Skills exchange projects for the elderly in the Netherlands, started in 1984 in Amsterdam.

global learning   A technique of learning in which the totality of something is studied rather than the parts.

global marking   A marking technique in which the assessor seeks to assess a piece of work holistically rather than analytically. See *analytic marking*, *impression marking*.

global teaching   See *integrated teaching*.

globalization   The growing compression of the world and the increasing consciousness of the whole, resulting in an increasing level of interdependence across the world.

goal   1. End result aimed for in action. 2. In curriculum development goals are either high-level generalizations (*aims*) or specific statements of behaviour which students are expected to display (*objectives*). 3. This is the immediate aim of a lesson or educational course. Used very widely, often synonymously with aim, especially in the United States.

goal-oriented learning   An instrumental approach to formal learning. One of Houle's three approaches to learning. See also *activity-oriented learner* and *learning-oriented learner*.

golden age 4-H club   The Four H (head, heart, hand, health) concept has been adapted from its original usage with young people in *co-operative extension* and is now used in some areas with adults and the elderly. See *4-H Club*.

grade   1. A position or level on a scale. 2. A mark awarded as a result of an *assessment*. 3. A year level in a school or a college. See *mark*.

grade inflation   The idea that the value of grades is lowered as courses become open to more people, so that it becomes necessary to gain a higher grade to gain a similar status.

graduand   One who has been awarded a degree or a diploma from a college or university and who is in the process of graduating.

graduate   To complete a college or university course and gain its award.

graduate assistant   A research or teaching assistant.

graduate education   In the United States this term is used for education beyond undergraduate level. It is synonymous to the idea of postgraduate education in the United Kingdom.

graduate equivalent   An award, such as a professional qualification, which is treated as equivalent to a *first degree* for the purposes of entry to a postgraduate course.

graduate school   An educational institution devoted to post-graduate work.

graduate student   A student studying for a postgraduate award.

graduate study   Postgraduate education.

Great Books Foundation   Established by the University of Chicago in 1947. It published major books in paperback, trained discussion group leaders and published training manuals.

Great Books Movement   Originated in 1921 with John Erskine, Professor of English at Columbia University where he ran a programme on great books. This eventually led to the Chicago course and from there to the *Great Books Foundation*.

Great Decisions Program   Launched in 1955 by the Foreign Policy Association in the United States, this was a programme aimed at raising citizen awareness about foreign policy through discussion group. See also *National Issues Forum*.

great tradition   A term first used by Harold Wiltshire to describe what *adult*

education offered the nation: a humane curriculum, provision for reflective citizenship, non-vocational learning, and democratic and Socratic approaches to teaching.

group   A number of people associating for a common purpose.

group counselling   Counselling undertaken in a group rather than individually.

group development   The stages of a group's existence.

group discussion   A teaching method whereby students are put together in a group to discuss a specific subject.

group dynamics   1. The way in which a group functions, and the processes of interaction among its members. 2. The study of the ways in which a group functions.

group need   The deficiency a group has that needs to be satisfied in order to make it function efficiently.

group norm   The generally expected pattern of behaviour that evolves when a number of people associate over a period of time for a common purpose.

group pacing   The pace of learning set by the group, as a whole, as opposed to *self-pacing* or set by the teacher.

group process   The patterns of behaviour that evolve and change in the life of a group. See *group dynamics*.

group selection technique   A method that involves setting the candidates for a particular post or position an activity to be undertaken together in order to assess their ability or willingness to function within a group setting.

group structure The patterns of relationship that emerge among members of a group.

group teaching The practice of subdividing a class by interest or some other criterion and teaching the subgroups separately.

group test A test administered to the members of a group simultaneously.

group therapy The process in which a group of people having similar needs assist each other through the group processes of interaction and the sharing of common problems, experiences, etc.

group training scheme 1. A scheme whereby a number of small employing organizations join together to provide training for their employees. 2. A training scheme organized for the employees of all the companies within the same group.

group tutorial The process of several students having a *tutorial* with the same tutor simultaneously.

group work This occurs when a group of students are set an assignment to complete working together.

Groupe d'Etude et de Recherche pour l'Education des Adultes (GEREA) Established in France in 1965, this is a group of voluntary associations concerned with the study of education for adults.

Groupe de Recherche pour l'Education Permanente (GREP) Established in 1964 in association with the Ministry of Agriculture with the aim of contributing to the social advancement of farmers in France.

growth The development of a person or organization.

growth theory The theory that suggests that the aim of teaching is to assist in the growth and development of the learner. Consequently the teaching and learning transaction is regarded as learner-centred.

Guild A City of London livery company. The Guilds were among the early proponents of *vocational education*.

Grundtvig, Bishop Nokolai Frederik Severin (1783–1872) A priest, poet, philosopher, educationalist whose ideas contributed greatly to the development of the *folk high school* movement in Denmark.

guest lecturer A visiting speaker.

guest student In Germany, students who are not qualified to register for the whole of as degree but only part of it.

gynagogy The art of helping women learn, using feminist approaches.

Hh

half-timer A part-time student.

Hallenbeck, Wilbur C Awarded the first PhD in adult education in the United States, by Teachers College, Columbia University in 1935. He was a contributor to the *'black book'*. See *Yeaxlee* who was awarded the first PhD in the subject.

halo effect The process by which someone is assessed as being more competent than they are, as a result of previous good performances. The term was first used by L Thorndike.

Hampton Clubs Founded in England by Morse Cartwright in 1812 and popular with radicals. They were an early form of *study circles* in England in which radical texts were read and discussed.

handbooks of adult education Since 1934, the American associations have published a handbook every few years (now nearly every ten years) to review the state of the field. There have now been seven separate handbooks.

handicapped Persons who, for a variety of reasons, physical, mental or social, are unable to participate fully in normal activities and who might therefore have special needs in order to learn.

handout An aid to teaching and learning in which the learners are given a written or printed supplementary item from which they might learn.

hard-to-reach adult Adult member of the population who appears disinterested in adult and continuing education programmes. The target population for many forms of outreach education.

hardware Term used in the computer field to refer to electronic equipment. See also *software*.

Haret, Spiru (1851–1912) Founder of adult education in Romania through the network organization of adult education institutions.

Haycocks Reports Three reports issued in the 1970s in the United Kingdom concerned with the supply and training of teachers of adults. It proposed the three level scheme of training, leading to an award equivalent to a one-year full-time certificate, equivalent to one-third of an undergraduate degree. These reports were influential in the education and training of *part-time adult educators*.

Health and Safety at Work (1974) Legislation in the United Kingdom to ensure that the workplace is healthy and safe which has resulted in considerable work place education. There is similar legislation in the United States.

health education Any series of planned teaching and learning episodes aimed at increasing people's awareness of health and well-being.

health sciences   The study of a variety of different disciplines related to people's mental, physical, emotional, and social health.

health visitor   A trained nurse whose role in the community is preventative, rather than specifically orientated to nursing, so that the health visitor has an educative function.

hedonism   A philosophical theory claiming that pleasure is the sole good.

hegemony   The exercise of covert power in a non-formal manner, eg without the threat of physical force, so that the ideas of the dominant group are assumed to be correct and become taken-for-granted.

hemgard   Swedish discussion centre.

hermeneutics   Originally this involved the study of biblical texts, seeking to understand the meaning that the writers of the words gave to the text, rather than meaning imputed into the text by later interpreters. Hermeneutics has now taken a more secular meaning, still seeking to understand the meaning that the writers gave to their writings. In general, the meaning and interpretations and the relationship between author, text and reader.

heteronomy   The act of depending on the authority of another – the opposite of *autonomous*.

heuristic methods   1. Guiding, helping others to learn by stimulating interest. 2. Encouraging learners to learn things for themselves.

hidden curriculum   Those aspects of the curriculum that are hidden either to the learners or the teachers, which influence the learners in certain ways.

hierarchy of needs   Formulated by Abraham Maslow, it claims that human needs start with the basic physical ones and move up a hierarchy of five levels to self-actualization. See also *need*.

high school   Senior school for children in the United States.

high school diploma   The award for satisfactory completion of high school.

high school equivalency diploma   The award signifying satisfactory completion of the high school equivalency examinations. See *General Educational Development Tests*.

higher degree   Any category of degree above bachelors level.

higher doctorate   Categories of doctorate beyond PhD, eg DSc.

higher education   Education beyond compulsory schooling, eg university education.

higher preparatory examination Introduced in 1968 in Denmark, it is the adult equivalent to the Danish upper secondary school examinations.

Highlander   A *folk high school* in Tennessee, founded by Myles Horton. Famous for its having espoused radical Christian principles but regarded as too left-wing by many politicians in that state in its earliest years who closed it. Horton immediately re-opened it on a different site with a different mission statement. It is best known for its work with civil rights and workers.

Highway   The magazine of the *Workers' Educational Association* for many years.

Hillcroft College   Founded in 1920, this is the only residential college for women in the United Kingdom. Located in Surbiton.

Hinukh Mevugarim Be-Yisrael   Adult Education in Israel – the magazine was founded in 1972 and is published twice a year.

Histadrut Na'amnat This is a movement for working women in Israel, devoted to providing every woman in the country with *continuing education*.

histogram Similar to a graph, but in which frequency data are presented in the form of a series of rectangles touching each other. Often incorrectly called a bar chart.

Historical Foundations of Adult Education: A Bulletin of Research and Information Started in 1985–6 by the National College of Education in the United States.

History of the Origin and Progress of Adult Schools Written by Thomas Pole and published in 1816; the earliest known book in English about adult education.

Holbrook, Josiah (1788–1854) The founder of the US *lyceum* movement in nineteenth century adult education, originally called *Society for Mutual Education*.

Holiday Fellowship A UK study organization in the *liberal adult education* tradition.

holism A *learning style* in which the learner seeks to complete the task and fit the learning in a global context; opposite of the serialist style. Gestalt psychology is based on a holistic principle. See also *holistic education*.

holistic education An approach to teaching and learning focusing upon the whole situation and seeking to respond to the needs of both in order to develop the whole person.

holistic learning See *holism*.

home demonstration agent An *extension agent* in the *co-operative extension* movement in the United States whose main responsibilities lie in organizing education in the areas of home making.

home economics A body of subject matter and the study of subjects related to the home and family. Subject commonly studied through the *Co-operative Extension Service* in the United States, although it is also studied widely in other countries.

home economics schools Residential schools in Denmark for those over the age of 16 years, studying subjects specializing in *home economics*.

home groups The *adult school* movement introduced the idea of organizing adult schools in the home in 1954, following the ideas of the early church. See also *house group*.

home study education Education designed for students to undertake at home and away from the educational institution. See *distance education*.

homework Assignments undertaken by learners in their own time and away from the educational institution.

homily A form of *instruction*, usually used within the context of the Christian churches, although sometimes used within an educational setting.

honorary degree A degree awarded by a college or university to a person who has undertaken meritorious work – not always academic; the honorary doctorate is the highest honour a university can bestow.

honours degree A degree taken at a higher level, or a degree obtained with excellence. See *ordinary degree*.

hook and loop board A board with lots of small loops on it, which can be used to hook visual display objects.

horizontal learning Learning from and teaching others through group discussion by sharing experiences.

Horton, Myles (1905–90) Founder of the *Highlander Folk High School* in Tennessee.

Høsjskolebladet The magazine of the *folk high schools* in Denmark.

Houle Award The C O Houle World Award for Literature in Adult Education is an annual award administered by the American Association of Adult and Continuing Education for a piece of scholarly work in the English language considered as a principal contribution to the whole field.

Houle, C O (1912–1998) Distinguished writer in the field of adult education in the United States. See *Houle Award*.

hourly rate The hourly rate of payment made to teachers – this usually refers to those who are working on a part-time basis.

house group A study group meeting in people's homes – used in the Christian churches. This is usually considered the origin of the *study circle*s.

house journal The magazine or journal published for members of an organization or department. It is sometimes referred to as an in-house journal. Also called a newsletter.

house of discussion Forerunner of the *study circle*, the traditional method of adult education in Sweden in which public meeting places were employed to encourage cultural and intellectual pursuits.

house style The style and format adopted by a publishing organization for all its publications.

human biology The branch of biology concerned with the human body.

human capital theory The theory maintaining that investment in human resources to improve the level of knowledge and skill in a society is the most effective method by which a society can encourage

growth and development. See also *screen hypothesis, human resource development*.

Human Employment and Resource Trust (HEART) A non-formal *skills* training board in Jamaica.

human engineering The idea of ensuring that the human being is in harmony with the environment. See *ergonomics*.

human potential development The development of the potential that exists in all human beings. It has recently been recognized that this is one of the functions of education and training.

human relations Term used to refer to social relationships.

human resource The potential available in an organization from its employees.

human resource cycle A cycle that management might employ in *human resource development* consisting of recruitment, selection, placement, socialization, evaluation, training and development, promotion and transfer.

human resource developer A person involved in *human resource development* programmes as a trainer, instructor or staff developer.

human resource development (HRD) The education and training provided by an organization for its employees. See also *staff development*.

human rights Rights contained in the United Nations declaration of 1948, which exist by virtue of being a human being.

humanagogy Pedagogy and andragogy combined, trying to reflect that it is neither children nor adults who learn only human beings. It was suggested as a solution to the andragogy-pedagogy debate in the 1970s–1980s in the United States, by R Knudson.

humanism   A philosophical position having two variants: the first rejecting all beliefs in a divine force; second, it is sometimes used to refer to a humanistic position. See *humanistic psychology*.

humanistic psychology   A school of psychology which affirms the human qualities of the person, such as autonomy, freedom, and subjective experience. It has been very influential in adult education with such thinkers as A H Maslow and Carl Rogers.

humanistic research   A qualitative approach to research, which seeks to make sense of human action and experience by employing more naturalistic methods. See *naturalistic research*.

humanities   Those academic disciplines concerned with human culture.

hypermedia   Multimedia interactive systems. The opportunity to gain access to and combine, edit and orchestrate a wide range of material from different media.

hypothesis   An untested assertion to be examined during research.

hypothetical-deductive reasoning   A rational thought process that starts from a theoretical proposition and seeks to deduce fact.

Ii

ice-breaker A group technique to enable people to relate to each other in a group, usually used at the start of a course or a session.

idea In Plato's writing this is the intellectual equivalent of the form. Later it became something that was perceived directly in the mind, and more recently it has come to refer to an *hypothesis* or a plan in the mind, or a thought.

idea inventory The construction of a list of ideas as a result of a brainstorming session.

ideal 1. A desirable state which is not usually achievable. 2. A moral value that should be striven for. 3. An abstract representation of the basic characteristics of a phenomenon, eg *ideal type*.

ideal self The image, value, or type of person that people think that they could or should be. It is an element in the *self-concept*.

ideal speech act A notion in the theory of Habermas that suggests that perfect communication has occurred if four conditions have been met. Communicative competence depends on sincerity, comprehensibility, legitimacy and truthfulness.

ideal type A representation of a phenomenon symbolizing it by its salient features only.

idealism A complex concept with a variety of meanings, some of which are relevant to adult education. 1. People's ideas are the sole cause of social behaviour. 2. In order for people to alleviate their dissatisfaction all that they have to do is to change their ideas about their selves and their behaviour. 3. People are willing to listen to rational thought and act upon it.

idealized self A perfected characterization of the self; what an individual would like to become.

identify To feel affinity with a person or phenomenon. In Freudian psychology, this is used to indicate that a person has incorporated certain characteristics of another into their own *identity*.

identity 1. A social construction in which a person comes to see how they are seen in the social world. 2. How each person sees themself. Hence there are both social and self-identities.

identity crisis An acute sensation of doubt about one's identity. It often calls for people to redefine their identity. Some research in adult education has been undertaken on transition periods in the life cycle.

ideographic A psychological system relating to the concrete or to the individual. See also *nomothetic approach*.

ideological state apparatus A Marxist concept, formulated by Althusser, to refer to those social institutions, including education, that uphold the dominant ideology within society.

ideology 1. A world-view or system of meaning accepted by a social group. 2. An individual's belief system. 3. It is also used in a derogatory manner to refer to a system of belief that is not acceptable to the person employing the term. See also *sociology of knowledge*.

illiteracy The definition has altered on a number of occasions in both the United Kingdom and the United States, so that it is probably best regarded as the inability to cope with the basic skills of reading, writing and numeracy in daily life. See also *functional literacy, semi-illiterate*.

illusion A false perception of reality.

image A picture in the mind, often a construction of reality.

imagery Descriptive language.

imagination The process of combining memories of previous experiences with current thoughts and experiences in order to create new ideas or pictures in the mind.

imitation A form of social learning, where the learner copies the behaviour of a *role model*.

immediate experience Direct or first-hand experience. See *primary experience*.

immigrant education The process of teaching immigrants the language and customs of the country in which they are about to reside. It is a major component of the adult education programmes of many countries that have been recipients of immigrants. See *Americanization education*.

immigrant language centre An educational establishment where the language of the host community is taught to immigrants.

Imogene Okes Award An annual award made at the *American Association for Adult and Continuing Education* by the Commission on Research for outstanding research in adult education.

impact evaluation An evaluative process seeking to assess the effects of a course of education or training, usually, on the workplace or on the learner's performance. See *evaluation*.

impression marking A holistic approach to grading, rather than an analytical approach. See *global marking*.

imprinting A special social attachment that is created between the young and usually the significant other members of the older generation who care for them.

improvident orientation An approach to learning in which the learner places more emphasis upon the detail and less upon the context.

impulsive learning A learning style in which the learner responds rapidly to a potential learning situation, usually accepting the first possible response, rather than reflectively examining many more possibilities before choosing which response to make. See *reflectivity*.

in absentia In his/her absence. For example, a university award can be made to a candidate *in absentia*.

inaugural lecture A lecture given by a new professor to commemorate the assumption of the appointment.

in-basket exercise An exercise given to management trainees to help them consider priorities. See also *in-tray exercise*.

incidental learning The unintended learning that occurs through personal experience or interaction.

inclusive understanding Sometimes used to refer to deep processing of information, resulting in reasoning, reflection and new insights.

in-company training See *in-house training*.

independent learner One who seeks to learn in an autonomous manner. See *self-directed learner*. See also *self-pacing*.

independent study 1. Programmes of study constructed by educational institutions for learners who do not join classes. 2. A self-initiated programme of study. See *correspondence education, self-directed learning*.

independent variable A variable in a phenomenon under investigation that affects some other one; an antecedent condition prior to manipulation and or observation of the dependent variable.

Indian National Adult Education Programme Initiated in 1978 to enable the mass of the population to play an active role in social and cultural change.

indicator A phenomenon or variable whose presence and qualitative measurement are crucial for a judgement on the effectiveness of a programme in terms of specified criteria.

Indira Gandhi National Open University The Open University of India, established by Act of Parliament. The stone-laying ceremony was held in November 1985.

indirect teaching methods See *facilitative teaching*.

individual entitlement A concept proposed by some exponents of recurrent education who argue that everybody should have the right to a specific amount of post-compulsory education and that they should be able to draw upon it throughout their lifetime. See *drawing rights*. There is some similarity between this and *voucher* schemes.

individual learning account An idea being promulgated in the UK whereby people have a bank account through which they fund their own learning, government will contribute an initial sum and thereafter individuals are expected to contribute and gain other finances that will enable them to fund continuing learning. See *educational vouchers*.

individualism 1. Personality traits that distinguish one individual from another. 2. A social philosophy that emphasizes the importance of the individual over the social or the collective.

individualized instruction An approach to teaching and learning that seeks to meet the needs of each learner. See also *customized instruction*.

individualized study A programme of study designed to meet the demands of an individual learner. See *individualized instruction*.

individuation A process whereby a person forms a clear boundary between the self and the social during personal development.

indoctrination A process of forcing a person to learn beliefs and knowledge held by another or a group.

induction 1. A planned programme in which new students or staff are introduced to the ways in which an educational establishment, or a new course, functions. 2. A method of thought and reasoning in which a general law is inferred from the analysis of specific instances; primarily an analytical process in qualitative research.

inductive reasoning The process of *induction*.

industrial education 1. Provision of educational opportunities for workers. 2. The study of vocational education.

industrial studies   The study of work in society, especially from a non-management perspective.

industrial tutor   1. A member of the teaching staff of an educational institution who is responsible for preparing students to enter a work-based placement. 2. The title of the journal of the Society of Industrial tutors.

inferiority complex   A collection of repressed fears in an individual which gives rise to feelings of a more general inferiority.

informal curriculum   An informal process of learning developed by groups of students.

informal education   This often refers to the form of education that occurs when people learn informally from their environment. However, there has been confusion between the concepts of education and learning. Hence another definition is where groups of people learn through planned activities in an informal manner, eg where there is no overt status role difference between learners.

informal learning   The type of learning that occurs when a person acquires knowledge, skill, or attitudes through interaction in an informal situation.

information   1. Knowledge to be presented to other people. 2. News. 3. Knowledge that is stored but which can be accessed. It should be recognized that most information is mediated knowledge and interpretation of phenomena even though it might be presented as if it were fact. See *theory*.

information brief   A teaching aid consisting of a summary of specific information about a given topic. This summary is distributed to participants prior to a session so that they can prepare themselves.

information retrieval   A branch of computer science concerned with the classification and storage of large quantities of information.

information science   The study of information systems.

information society   1. A term used to describe contemporary society in which people are presented with information through a variety of media. 2. A society, the efficient functioning of which is dependent on knowledge. See also *knowledge society*.

information system   The methods, materials, media, personnel and recipients necessary to transfer information within a specified field of activity.

information technology (IT)   All forms of technology that assist in the storage and the rapid transmission of information, but the term is usually restricted to electronic forms of technology.

informatics   See *information science*. A term more frequently used in continental Europe.

Informecca   The newsletter of *Radio ECCA* in the Canary Islands.

in-group   Any group that seeks to distinguish itself from other groups and sees itself as superior to other groups.

in-house training   The training offered to employees by the employers and undertaken in the company premises by company employees.

initial education   The first formal education of a person's lifetime; it is completed when the person leaves school or college for the first time and enters work.

initial preparation   The pre-service vocational training provided by most occupations and professions.

initiation   The process of introducing people to a new situation – this frequently used to be through a ritual although now it is more frequently through an *induction* course.

ink-blot test   A generic term for a number of projective psychological tests, using shapes like ink-blots.

innate   A trait that exists, or is a potential, in the human being at birth as a result of genetic inheritance.

inquiry-based learning   Learning through projects and problems. See *discovery learning*.

inquiry methods   Activity teaching methods that use problems and projects. See *discovery learning* and *facilitative teaching*.

in-service training   Continuing education given to employees during the course of their working life, which may be in-house. It may also take the form of block release or even secondment (a form of temporary transfer of employment). See *on-the-job training*.

inspector   General term for officers who are appointed to inspect and supervise educators. It has partly been replaced in recent times by the less threatening term of advisor in the United Kingdom.

instinct   An unlearned process characteristic of a species as a whole. Used less precisely in everyday speech to refer to basic human drives.

institute   1. An educational, or research organization. 2. A professional organization or accrediting body.

Institute for Learning in Retirement   An American network of non-formal educational institutions that developed from the mid-1960s to provide education and learning opportunities for third agers. In 1988, Elderhostel merged with the loose federation of institutes and created the *Elderhostel Institute Network*.

Institute for Retired Professionals
Founded in 1962 under the sponsorship of the New School for Social Research in New York City, this became the first *institute for learning in retirement*. It was first institute for seniors' learning in the world. See *University of the Third Age*.

institution   1. An organization. 2. A patterned and socially regulated form of behaviour. 3. A total institution is a closed organization, such as a prison.

instruct   1. To direct or order. 2. Teaching method of a didactic nature. 3. To authorize.

instruction   The process of teaching, but often used in relation to training.

instructional design   The process of preparing a programme or a course in a specific manner, utilizing educational technology in order to achieve specific objectives.

instructional games   See *gaming*.

instructional material   Teaching aids.

instructional objectives   The instructor's specific aims for a teaching and learning session. They are usually non-negotiable and behavioural in orientation.

instructional technology   The development and design of teaching aids.

instructor   One who instructs; a teacher. However, the term is often associated with teaching at a low level, including helping students to acquire skills. Occasionally, in the United States it is used with wider connotations of teaching to include all that the teacher does to help adults learn.

instrument   1. A tool. 2. Often used in the language of US research to refer to an accepted and validated research tool, such as a questionnaire, attitude inventory, which is utilized in a research process. 3. A musical instrument.

instrumentalism   A system of pragmatic philosophy that holds that ideas are instruments that should guide actions to bring about change. Hence, for some liberal adult educators instrumentalism in education is the very antithesis of the purposes of liberal education and even of education itself. See also *technical rationality*.

integrated course   1. A course, or a programme, in which the theoretical and the practical are combined. 2. An *interdisciplinary* course.

integrated curriculum   1. A *curriculum* in which all the parts fit into a meaningful whole. 2. A curriculum in which all the subjects are taught in a multi-disciplinary manner.

integrated education   A term used to signify that different races, ages, religious or gender groups are taught together.

integrated learning systems   A planned use of a number of different approaches to learning and modes of delivering teaching in order to achieve specified learning outcomes.

integrated teaching   The teaching of different subject areas in a thematic manner, so that the different disciplines are not emphasized. See also *global teaching*.

intellect   The cognitive ability of the person is usually the subject of this term, although it originally referred to rational ability. However, there would be some debate about the extent to which it should be restricted to the cognitive. See *multiple intelligences*.

intellectual   1. A member of a social stratum to which society has ascribed the dominant role of providing it with the

solutions to its problems, explications of its dominant world-view, ideology, etc. 2. One who is employed in an occupation usually considered to be intellectual. 3. One who is learned and has the ability to think critically. Intellectuals should be seen as separate from the knowledge class, which is orientated to the fact that an increasing number of jobs might be regarded as knowledge-based occupations.

intellectual development   The process of developing the cognitive skills of individuals.

intelligence   The ability to respond to the variety of experiences of everyday life. There are, however, many theories of intelligence. See, for instance *crystallized intelligence, fluid intelligence, multiple intelligences*.

intelligence quotient (IQ)   A numerical measure of intelligence, based on the assumption that there is a single intelligence that can be measured. Not all scholars accept that this is a realistic undertaking and there is a greater emphasis being placed on *multiple intelligences*.

intelligence test   A technique devised to assess the level of intelligence that an individual possesses, based on the assumption that there is a single form of intelligence that can be measured.

intelligentsia   A term that emerged in nineteenth-century Central and Eastern Europe to refer to radical or revolutionary thinkers. In contemporary society it tends to have the same meaning as *intellectual*.

interaction analysis   1. The study of group processes. 2. A statistical process for gauging effects between variables.

interactionism   A sociological approach to the study of human behaviour, based on the idea that individuals are influenced by the social pressures exerted upon them in social interaction. See *symbolic interactionism*.

interactive learner   One who learns most effectively through participation and discussion.

interactive skills   See *interpersonal skills.*

interactive technology   Technological systems that are being introduced in which the learner is able to interact with others through the media. It is being used in distance education so that the learners can interact with teachers, fellow learners or learning programmes through electronic systems, teleconferencing, etc.

interactive video system   Through the use of a computer, these systems allow the user/learner to gain access to material stored on videodisk, or access to video computer based learning programmes.

interdisciplinary   Knowledge or data about a phenomenon that combines two or more academic disciplines simultaneously.

interest   1. A freely chosen activity. 2. An activity that provides satisfaction, or pleasure. 3. A disposition to engage in certain activities, which are appropriate to specific ends. See *motivation.* 4. Used as 'best interest' to refer to the benefit to be gained from a specific action. Hence critical theorists suggest that those people whom they claim to have a false consciousness do not know what their interests are. See also *need* and *want.*

interest group   A group of people who meet to pursue the same or similar activities; such groups often form pressure groups that seek social change.

interest inventory   An attitude test used to assess people's likes and dislikes.

interest test   A test used in personnel guidance and selection to investigate people's interests and aptitudes.

interface   A meeting point.

interference   1. A conflict between associations formed between stimuli and responses. 2. A conflict between learning new information and the memory of previous phenomena or events. This inhibits memorizing the new information. See *cognitive dissonance.* 3. A situation in which old information is difficult to recall because new information is distorting it.

inter-cultural   The study of phenomena from the perspective of more than one culture.

inter-generational   Differences between people of different generations. Previously used in child psychology but now becoming more prevalent in *lifelong education.*

intern   An American expression for a new recruit to a profession preparing for a professional position, who spends time performing the practical elements of professional role as part of that preparation, under supervision. See also *probation, professional placement, teaching practice.*

internal consistency   1. The logical sequence of an argument. 2. In questionnaire design, it refers to the extent to which all the items are consistent with each other in measuring precisely the same phenomenon.

internal degree   An award of a college or university to students who have successfully completed a course of study as a registered student of the institution.

internal validity   The internal consistency of a research instrument. The extent to which causal interpretation of the findings result from the manipulation of study variables. See *external validity.*

internalization   The process of learning and taking for granted information, beliefs and cultural practices.

International Andragogy Institute   An adult education association established in

South America, enabling the international co-operation between those universities and Florida State University.

International Associates   Created in 1975 to further the aims of the *Coalition of Adult Education Organizations* in the United States of America on an international basis.

International Association for Continuing Education in Engineering   An international non-governmental association with the objective of supporting and enhancing lifelong technical education and training and advanced engineering education world-wide.

International Association of Universities of the Third Age   This is the association on which all national *Universities of the Third Age* are represented. It holds a bi-annual conference.

International Centre for Advanced Technical and Vocational Training Established in Turin by the International Labour Office.

International Charter of Workers' Education   Prepared and published by the *International Federation of Workers' Educational Associations*, this charter describes *adult* and *continuing education* as a necessary part of the democratic process. It also calls for more *vocational* education and a widening of *general education*.

International Community Education Association   A voluntary independent association seeking to draw together those working in *community education*. Based in the United Kingdom, it holds a conference every four years and publishes its own newsletter.

International Congress of University Adult Education   Established in 1960 at Syracuse University, after the UNESCO conference on adult education in Montreal to develop and maintain contact with *adult educators* working in universities.

International Correspondence Bureau Established in 1920 by the adult school movement as part of its international activities. In 1956 its activities were transferred to the International Friendship League, but it resumed its activities for a brief period in the 1970s.

International Council for Adult Education   Founded in 1973 by the Canadian adult educator, Roby Kidd. It is a non-governmental international organization, having membership from many national *adult education* organizations. Still based in Toronto, Canada.

International Council for Correspondence Education   See *International Council for Distance Education*.

International Council for Distance Education   Adopted this name in 1982, previously called *International Council for Correspondence Education*, this is a body concerned to promote research and provide information about distance education.

international education   The study of education in different countries, but it need not be comparative education.

International ESVA Foundation A foundation supporting the *European Symposium on Voluntary Associations*.

International Federation of Workers' Educational Associations   Established in 1947, an association of *Workers' Educational Associations* to improve workers' educational opportunities.

International Handbook on Adult Education   Published in 1929, in conjunction with the first *World Conference on Adult Education*.

International Institute for Adult Literacy Methods   Established by UNESCO in 1968 and supported by the government of Iran.

International Journal of Lifelong Education Established in 1982, a referred journal providing a forum of scholars to examine all aspects of *lifelong education*. Currently published six times a year.

International Journal of University Adult Education Founded in 1962 by the *International Congress of University Adult Education*.

International Hall of Fame of Adult and Continuing Education Based at the University of Oklahoma, USA, this Hall of Fame was inaugurated in 1996.

International League for Social Commitment in Adult Education Founded in 1984 by *adult educators* who shared a concern for social justice, the League has organized a number of meetings in different countries throughout the world.

International Literacy Day Established in 1966, it has been celebrated on 8 September each year ever since.

International Literacy Prize Jury UNESCO administers four literacy awards: Iraq Literacy Prize, Nadezhda K Krupskaya Prize, International Reading Association Literacy Award and the Noma Prize – one jury decides upon these awards each year.

International Literacy Year The United National General Assembly proclaimed this to be 1990.

International Network for Adult Educators Serving the Disabled Person This is an *International Council for Adult Education* network.

International People's College Danish *folk high school* founded, in 1921, by *Peter Manniche* to promote international understanding. It is at 1 Montebello Alle, Elsinsore, Dk-3000 Denmark.

International Review of Education A referred journal published by the UNESCO Institute for Education in Hamburg.

International Yearbook of Adult Education Published annually in Germany, with papers in either English or German.

Internet Decentralized world-wide computer network through which information can be accessed.

internship A probationary period of practice, conducted under supervision.

interpersonal skills The skills necessary to communicate with a person or a group while remaining sensitive to their feelings. See also *interactive skills.*

intervention The action taken by a third party or change agent in order to influence the proceedings of a group or a meeting or the processes of an organization.

intervention style The approach a teacher or trainer adopts when intervening in a group activity, eg telling, encouraging, testing, consulting or joining.

interview 1. A formal process in which the aptitude, ability, etc of an individual is assessed by one or more people through a process of questioning. 2. A teaching technique in which an individual or an expert is questioned about their area of expertise in order to allow others to learn about it. 3. A research technique in which a researcher questions respondents about the phenomenon under investigation.

interview schedule A list of questions that are to be used during an interview. Sometimes called a *protocol.*

in-tray exercise See *in-basket exercise.*

introversion A psychological state in which people turn in upon themselves, do not seek social interaction, and become preoccupied with their own thoughts.

introvert   One who exhibits the characteristics of *introversion*.

intuition   A perception or belief, which has not been acquired through the conscious use of reason and intelligence.

intuitive thought   A process of arriving at conclusions without using reasoning and *reflection*.

Investors in People   National UK award to employers involved in offering good opportunity for their employees' own human development. See also *national training awards*.

invigilator   The supervisor of a written examination; sometimes called a *proctor* in the United States.

itinerant teacher   A teacher who moves from one school to another.

Ivy League   A small number of elite college and universities in America are known by this phrase. It is both a laudatory and divisive term – laudatory because of the academic achievement of many of its students, divisive because they are more easily entered by young people from the privileged social strata of society.

Jj

Jago aur Jago Hindi adult education monthly magazine published by the Indian Adult Education Association since 1982.

job analysis Identification of component tasks of a job, often undertaken in order to plan a training programme.

job club Established in Canada and later introduced into the United Kingdom. The job club is both a formal and an informal opportunity for unemployed people to meet, to learn about each other's experiences, and to receive some education relevant to their needs.

job club counsellor A counsellor employed in a job club to offer support and guidance to the unemployed who come within the ambit of the job club.

Job Corps Administered in the United States by the Department of Labor. It offers residential education and training programmes to disadvantaged young people, and has over 100 residential establishments nation-wide.

job description A statement of the main components of an occupational plan.

job development Identification and creation of employment opportunities within the work environment for persons participating in *staff development* programmes.

job enrichment The process of adding variation to a job to make it more satisfying.

job entry level of employment The occupational level at which a person is equipped to be employed as a result of *training*.

job evaluation The process of deciding upon the significance of an occupation within an organizational context.

Job Opportunities for the Business Sector (JOBS) An American plan to finance the training of the long-term unemployed. It was introduced in 1968, by the National Alliance of Businessmen.

job placement An internship undertaken simultaneously with professional preparation.

job readiness The possession of the necessary *knowledge, skills* and *attitudes* necessary to enter employment.

job satisfaction The satisfaction gained from undertaking a certain occupation. There are two types of job satisfaction: that which is intrinsic to the actual work process, and that which is extrinsic to it, such as financial reward or personal status.

Jodh, Frederick (1849–1914) Austrian philosopher and leader of the *popular education* movement, especially influential in Vienna.

Johnson, Alvin Early American *adult educator* and writer about adult education and the *library* movement.

Joint Commission for the Study of Adult Education Formerly the *Joint Committee for* the *Study of Adult Education Policies, Principles and Practices*, this commission recommended that the *American Association for Adult Education* and the *National Education Association* explore closer ties. As a result the *Adult Education Association of the United States of America* was founded in 1951.

Joint Commission for the Study of Adult Education Policies, Principles and Practices   Established in 1946, as a joint conference of the five largest adult education associations in the United States; it became the *Joint Commission for the Study of Adult Education* in 1948.

joint course provision   See *joint provision*.

joint provision   When two or more providers of educational courses make the same provision.

Jones, Reverend Griffith (1683–1761) Founder of the *Welsh Circulating Schools*. He was Rector of Llanddowrorin.

Jones, Thomas (1870–1955)   Founder of Coleg Harlech in 1927 – influential in the *Workers' Educational Association*.

journal   1. An academic publication. 2. A learning journal is a record of learning events recorded by students or practitioners during a course, professional placement etc. This approach to learning is being used more frequently with the growing emphasis on experiential learning. See also *diary, learning log*.

Journal of Access Studies   A quarterly journal published by the *Forum for Access Studies*.

Journal of Adult Education   1. First published in September 1926 in Britain, it soon became *Adult Education* – the longest running journal in the adult education movement. 2. The original title of the *American Association for Adult Education's* journal that was started in 1929 – changed its

name to Adult Education Journal in 1942. 3. The title of the journal of the Mountain Plains Adult Education Association, in the United States. 4. The title of the journal of the adult education movement in Zambia, it was launched in 1982.

Journal of Educational Gerontology Launched in 1986 as the journal of the *Association of Educational Gerontology*. Changed its name to *Ageing Education and Society* a decade later.

Journal of Extension   A journal about university extension in the United States, published since 1962.

Journal of Lifelong Learning Initiatives (JOLLI)   Journal started in July 1997 in the United Kingdom, aimed at recording practical case studies and key practitioners in *lifelong learning*.

junior college   US college that teaches only the first two years of a four-year college course; first established by the University of Chicago. More commonly referred to as a *community college*.

junior year   The third year of a four-year college course.

junto   Formerly called the *Leather Apron Club – a Workingmen's Social and Debating Club*, started as early as in 1727 by 21-year-old Benjamin Franklin and 11 friends in Philadelphia, to debate societal and scientific issues. The word junto actually means a group of people joined for a common purpose. The juntos also initiated social action, eg establishing a public library. This form of meeting was briefly resurrected by the *American Association for Adult and Continuing Education*, at its annual meeting in 1983 in Philadelphia.

Kk

Kapp, Alexander In 1833 Kapp, a German school teacher, is reputed to have introduced the word *andragogy* into the educational vocabulary.

Kawamoto, Unosuke (1888–1960) A leading theorist of social education in Japan, concentrating upon the richness of leisure.

Kekkonen, Helena Finnish adult education who has specialized in peace education. Winner of the UNESCO Peace Prize in 1981.

Keller Plan A programmed learning plan in which the student studies prepared material at their own pace and then must complete the unit test successfully before moving on to the next one. See *mastery learning, personalized system of instruction.*

Kellogg Foundation Established in 1930 by W K Kellogg with the intention of helping people to help themselves. Consequently, institutional and community-based *adult education* has actually been the recipient of a great deal of support from the Foundation.

Kelly's Personal Construct A system constructed by the psychologist George Kelly, which assumes that human behaviour is based upon experimentation and that people construe their world by bipolar opposites, eg black and white, good and bad, etc.

key participants The use of significant personnel in the *evaluation* of training.

keynote lecture A major, or opening, lecture of a conference or a course.

keystoning The effect produced when the image from an overhead projector is not square, but wider at the top than at the bottom. This distortion is produced because the angle of projection is not perpendicular to the angle of the screen.

khaki college A Canadian *adult education* movement during the First World War for the education of men in the armed forces.

khit-pen 1. Term used in Thailand, meaning 'to know how to think'; it describes the philosophy of that country's *adult/non-formal education* service. It involves three forms of *knowledge* – of self, society and the environment. 2. The title of Thailand's *non-formal education* journal, that was established in 1980.

Kidd, J Roby (1915–82) Canadian adult educator, first secretary-general of the International Council for Adult Education.

Kidd, J Roby Award Annual award of $1,500 Canadian, to individual or individuals who have made a significant contribution to *adult education*. The award is made in association with the *International Council for Adult Education* that administers the award.

Kidd, J Roby Trust Fund Established in memory of Roby Kidd and administered by the *International Council for Adult Education.*

kinesthetic learner   One who learns best while moving around and through tactile engagement.

kite mark   An official mark of quality, so that kite marked educational courses are those that have been approved by the kite marking agency.

Kjellberg, Knut (1867–1921)   First chairman of the Popular Education Association in Sweden.

know-how   The ability to do things. See *practical knowledge*.

Know-how Fund   A UK government fund, giving grants to help initiatives, usually initiatives abroad.

knowledge   1. The certainty that phenomena are real and that they possess certain characteristics. 2. The domain of truth propositions. 3. Mastery of principles. 4. Fundamentally, knowledge is subjective, although the idea of objective scientific knowledge has prevailed since the Enlightenment, although it is now being called into question. 5. Knowledge can be classified according to the manner in which it is legitimated – empirical, logical or pragmatic.

knowledge class   A concept that has become familiar within the social sciences, especially since the emergence of post-industrial society, to refer to four distinct groupings of people: the scientific, the technological, the administrative, and the cultural sections of modern society. This group should be seen as separate from intellectuals and the intelligentsia.

knowledge industry   Industry in which *knowledge* is the commodity traded.

knowledge manager   An occupational professional in the knowledge-based industries whose function is to ensure that the essential knowledge required by the company is stored and managed so that it can be used efficiently by all its employees. The knowledge is usually stored electronically.

knowledge manufacture   The creation of information in such a manner as to produce it as socially accepted knowledge; this usually reflects the biases of those who control the process. See *hegemony*.

Knowledge Network   A learning network in Canada.

knowledge production (mode 1)   Knowledge that is produced in accordance with scientific practice.

knowledge production (mode 2)   Knowledge produced in the context of application, through the process of continuous negotiation in which the interests of all the actors are incorporated.

knowledge society   A society that is dependent upon the supply of information and knowledge in order to function efficiently. See *information society*.

knowledge worker   An employee who uses *knowledge* or *information* as the basis of their work. Some 30 per cent of the work force, it is estimated will fall into this category. See *symbolic analysts*.

Knowles, Malcolm (1913–1997)   American adult educator; best known for his writings on *andragogy*. He was executive director of the *Adult Education Association of the United States of America*, and thereafter a professor of adult education.

Knowles Award   The Malcolm Knowles Award is made by the American Association of Adult and Continuing Education for outstanding adult education programme leadership.

Kohlberg, Lawrence   American psychologist whose work on moral development grew out of the work of Piaget – he recognized that moral development continued beyond young adulthood and so his studies are relevant to *adult education*.

Kolb's learning cycle   D A Kolb postulated an experiential learning process of four elements: concrete experience; reflection and observation; generalization and conceptualization; experimentation.

Kolb's learning style inventory   Consists of nine items with four preferences to each – based on his *learning cycle*, purporting to demonstrate four distinct learning styles.

Kold, Christian (1816–1870)   A leading Danish adult educator involved in the formation of some of the early *folk high schools*.

Kom   Newsletter of *Komvux* in Sweden.

kominkan   An adult learning centre, based in local communities, in Japan – similar to a community school.

Kominkan Geppo   The journal of the *kominkan*.

Komvux   Municipality adult education in Sweden, instituted in 1968.

Krant   Dutch magazine for those involved in *adult literacy* work.

kyoiku   Japanese *adult education* institution.

Ll

laboratory   Room especially designed and equipped for specialist practical teaching and scientific research.

Labour College   1. The first labour college was founded in the UK in 1909, as a result of disputes at *Ruskin College*. With the increase in the trade union movement in England in the inter-war years, more colleges were founded. See also *Plebs League*. 2. American college for trade unionists.

Labour Education   Established in 1964, quarterly journal of the *International Labour Office*.

labour education   Workers' education, sponsored by the trades unions.

Labour International   Quarterly journal of the International Labour Office.

labour studies   The study of work in America, its history, problems and future development.

labourer-teacher   Employed by *Frontier College*, highly educated men and women who worked as labourers in the frontier camps and offered basic education classes in the evenings. See *lecturer practitioner, teacher practitioner*.

land grant college   The land grant colleges were established under the *Morrill Land Grant Act* of 1862 in the United States, when certain colleges were given grants to establish the study of practical subjects, such as agriculture and engineering. Most of them

have subsequently expanded their activities and offer a full university curriculum, but they have retained their extension activities.

Land Grant College Act   The Morrill Act of 1862 provided a grant of 30,000 acres of public land to each state for each senator or representative that it had in Congress to endow colleges of agriculture and mechanical arts. Research was not allowed in these colleges until the Hatch Act of 1887.

language   A system of symbols, usual verbal (although non-verbal communication might be conceived of as a form of language) which expresses ideas, knowledge, feelings, sensations, values and beliefs, and so on.

language circle   A *study circle* studying a language.

language code   Forms of speech used by people from different social backgrounds. See *elaborated code* and *restricted code*.

language deficit   Deficiency in language use, often caused by cultural deprivation.

language laboratory   Laboratory specially equipped with teaching machines, audio cassette equipment, etc so that students can study speech and learn languages.

large type reading materials   Materials prepared in a large font for the partially sighted.

Last Post   The name given to the newspaper of the *University of the Third Age* in the United Kingdom; the title was not appreciated and was changed to *Third Age News*.

late adolescence   Stage in human development, often regarded as the period between 16 and 20 years of age.

late adult transition   Period of transition from the dominant period in adult life to the time of late adulthood – often regarded as the period between 60 and 65 years of age.

late adulthood   Usually regarded as the period over the age of 65 years, when one moves from the world of work.

late bloomer   See *late developer*.

late developer   Term used to describe a person who appears to develop academic, or other, ability after having left school. However, such a person may have been an *underachiever* at school.

late modernity   The theory that suggests that the period of modernity is changing and that, while society is still experiencing its consequences, a new phase is also emerging. See *postmodern*.

latent function   A consequence of the existence of a phenomenon that was neither intended nor initially recognized. However, some latent functions are recognized and used in certain situations. It might be claimed, for instance, that the *hidden curriculum* is about the latent functions of attending an educational institution. See also *manifest function*.

latent learning   Learning that occurs without there being any evidence in the learner's performance at the time. See *pre-conscious learning*.

lateral thinking   Restructuring the knowledge that a person already has in order to bring about new insights and ideas. This involves thinking across a range of academic disciplines rather than pursuing one approach systematically. See also *vertical thinking*.

Laubach, Frank (1884–1970)   American founder of the *literacy* movement that bears his name. A former Christian missionary of the Congregational Church, his method is perhaps epitomized by the phrase, *each one teach one*.

Laubach Literacy Action (LLA)   The US domestic arm of *Laubach Literacy International*, it trains and certifies volunteer tutors to teach reading and writing, including English as second language. It operates many local programmes and prepares instructional material.

Laubach Literacy International   A non-profit making educational corporation, founded in 1950 by Frank Laubach, to help illiterate adults to acquire the listening, speaking, reading, writing and number skills necessary to solve the problems that they encounter in their daily living.

Laubach Literacy International News   The quarterly newsletter of *Laubach Literacy International*.

law of effect   One of Edward Thorndike's laws that states that satisfaction serves as a reinforcer of the stimulus-response bonds.

law of exercise   This is one of Thorndike's laws and refers to the process of strengthening the connection between stimulus and response through practice.

law of readiness   A law of Thorndike – that when a person is ready to act in a certain way, it is because it is a satisfying thing to do.

laws of learning   These are laws associated with the work of Edward Thorndike.

lay leader   1. An unordained leader in the Christian churches. 2. Term employed by C O Houle in his pyramid of leadership to refer to the volunteer leaders who are adult educators by virtue of their work, eg youth club leaders.

lay training   Term used in the Christian churches to refer to the education and training of unordained people, so that they can either become workers for the church, or in order to make them more effective Christians in their everyday lives.

lead lecture   A presentation designed to open up a subject, upon which a class or conference will then focus for further discussion.

leader   One who accepts responsibilities to guide, rule, or control a group or organization.

leadership   1. The ability of a person to influence the actions, behaviour, beliefs, and feelings of another person or persons and gain their co-operation. 2. The ability to attract followers to the performance of a task. 3. In US graduate programmes it is about researching and teaching the principles of administrative practice in educational institutions.

leadership style   The way in which leaders perform their role, eg *authoritarian, democratic.*

learn   There are many definitions of the process of learning, depending upon the perspective one adopts towards the study of learning: 1. A more or less permanent change in behaviour as a result of experience. 2. The acquisition of knowledge, skills and attitudes as a result of experience. 3. The transformation of experience into knowledge, skills, attitudes, values, beliefs, senses, etc. 4. The construction and transformation of experience into knowledge, skills, attitudes, beliefs, values, emotions, senses, etc. See *learning.*

learned goal   A goal which is itself acquired through learning.

learner   One who learns, a student.

learner analysis   The identification of an intended audience for a learning activity and the significant characteristics of those learners.

learner-centred education   Teaching and learning which focuses upon the students' learning needs and processes rather than teaching and the teachers' aims. A great deal of the early theory for this approach is to be found in the work of *John Dewey.* See *student-centred learning, Eduard Lindeman.*

learner-controlled instruction   The process in which the learner assumes responsibility for setting the educational objectives of a teaching and learning session so that the responsibility for self-development lies with the learner. Used in certain work situations.

learnership   Formal training arrangement between employer and employee, but not involving an *apprenticeship.*

learning   There are many definitions of learning, all reflecting the academic specialisms from which the study is conducted. 1. The process of acquiring knowledge, skills, attitudes, values, beliefs, emotions, senses, etc. 2. The sum total of the process of acquiring knowledge, skills etc, eg a learned person. 3. Sometimes it is wrongly used as a synonym for education, eg adult learning. Significantly, it is replacing the term education in the educational vocabulary. See *learn.*

Learning   A quarterly journal, published by the Canadian Association for Adult Education.

learning account   A financial account established by individuals to fund their learning – it is a proposal espoused by the Labour government's plans for lifelong learning in the United Kingdom in 1997–98.

Learning Activity Centre   Centre in the *non-formal education* programme in Sri Lanka providing learning opportunities to *non-schoolers* in remote parts of the country.

learning activity package   A self-contained set of learning materials designed to assist learners master some specific area of *knowledge* or *skill*.

Learning Age   The title of the UK Labour government's Green Paper on *lifelong learning*.

learning block   Something that prevents a person from learning – it may be psychological or situational.

learning by immersion   Used in language teaching, when students live in a community where only the language they are to learn is spoken all the time; they are immersed in the language.

Learning Campaign   An educational project in UK, sponsored by the Royal Society of Arts to encourage a greater awareness of the need to learn.

learning centre   A place where individuals can go to learn; often it will now be a centre where the learners can use electronic technology in order to access learning material.

learning community   An organized group of individuals working together in order to increase their *knowledge, skills*, or sensitivity.

learning contract   A contract between two or more persons (usually involving a tutor) to learn certain *knowledge* or *skill* within a specified time. The contract is often made in writing, although there are probably many more informal contracts made between tutors and learners. *Knowles* suggested that it was learner-designed, planned, implemented and evaluated.

learning culture   The overall environment of a group or an organization committed to

learning – it involves: the physical design and layout; the emotional culture with a supportive attitude towards risk; a mental culture which stimulates learning; a macro culture which is the organization's own vision and values, often laid down by the leadership of the organization.

learning curve   A graphic representation of the actual or expected rate of acquisition of *knowledge* or *skill*.

learning cycle   A cyclic model of the learning process. See, for instance, *Kolb's learning cycle*.

learning diary   See *learning log*.

learning difficulty   The failure to make satisfactory progress through a course of study. See *learning block*.

Learning Direct   A telephone educational guidance service established in the United Kingdom as part the Labour government's initiative in lifelong learning in the latter part of the 1990s.

learning disability   An inability to learn something as a result of a sensory handicap or cultural deprivation. An improper neurological process that inhibits learning capability in otherwise normally functioning people.

learning environment   The total set of conditions that influence learning.

learning episode   A defined period of time in which learning occurs or is planned. The period of time may vary from a moment to a much longer period, although it is unwise to specify time length, except for specific purposes. See *learning project*.

learning exchange   1. An educational brokering agency whose task is to match those who wish to teach something with those who wish to learn the same topic. See *free university*. 2. Freely available educational institute for adults, occurs in Australia.

learning exchange network A *learning exchange* developed in the United States to cater for rural populations. They are locally organized.

Learning for All UNESCO conference held in Thailand.

Learning for the Twenty-First Century The title of the first report of the UK government's advisory committee on lifelong learning. See *Fryer Report*.

learning from experience 1. Term used to refer to the type of learning that is facilitated by teachers providing primary experiences from which the learners can learn through induction. 2. Learning from all the experiences of everyday living, stemming from the work of *John Dewey*. See *experiential learning*.

Learning from Experience Trust An educational charity established in the United Kingdom to promote *experiential learning*.

learning how to learn The recognition that people need to learn how to learn to cope with the rapidly changing world, especially true of the world of work where courses are now run in order to help people acquire the skills of learning.

Learning in Later Life A European network about third age learning, based at the University of Ulm.

learning journal See *journal, learning log*.

learning laboratory Specially equipped room for learners with either programmed or other *self-instructional* materials for *independent study*.

learning log A record of learning undertaken, or a record of learning needs, discovered as a result of experience. This is used in professional preparation, especially during the practical placement. See also *diary, journal*.

learning material A package containing information to be learned.

learning need A deficiency in *knowledge* or *skill* that can be remedied through learning.

learning needs assessment The identification of learner, provider, and community needs and the synthesis of these into a specification of the problem.

learning network 1. A matching service of people who wish to learn and those who wish to teach a subject, skill, or topic in a formal or informal manner. The networks are sometimes established through educational brokering agencies, or through some other organization. See *learning exchange*. 2. An Australian organization that seeks to provide educational broadcasting. Established in the mid-1980s.

Learning Opportunities for All A report issued by the Organization for Economic Co-operation and Development between 1971 and 1981 in five volumes. See *Lifelong Learning for All*.

learning organization A team working together towards its collective performance, committed to continuing learning and adaptation to changing circumstances.

learning-oriented learner One who learns for learning's sake – one of Houle's three types of learners. See also *activity-oriented learner, goal-oriented learning*.

learning outcome The end-product, or the intended end-product, of a course of learning. See *objective*.

learning package A collection of materials prepared by a teacher or an educational institution to be used in *self-directed learning*.

learning plateau A period in the learning process where progress seems slow and the acquisition of new *knowledge* and *skill* seems difficult.

learning project   A scheme, or plan, of learning. It can vary in duration, although Tough suggests that it should take at least seven hours.

learning resource   Anything that can be used for learning.

learning resource centre   A centre that stores books and other learning material, usually in a specialist topic, in order to be of service to learners.

Learning Resources Kit   Formerly called *Tie Lines* when it was first established in 1966. Published by the Canadian Association of Adult Education in English and French.

Learning Resources Network (LERN)   Established in 1974, this is an American national technical assistance network in *non-credit* programming.

learning set   A group of learners who begin a course of study together and usually progress through the course together.

learning setting analysis   The identification of contextual factors relevant to the design of learning activities.

learning society   There is no agreed definition, but the term is used in a number of ways, namely: 1. An ideal democratic society in which all are able to acquire all the necessary *knowledge* and *skill* to play their full part in society and realize their human potential. 2. A society that is changing rapidly, so that all its members are forced to learn all the time to keep abreast with these changes. 3. A consumer society in which all forms of learning material may be purchased and in which it is fashionable so to do.

learning structure   The way that a teacher organizes the learning process for the learners.

learning style   The characteristic manner by which a learner approaches a learning task. A variety of styles have been identified, usually in terms of opposites, eg convergent/divergent. The relationship between learning style and *cognitive style* is a debatable question.

learning style inventory   A research instrument seeking to investigate people's preferred *learning styles* through a self-description *questionnaire*.

learning task analysis   An identification of the main *skills, knowledge* and/or *attitudes* required by a learner.

learning theory   There are a number of theories about the way people learn – *behaviourist, cognitivist, social* and *experiential*; their development reflects the changes in the wider society.

Learning To Be   The *Faure Report*, published by UNESCO in 1972.

learning to learn   See *learning how to learn*.

Learning Works   The title of the Kennedy Report on Further Education in the United Kingdom, published in 1997.

Learning Zone   Adult education programmes broadcast by the BBC each night.

Leather Apron Club   The original title of the *junto*.

leave of absence   Period of time a person is away either from work or study. See *paid educational leave*.

leaving certificate   A certificate awarded to successful students at the end of schooling, usually as a result of sitting national examinations.

lecture   1. A method of teaching. 2. A discourse on a specific topic. 3. To scold or reprimand.

lecture theatre   Large, especially equipped room, usually with ranked seats so that all learners can see the lecturer.

lecturer   1. One who gives a lecture. 2. An occupational teaching position in further and higher education in the United Kingdom.

lecturer practitioner   A teacher who also undertakes a practice role and teaches the subject of the practice. See *labourer-teacher, teacher practitioner.*

lecturette   A short lecture, sometimes referred to as a mini-lecture.

legal adult   A person who has reached the legally specified age of adulthood.

legibility   The clarity of written work for reading or deciphering.

leisure centre   Specially equipped centre for sports and other leisure activities; often a venue for *adult education.*

leisure class   1. An educational activity that takes place in people's spare time. See *leisure education.* 2. The socio-economic group which can afford to live on its wealth rather than its earned income.

leisure counselling   Assistance to help people use their leisure time.

leisure education   1. Education that occurs during leisure time. 2. Education into the use of leisure. See *pre-retirement education.*

Leisure Learning   A programme initiated by the Scottish Museums Council to attract wider audiences than museums tend to attract.

Lengrand, Paul (b. 1910)   Active proponent of *lifelong education.* Member of the UNESCO secretariat from 1948 and in 1951 he was appointed head of the Adult Education Division of UNESCO.

Léo Légrange Federation   An organization providing *socio-cultural animation* in France, jointly funded by the French government and the local municipalities.

lesson   1. A specified period of teaching and learning. 2. Something learned.

Lesson Handbook   The original title of the annual study notes of the adult school movement which started in 1911; in 1919 the title was changed to *Study Handbook.*

lesson plan   The teacher's outline of a proposed lesson.

Let's Read   The quarterly publication of the Jamaican Movement for the Advancement of Literacy: publication started in 1974.

letters   Sometimes used as a synonym for arts.

liberal adult education   A specifically adult form of *liberal education.*

liberal arts   The study of fine arts, humanities and the social sciences.

liberal arts college   American college that provides a four-year degree course in *non-vocational education.*

liberal education   A form of education not orientated to work and employment. It stems from the idea that education frees the individual – which is at the heart of the liberal ideological system. See also *general education, non-vocational education, liberalism.*

liberal studies   1. A *liberal arts* education. 2. A non-vocational element introduced into the *vocational education* programme in order to broaden the curriculum.

liberalism   An ideology that suggests that individuals are independent, rational and free to pursue their own interests. This ideology which is to be found in Greek literature achieved prominence in the West with the Enlightenment thinkers, so that it forms the basis of much thinking about *modernity*.

liberation education In some ways this is a term similar to *popular education*, especially in its Latin American context. It is associated with the work of *Paulo Freire* and has the following characteristics: it is associated with the people, organized by the people, and critical of the more established forms of education which are provided by the state for purposes other than that of emancipating the people. It is also associated with liberation theology – a radical theological movement. See *emancipatory education*.

liberty The freedom of the will, or political freedom. See *liberal education*.

library 1. Collection of books, and other learning resources. 2. The building in which such a collection is stored. See *public library*.

Library of Congress The national library of America.

Library of Congress classification A system of classification of books, developed in the Library of Congress.

Library of Continuing Education Based in Syracuse University, this is a collection of adult education materials. It was later called *Syracuse University Resources for Educators of Adults (SUREA)*. Recently renamed the Alexander Charters Library.

library science The study and skill of collecting, organizing and utilizing books and other learning materials.

library time A period of time on an academic timetable when the learners are expected to work in a self-directed manner in the library.

licence A legal document authorizing a person or organization to perform specific services.

licentiate in education An academic qualification in education. In the United Kingdom, this is usually sub-degree level, but in other European countries where there is a five-year first degree, the licentiate is the qualification awarded.

licentiture The final three years of a five-year degree course in some European countries.

life change See *life cycle*.

life class Art class using a live model.

life crisis A major change in the pattern of a person's life. See *life cycle transition*.

life cycle The series of changes that occur in the life of a person, a living organism or an organization between one stage of development and the identical stage in the next generation.

life cycle transition Periods of major change in the course of life, sometimes associated with age but often with circumstances. See *life crisis*.

life experience credit Academic credit that is awarded for experiential lifelong learning. See *accreditation of prior experiential learning*.

life history The study of the course of an individual's or a community's life.

life history method Research into people and their learning through the study of their biographies. See *biographical method*.

life passage The patterned pathways through aspects of social living. See *career*.

life review A normal process in older adulthood of looking back over life, taking stock, and confronting mortality. This type of review has been formalized by some educational gerontologists who run workshops to help people undertake their life reviews in a more systematic manner. There are some similarities to *life history* methods.

life satisfaction   A concept found in gerontological literature that refers to a cognitive assessment of one's progress towards desired goals.

life sciences   Biological and related sciences.

life skills   Those skills necessary to live and interact successfully in the context of social living. Sometimes referred to as *coping skills*. See also *common skills*.

life style   The way of life adopted by an individual, often related to socio-economic position.

life world   A sociological or phenomenological concept about the way people see their own world. It underlies the way people interpret their own experiences. It refers to a frame of reference, stock of knowledge etc that provides meaning for an individual's aspirations and actions.

lifelong education   The concept that education should be a lifelong process. There have been two ways of looking at this process in the literature: the first has started from *initial education* and continued it throughout life; the second has started from an *adult education* perspective and stretched it backwards.

Lifelong Education, Assessment and Referral Network (LEARN)   A network of the *Council for Adult and Experiential Learning*.

Lifelong Education Bibliography   Published by the UNESCO Institute for Education and regularly updated.

lifelong learning   Until recently, there has been a tendency to treat this term as being synonymous with lifelong education.

However, there are distinct conceptual differences. 1. The process of learning which occurs throughout the life span. 2. The learning that occurs variously in formal institutions or education and training, and informally, at home, at work or in the wider community.

Lifelong Learning   A report by the Commission of Education in Eire in 1983.

Lifelong Learning Act   Title 1, Part B of the Amendments to the Higher Education Act (Public Law 94-482) passed by the US Congress in October 1976. This constituted a manifesto of the types of services Congress considered should be made available and funds were voted in order to make them available.

Lifelong Learning: An Omnibus of Practice and Research   A practitioner journal published eight times a year in the United States between 1983 and 1989. It was previously called Lifelong Learning: The Adult Years, and it has been superseded by Adult Learning.

Lifelong Learning for All   A report issued by the Organization for Economic Co-operation and Development in 1996. See also *Learning Opportunities for All*.

Lifelong Learning in Europe (LLinE)   Journal started in Finland in 1996 aimed at providing a forum for scholars and practitioners to examine lifelong learning in Europe.

Lifelong Learning: The Adult Years   Established in 1977 this journal was published until 1983 when it changed its name to Lifelong Learning: An Omnibus of Research and Practice. It was published by the Adult Education Association of the United States of America.

lifespan development   The progress of an individual through the *life passage*.

Ligue Français de l'Enseignement et l'Education Permanente   The Ligue de l'Enseignement (The League of Teaching) was formed in France in 1866 and in 1967 it changed its name to the French League of Teaching and Lifelong Education.

Likert scale   Scale used in attitude measurement tests.

limited English-speaking ability   Term used in the United States to refer to those whose proficiency in English is limited.

Lindeman, Eduard (1885–1953)   One of the founding fathers of adult education in the United States. He was an early proponent of *Dewey's* ideas of *experiential learning* in *adult education*.

linear relationship   In statistics, this refers to a specific form of relationship between two variables.

linguistic code   See *language code*.

linguistic context   The speech context within which a word or phrase is used.

linguistic philosophy   A school of philosophy that concentrates on the meaning of language.

LinkAge   Founded in the United Kingdom in 1988, with the idea of trying to link generations in different ways, such as recruiting seniors to go into schools. In 1990, it was incorporated into the Community Service Trust.

linked courses   Academic courses run jointly by two or more educational institutions. This is becoming more possible through the use of *teleconferencing*.

lip reading   The ability to understand the meaning of words from the shape made by the lips, without necessarily being able to hear the words.

listening group   A group of people organized to listen to a lecture, or a radio or television programme, and discuss it afterwards. Used in *community education*.

listening skill   The ability to listen carefully with insight and understanding. A skill taught to those involved in counselling.

literacy   1. The reading and writing ability for a person to engage effectively in those activities normally expected from an adult member of a culture group. 2. It is often defined as a reading age of 9.5 years or 5 years of schooling, although there is considerable variation between different authorities. See *functional literacy, computer literacy*.

literacy centre   Centre that provides non-school children with opportunities for basic education.

literacy education   See *adult basic education*.

Literacy Volunteers of America Established in 1962, it operates many programmes in adult *literacy* with volunteer tutors.

literary association   Historical voluntary association offering adult education opportunities, similar to *Mechanics Institutes* although not necessarily orientated to the working people in quite the same way.

literature   1. Written material. 2. Body of writing about a specific topic.

literature review   An overall assessment and analysis of the published research and scholarship on a specific area of study.

LittD   Degree of Doctor of Letters.

Local Authority advisor   In the United Kingdom, local government education authorities have traditionally employed advisors, or formerly inspectors, to advise educational practitioners about their work.

Local Development Council The *Russell Report* led to the growth of the idea that there should be development councils, with representatives drawn from a wide range of educational providers, to develop *adult education* provision in local areas. The idea was not widely accepted.

local education agency (LEA) 1. US term used to refer to agencies in specific localities to which educational services may be contracted. 2. In Federal legislation, the local education agency is a legally constituted board of education, or other educational authority.

Local Education Authority (LEA) Local government education authority in the United Kingdom. See *Training and Enterprise Council*.

local history The historical study of a specific geographical area: a popular subject in liberal adult education.

local learning centre Centres where adults can have their learning needs assessed and be given advice and guidance. See *education shop*.

local school district US *local education agency*.

logical positivism A scientific analysis of natural human phenomena that uses a deductive-nomological approach in which causality is imputed from the constant conjunction of events, as measured by 'sense' or 'experiential' data. Typically held in disrepute by philosophers of science, but it still dominates educational research.

long-term goal The predetermined outcome of a course of study. See *aim* and *short-term goal*.

long-term memory Having processed input information, it is stored away in the memory system known as the long-term memory. See *short-term memory*.

longitudinal study A research technique that studies one or more groups or categories over a period of time. See *cross-sectional study*.

looking-glass self The American sociologist C H Cooley, first used this term to refer to the type of self-concept that emerges as a result of seeing oneself as others do as a result of interaction.

low achiever One who under-performs.

lyceum Self-help adult education organizations, in which members were both learners and teachers. Josiah Holbrook started the lyceum movement in Massachusetts in 1826. The associations, normally town-based, were usually for working people. They were formed for mutual improvement through the acquisition of useful knowledge by lecture, discussion or any other appropriate method. The movement grew to such an extent that there were over 3,500 lyceums in different towns within a decade of the start of the movement. By 1850 the national movement had disintegrated, although individual lyceums continued to function. The lyceum was originally called the Society for Mutual Education and it then became known as the *Society for the Improvement of Schools and Diffusion of Useful Knowledge*.

Mm

MA Master of Arts degree.

machine learning The emulation of human knowledge-acquisition processes by digital computer systems. The significance of machines being able to learn from and control their environment has been a significant feature in engineering for many years. These systems have recently begun to appear in adult education studies. They are also significant in forms of education and training.

MAdEd Master of Adult Education degree.

magnetic board A board covered with magnetic material, which can be used for visual display using display objects which are backed with a magnet so that they stick to the board.

mainstreaming 1. The process whereby non-award, or non-credit, bearing educational courses are incorporated into the normal award-bearing programme. This has recently occurred with extra-mural courses in the United Kingdom. 2. In the United States, this term also refers to the process of incorporating all 'non-normal' students into the normal educational programmes.

maintenance learning Learning that is designed to maintain the system and the established way of life.

Maison de la Culture French community centre, in which a great deal of adult education is conducted.

major The main subject studied by a student in a US university.

major adviser The academic member of staff responsible for advising students on their major course of study in a US university.

major award A high-value financial scholarship.

major premise A term used in logic having greater generality or scope than the *minor premise*.

make-up class US term for students wishing to catch up on their academic programme, or a replacement class because of a prior cancellation.

management committee The governing body of an institution.

management development A strategy to promote the effectiveness of management through learning events.

management education Instruction in the principles of management.

management game *Gaming* is a teaching technique used in education, including *management education*.

mandatory continuing education The practice by which the members of a profession are compelled to attend continuing professional education – either through legislation or through the regulations of professional associations, in order to retain their licence, or accreditation, to practise. See *compulsory continuing education, continuing professional development.*

mandatory grant   The financial assistance paid to students in the United Kingdom by local government as a result of government regulations.

mandatory periodic refreshment   See *mandatory continuing education.*

manifest function   A consequence of the existence of a phenomenon that was both intended and is recognized. See *latent function.*

manipulation   1. The management of people for ends other than of their own choosing. 2. The way that different variables are related to each other in statistical analysis is sometimes referred to as the manipulation of variables.

Manniche, Peter (1889–1981)   Danish adult educator. Founder of the *International People's College* in 1921 and its principal for 33 years.

manpower analysis   Analysis of the characteristics of the workforce.

manpower planning   Analysis of the present and future needs of the workforce.

Manpower Services Commission (MSC)   Established in 1973 to run public employment and training services in the United Kingdom.

manpower studies   The study of the supply and demand of the workforce.

Mansbridge, Albert (1876–1952)   Founder and first secretary of the *Workers' Educational Association.* Pre-eminent in England as an advocate of adult education, in the early years of the twentieth century.

manual ability   See *manual dexterity.*

manual dexterity   The ability to control and co-ordinate the physical body, especially in relation to perception.

manual dexterity test   An investigation into the extent of a person's *manual dexterity.*

manual training   *Training* in *skills.*

marginality   Something which is not a core activity of an organization is regarded as marginal; adult education programmes have traditionally been seen to be marginal to a university's main educational functions.

marginalization   The exclusion of sectors of a population from central and crucial areas of the economic and power positions. See *social exclusion.*

mark   The grade awarded for a piece of work. See *grade.*

market research   The process of identifying and assessing potential markets. Becoming more common in education as it is becoming commodified.

marking   The process of assessing a piece of academic work.

marking criteria   Guidance given to those marking academic work, indicating what should be included in order to gain a specific grade. See also *tutor notes.*

marking scales   Scales established to order to try to lessen the subjective element in *marking* examination papers and other pieces of academic work.

marking scheme   A set of notes to guide *tutors* (and students) about the specific criteria that should guide the assessing of a specific piece of academic work.

mass communication   Communication to large numbers of people.

mass education   Education for large proportions of the population, as opposed to education for an elite. UK higher education has recently moved in this direction.

mass media   The means of communicating to large groups of people. Used in some forms of *distance education*.

massification   The creation of a mass education system in higher education.

Masters degree   The academic award above a bachelors degree. In the United Kingdom there are two forms: a masters degree by being taught (taught masters) and another by research.

mastery   Demonstrated proficiency of specified *knowledge* or *skill*.

mastery learning   A form of learning that entails the successful completion of a learning unit before proceeding to the next ones.

mastery test   An examination designed to assess the extent to which the requisite knowledge or skill has been mastered.

matched groups   In educational research it is sometimes useful to match people on all variables relevant to the research except the one under investigation.

matched sample   Samples selected because they share the same characteristics relevant to the study.

matching funding   System of funding, whereby the funding agency will provide funding on a fixed, or equal, proportion to the amount raised by the host institution.

matching type question   A variant of the *multiple choice question*, in which candidates are asked to match a given response to a set question from a number of options.

material self   Elements of the *self-concept*, which relate to material objects.

mathetics   The study of students' behaviour in the learning process, contrasted to pedagogy which is the study of teachers' behaviour. The term was first introduced by *Roby Kidd*.

Matna   An Israeli centre of culture, youth and sports – a form of *community centre*.

matriculate   To pass the school leaving examinations and to enrol in an educational course in an institution of higher education.

matrix   A rectangular display of research results in rows and columns to facilitate comparison of variables.

maturation   The process of physiological and psychological change that occurs with ageing.

mature student   In the United Kingdom, a mature student in an institution of higher education is one who enters it over the age of 21 years – it used to be 23 years – of age, usually after having undertaken a period of employment.

Mature Students' Union   A student union formed in UK in 1975 in order to look after the interests of *mature students*.

maturity   The state of being relatively advanced physically, mentally or emotionally. Having achieved a state of adulthood.

MBA   Master of Business Administration degree.

McClusky, Howard (1900–1982)   Adult educator at the University of Michigan. He was first president of the *Adult Education Association of the United States of America*, and the author of the paper on *educational gerontology* for the White House Conference on Aging in 1971.

McClusky Symposium A symposium held each year at the *American Association for Adult and Continuing Education* conference on *educational gerontology*.

McClune Award The Donald McClune Award for Collaborative Efforts in Adult Education is sponsored by the *American Association for Adult and Continuing Education* and awarded to the individual or group that has promoted collaboration in *adult education*.

McClune, Donald (d. 1986) Californian State Director of Adult Education. There is a State award in his name as well as the national one.

Mead, George Herbert (1863–1931) American psychologist and founder of *interactionism*. His work on the *self* has had a considerable impact on the social sciences.

Mead, Margaret (1901–1978) American anthropologist whose work on adolescence has had considerable effect on education.

mean Measure of central tendency, determined by adding all the scores together and dividing the sum by the number of items. It is often called an average.

meaning-orientation An approach to learning in which the *learner* seeks to comprehend the whole meaning rather than just the facts.

meaning perspective The structure of psycho-cultural assumptions within which new experience is assimilated and transformed by one's past experiences. See *transformative learning*.

meaning scheme Symbolic models, which are projected upon sense impressions of the world, in order to construe meaning and habitual expectations. See *transformative learning*.

means test Process of assessing whether a student's family earns sufficient income to pay the requisite fees of a college or university.

Measure of English Language Proficiency (MELP) A written literacy test consisting of 26 questions which assess the candidate's ability to identify key words and phrases and to match these with one of four fixed-choice alternatives.

mechanical ability The *skills* required to employ, and diagnose the malfunctioning of, mechanical equipment.

mechanical arts US phrase for engineering.

mechanics institutes Institutes founded to offer working class people a scientific and mechanical education. They were democratic institutions, offering lectures and reading facilities to their members. The movement started about 1823 in Glasgow and rapidly spread throughout Britain and the rest of the world.

Mechanics Institution Founded in London in 1817 by Thomas Claxton. Predated the *mechanics institutes*. It was a weekly discussion group at which members were expected to deliver a lecture, followed by discussion.

mechanistic learning model The *behavioural* approach to learning.

MEd Master of Education degree. See also *EdM*.

media The means of transmitting information to people. See *mass media*.

media analysis Analysis of aims, content and method of media presentations.

media centre An area in an institution in which a full range of materials, equipment and associated staff are available.

media research Analysis of all ways by which the media are used in society.

media university   A distance teaching university.

median   The mid-value in a frequency distribution.

mediated experience   Experience of a phenomenon at second hand, eg through a book, mass media, etc. In all of these cases it is the transmission of another's *primary experience* to the recipient. See *secondary experience*.

mediated self-instruction   A form of *self-directed learning* in which guidance is provided as to mastering the information provided.

Meeting in Finland   The Association of Finnish Adult Education Associations has organized this annual gathering of adult educators since 1970 to discuss important educational and political concerns.

mega-university   A very large, usually global, university having in excess of 100,000 students.

membership group   The group with whom an individual identifies and by whom they are accepted as a member.

memorizing   The process of committing to memory. It is a form of non-reflective learning. See also *rote learning*.

memory   1. An individual's conscious and unconscious record of past experiences. See *rote memory*. 2. The storage system within the brain in which past experiences are retained.

memory span   The number of items that are actually reproducible after a presentation.

mental ability   The ability to think and reason.

mental ability test   An examination of a person's general ability to adapt to new situations and to learn from experience.

mental coaching   A technique employed by *Peuple et Culture* to assist people in developing the art of critical thought. It has three phases: a number of exercises to help participants express themselves, a number of exercises to practise in order to become more aware; and the recreation of the first phase with the implementation of the skills of the second.

mental disorder   A form of abnormality or illness of the mind.

mental health   The neurological or psychological condition of the mind.

mental illness   Person having certain forms of *mental disorder*.

mentality   The state or quality of the mental or intellectual ability.

mentally handicapped person   Person who has been classified as mentally ill.

mentally retarded person   Person who has been classified as mentally subnormal or who is significantly below average ability.

mentor   One who advises, guides or counsels. In adult education this is not normally the official teacher, but one who advises on how skills should be performed in the workplace. There are both formal systems in organizations for mentoring, but there is an informal system whereby a younger person seeks the advice of an older colleague informally. Often the mentor is assumed to be the advocate as well.

meritocracy   Term used to suggest that in such a society the most able raise to the top of the social hierarchy.

metaphysics   The study of human existence and phenomena as a whole, instead of through the study of elements of it empirically through the natural sciences.

meta-theory   1. The critical study of the nature and purpose of philosophy. 2. A theoretical perspective behind the *theory* of a phenomenon.

method   An established or systematic order of performing any act or procedure.

methodology   1. The study of methods employed in research. Often wrongly used to refer to the method of a particular piece of research. 2. Sometimes used to refer to courses in teaching methods, but only rarely since this is now often included with curriculum studies.

Mezirow, Jack   Professor of adult education in Teacher's College, Columbia University in New York. Major exponent of *transformative learning* theory.

micro-didactical work (mikrodidaktische Tätigkeiten)   Term used in Germany to describe some of the special features of adult education: direct communication in small groups and discussion methods. See *micro-teaching*.

microfilm   A general term for material carrying micro-images. Can be used for teaching, or in the construction of data banks.

micro-teaching   Literally a scaled-down approach to teaching eg teaching a very short lesson to a small class in a limited period of time. It provides opportunities to practise new and different skills in a safe environment.

mid-life counselling   Counselling offered to people experiencing mid-life crisis. See also *mid-life planning*.

mid-life crisis   The apparent psychological crisis that many people experience in early middle age, which can result in depression or change in life style.

mid-life planning   Assistance at the time of mid-life in planning for old age.

mid-life transition   The period between about 40 and 45 years of age when the adult passes from early adulthood to middle adulthood. It is sometimes associated with *mid-life crisis*.

Midwest Research to Practice Conference   Started in 1981 at the University of Northern Illinois, this is a regional *adult education* conference.

migrant education   A form of education offered in immigrants soon after their arrival by some societies in order to teach them the culture of their new country.

Ministry of Reconstruction   A British government ministry established after the First World War that prepared the famous *1919 Report*. See *Final Report of the Adult Education Committee of the Ministry of Reconstruction, 1919*.

minor award   A low value financial scholarship.

minor premise   Used in logic, it is less general than the *major premise*.

minor subject   The second subject in a student's programme. See *major*.

minority group   Any small group in a society, usually an ethnic group. See also *social exclusion*.

mission   A mission statement is a statement of an organization's purpose or aspiration.

mixed ability group   Group of people who are not streamed for their ability. Sometimes there is confusion between ability and achievement within this context.

mixed ability teaching   Teaching a group of people with different abilities simultaneously.

mixed mode of delivery   When the educational process is offered to learners through a variety of systems, eg distance teaching, face-to-face teaching, etc.

mobile   Visual display where two- or three-dimensional objects are hung from the ceiling of a classroom.

mobile classroom   Temporary classroom that can be located in different sites.

mobile library   Library that can be transported to different locations. See *bookmobile*.

mode   The most common value in a frequency distribution.

mode of delivery   Term used to refer to the manner in which learners receive their learning materials, eg distance education, face-to-face teaching, etc.

model   A two- or three-dimensional representation. 1. As a two-dimensional representation, a model usually seeks to incorporate the salient points of a complex theory. 2. A three-dimensional model is a structure that represents a larger phenomenon. 3. A theoretical construction of a complex process, depicting its salient features.

model answer   A prepared answer to a set question; used as a model for teaching purposes.

model learning   Learning through observing and imitating.

modelling   *Imitating* another person in order to learn to play a role. See *role modelling*.

modem   A system that can be installed into a computer to enable it to function interactively electronically.

moderator   1. One who introduces and guides discussion and audience participation during a panel, colloquy, or forum. Sometimes called a *facilitator*. 2. An advisor to an educational course team. That advisor may represent the body that is validating the course or making the award.

modernism   An aesthetic culture reflecting the post-Enlightenment period.

modernity   A philosophical and sociological concept used to describe the post-traditional society, which emerged after the Enlightenment.

modernization   An economic and technological process that emerges with capitalism; this also has cultural and social implications. Sometimes called a theory of development.

modular course   A course comprising a selection of modules from which learners can select as appropriate to their *learning needs*.

module   A self-contained unit of teaching and learning that can be used in combination with other units to build a course or courses. An advantage of the modular approach is that the same unit can be used in different courses.

Mondale Act   The *Lifelong Learning Act* in the United States.

monism   A philosophical theory that maintains that there is one and only one substance, so that the mind-body relationship is not regarded as dualistic.

monitor   One who keeps check on a phenomenon or process. In the UK Open University, the monitor is one who checks on the part-time staff's grading of student assignments.

monotechnic   Term used to indicate that a course of programme prepares people for only one occupation. See *polytechnic*.

Montreal Mechanics Institute   Founded in 1828, the first *mechanics institute* in Canada. Ceased to function in 1835 and later re-opened. Is now the Atwater Library of Montreal.

moonlight school   Evening school for the poor in the United States in the nineteenth century. Only held when the moon was full, so that it would throw light on the paths and trails along which the learners came. See also *night school.*

moral development   A stage theory of development. Kohlberg's theory suggests people pass through six stages in order to become fully developed morally.

moral education   The teaching of moral ideas and practices.

moral philosophy   The study of ethics, or moral values.

moral relativism   The theory that there are no absolute values and that all values are relative.

mores   The customs and behaviour patterns by which people live and to which conformity is expected.

Morrill Land Grant Acts   The Federal Acts in the United States of 1862 and 1880 that made land and funds available for the creation of the land grant colleges.

motivate   1. To encourage someone to act in a specific direction. 2. To function as a goal or incentive.

motivation   The internal state or the intervening process that drives a person to act in a specific manner. It may be conscious or unconscious.

motive   The reason for acting in a specific manner. It may be conscious or unconscious.

motor skills   Physical skills.

moveable school   An *extension education* enterprise, where demonstration wagons were taken to farms in order to teach farmers about seed selection and other aspects of scientific farming.

MSc   Master of Science degree.

MSocSc   Master of Social Science degree.

MTech   Master of Technology degree.

multi-campus federal university   The provision of university level education through a number of different campuses and educational institutions, all co-operating to offer the provision over a large, often rural, area.

multi-cultural education   1. A system of education incorporating more than one culture. A preparation for the social, political, and economic realities that individuals experience in culturally diverse and complex societies. 2. A system of education that allows for all ethnic groups within a society to celebrate and learn about their own cultures.

multi-disciplinary   The use of more than one academic discipline but without integration of the disciplines, which would make it *inter-disciplinary.*

multi-ethnic   The involvement of more than one ethnic group. See *multi-cultural education.* However, ethnicity and culture are not synonymous concepts.

multi-factor tests   Tests seeking to measure a number of different factors.

multi-lingual database   Hans Hovenberg, in Sweden, has been building up a linguistic database of adult education terminology from across the world. He used the first edition of this dictionary as one of his initial sources.

multi-media interactive system   Through the use of a computer, these systems now enable the user/learner to gain access to and sometimes combine, edit and orchestrate a wide range of media. See *hypermedia*.

multi-skilling   Training workers in a variety of skills.

multiple choice question   A form of examination question in which the question is asked in the stem and a variety of answers are provided so that candidates can indicate which they consider to be correct. See *objective test*.

multiple intelligences   The theory that individuals are not born with a single intelligence but that they have, or acquire, different intelligences in their lives, such as a musical intelligence, etc.

multiple regression   Statistical technique for analysing the relationship between variables.

multivariate analysis   Statistical technique allowing for the simultaneous analysis of a number of variables.

multiversity   A concept in which the differing functions of the university, including teaching, pure and applied research, and service, are all given emphasis.

Mumbai Statement   Statement prepared in India in 1998 specifying the place of adults in the system of higher education.

Murikka Statement on Adult Education   Statement made in *Meeting in Finland* in 1979 when adult educators from 28 countries

stressed the importance of adult education in the contemporary world.

Murphy Report   Published in 1973 – a report on *adult education* in Ireland.

museum   A place where objects of artistic, historical, archaeological or scientific interest are exhibited. Regarded as an educational institution.

mutual improvement societies   Usually, small groups established on a self-help basis for the purpose of adult education, with the basic principle of the better educated helping the less well educated. The first mutual improvement societies were established in London towards the end of the seventeenth century and were middle class in origin. But during the period of their greatest popularity, in the nineteenth century, they were mostly working class in membership. They often met in members' homes but also in other premises, while they tended to be independent, there is some evidence of federations of societies. However, they did not only have an educational function, some of them undertook financial functions for their members. See also the *adult school* movement and the *workingmen's reading room* movement.

mutable self   The self that is able to accommodate change and progress and respond to the freedom so engendered.

myth   Cultural story conveying historical or metaphysical propositions. These stories often contained the world-view of a tribe or a people.

Nn

Nabila Brier Award   An award made to an outstanding woman *adult educator* in memory of Nabila Brier. The award was first made in October 1987.

Nabila Brier Fund   Administered by the *International Council for Adult Education*. The fund was established to assist in forging links between women educators in Arab countries and the remainder of the world.

Nadezhda K Krupskaya Prize   *Literacy* prize established in the USSR in 1970, and administered by *UNESCO*.

narrowcast   A form of transmission of *information* to specifically targeted audiences through media.

National Adult Education Clearinghouse
This *clearinghouse* disseminates information about a wide range of adult education in the United States.

National Adult Education Foundation
Established by the *American Association for Adult and Continuing Education* in order to provide support funding for projects in the field of continuing education.

National Adult Literacy Agency
Originally a sub-committee of *AONTAS* but in 1980 it became an independent national agency in the Republic of Ireland.

National Adult Literacy Project   As a result of the *Secretary's Initiative on Adult Literacy* this 14-month project was launched in late 1983 in the USA.

National Adult School Organization
The association of adult schools in the United Kingdom, which co-ordinates *self-study* groups. See *National Adult School Union*.

National Adult School Union   The name adopted by the National Council of Adult School Unions in 1914 and retained until 1982 when it became the *National Adult School Organization*.

National Advisory Council on Adult Education   Established in 1966 in the United States as the National Advisory Council on Adult Basic Education. It is a presidential advisory council whose members are appointed by the President. It adopted its present title in 1970. There are other National Advisory Councils on career education, continuing education, ethnic heritage studies, extension and continuing education, Indian education, radio in education, vocational education, and women's education programs.

National Advisory Council on Ageing
Canadian national advisory council.

National Affiliation for Literacy
American association concerned with *adult literacy*.

National Aging Policy Center on Education, Leisure and Continuing Opportunities for Older People
Established in the United States by the *National Council on Aging*, this is a focal point for the study of policy about the elderly.

National Agricultural Center for Advanced Study   Located at the University of Wisconsin, this is the national resource for research and development for the *Co-operative Extension Service*.

National Alliance of Business   An American organization, which seeks to improve *education, training* and job opportunities for the disadvantaged, disabled and displaced.

National Alliance of Voluntary Learning   Adult education organization, located at Northern Illinois University, seeking to emphasize the voluntary nature of *continuing professional education*.

National Association for Public Continuing and Adult Education (NAPCAE)   Association which merged with the *Adult Education Association of the United States of America* to form the *American Association for Adult and Continuing Education* in 1982.

National Association for the Teaching of English as a Second Language (NATESLA)   Founded in February 1978, this association aims to advance the education of UK residents whose first language is not English by helping organizers and teachers share their expertise in this area.

National Association of Adult Education   The adult education association or Eire. See *AONTAS*.

National Association of County Extension Agents   US association for *co-operative extension* workers.

National Association of County Home Demonstration Agents   Association of *extension* workers in the United States, working in the spheres of home and family life.

National Association of Development Education Centres   UK association, established in 1979, by development education centres to encourage mutual support and to act as a political lobby group for development.

National Association of Educational Guidance Services for Adults   This is a national association of educational guidance services for adults in the United Kingdom, formed in 1982, it is regarded as quite central to the development of *adult learning*.

National Association of 4-H Club Agents   American national association for those extension workers working with the *4-H clubs*.

National Association of State Universities and Land Grant Colleges   Established in 1908, this association functions as a lobby on behalf of the *co-operative extension* service.

National Association of Teachers in Further and Higher Education   A professional association in the United Kingdom for teachers working in post-compulsory education.

National Association of Youth and Community Education Officers   UK professional association for those engaged in youth and community education.

National Book League   UK body established to promote the publication and use of books.

National Catholic Adult Education Commission   Established in June 1956 by the Church of Rome in the United States.

National Catholic Educational Association   Established in 1904 in the United States.

National Center Clearinghouse   This US centre has three functions: to identify improvement projects and maintain a database of curriculum materials in *vocational* *education*, and to record innovations in military education.

National Center for Career Life Planning A clearinghouse of the American Management Association.

National Center for Community Education American *community education* clearinghouse.

National Center for Educational Brokering Established in 1976, this centre is for those involved in *educational guidance* and *counselling*. It promoted *educational brokering* through technical assistance, publications, policy studies and recommendations.

National Center for Educational Statistics US Dept of Education records all national educational statistics and government surveys into education in a central office.

National Center for Public Service Internships American clearinghouse concerned with internships in professional education.

National Center for Research in Vocational Education Based at Ohio State University, its mission is to increase the ability of diverse agencies to solve educational problems relating to individual career planning, preparation and progression.

National Centre for Developments in Nurse Education UK nurse education centre based in Sheffield.

National Centre for Popular and Adult Education A documentation centre established by the Danish government in Copenhagen in 1985 to monitor and record all *adult* and *popular education* in innovations in Denmark.

National Centre for Teaching Materials A national centre in Denmark that purchases,

prepares and lends teaching materials to teachers, including *adult educators*.

National Certificate in Training and Extension The certificate awarded to *adult educators* who have completed their training at one of the four residential training centres in Zimbabwe.

National Christian Education Council UK body concerned with education in the Christian churches.

National Clearinghouse on Aging The Administration on Aging of US State Department of Health, Education and Welfare runs this clearinghouse.

National Commission on Accrediting Official US body concerned with *accreditation* of colleges and universities.

National Commission on Co-operative Education This body provides a national forum for *co-operative education* throughout the United States.

National Commission of Vocational Education Established in 1913 to investigate the desirability of federal funding for *vocational education* – which it recommended in 1917.

National Community Education Association Founded in 1966 in Michigan, USA, as a non-profit-making organization, to advance and support community involvement in public education.

National Community Education Day Sponsored by the National Community Education Association and other organizations, the day was inaugurated in 1982, but not sponsored until 1986, and occurs during the American Education Week.

National Co-operative Education Association The educational association of the Co-operative movement that has long been involved in *adult education* activities in the United Kingdom.

National Council for Educational Awards Irish body that approves and validates educational courses.

National Council for Vocational Qualifications Established in October 1986 in the UK with a view to establishing a *national qualifications framework* based upon competency. The Council does not act for Scotland.

National Council of Adult School Associations Started in Leicester in 1899 to advance adult schools in Britain and to co-ordinate the work of local associations. Changed its name to *National Council of Adult School Unions* in 1907.

National Council of Adult School Unions See *National Council of Adult School Associations*. It only retained this name until 1914 when it became *National Adult School Union*.

National Council of Labour Colleges Established in 1921 to co-ordinate the *labour college* movement. It merged with the *Workers' Educational Trades Union Committee* in 1964.

National Council of Voluntary Literacy Schemes Established in 1977 in the United Kingdom to co-ordinate the voluntary work undertaken with *literacy*.

National Council on Adult Jewish Education American organization concerned with *adult education* among Jews.

National Council on Aging US council concerned with professionals and volunteers who work with all matters affecting older people.

National Department of Education Established in 1867, the United States Department of Education.

National Development Council The *Russell Report*, published in 1973, proposed the formation of such a council for the UK but the government only created the *Advisory Council of Adult and Continuing Education*.

National Distance Education University Established in Bangladesh in 1986, it offers higher education for *mature students* who were unable to enrol in universities in their youth.

National Education Association Established in 1857 as the National Teachers Association, but merged with other associations in 1970 and adopted its present name. In 1924, it became involved in the formation of the *American Association for Adult Education*.

National Education Crisis Committee Established in South Africa in 1986 to try to introduce education for blacks through a *night school* movement.

National Extension Centre for Trades Union Education Opened in October 1984 in London, it has become a major provider of trades union education.

National Extension College Founded in 1963 with four aims: to provide *second chance* education for adults; to use correspondence tuition and educational broadcasting; to be involved in development projects; to assist with Third World development. It has assumed a significant role in *adult education* in the United Kingdom.

National Farm Radio Forum Started in 1939 by the Canadian Association of Adult Education to encourage citizen involvement in Canadian public affairs.

National Federation of Settlements Established in 1911 to co-ordinate the work of *university settlements* in the United States.

National Federation of Social Education Japanese professional association for *adult education*.

National Federation of Voluntary Literacy Schemes Association of non-statutory bodies in the United Kingdom involved in *adult basic education.*

National Federation of Women's Institutes Voluntary women's association with *adult education* being a aspect of its remit.

National Federation of Adult Education Started in 1946 in Britain, merged with the *British Institute of Adult Education* in 1946 to become the *National Institute of Adult Education.*

National Foundation for Educational Research Non-statutory educational research body in the United Kingdom, which has undertaken some research into adult education.

National Foundation for the Education of Youngsters and Adults Brazilian *adult education* association.

National 4-H Club US association of *4-H Clubs.*

National Home Study Council Established in 1926 in the United States to raise the standards of private colleges.

National Indian Education Association Founded in 1976 in the United States, this is the national *adult education* association to promote, support and work for the improvement of the North American Indian peoples. Some people in the United States now consider it inappropriate to use such terms.

National Information Center for Volunteers American clearinghouse on volunteers.

National Institute of Adult Continuing Education (NIACE) UK national non-statutory body for adult and continuing education. It acts as a resource centre, research organization, a publishing company and a national lobby. Until 1983, it was called the *National Institute of Adult Education.*

National Institute of Adult Education Established in 1949 as a result of a merger between *British Institute of Adult Education* and the *National Federation of Adult Education.* See *National Institute of Adult Continuing Education.*

National Institute of Labor Education Established in 1957 to expand the scope of workers' education in the USA, and to encourage greater co-operation between workers organizations and other organizations in education.

National Institute of Social Education Founded in 1965, Japanese national institution of adult education involved in training, research and publication.

National Institutional Accrediting Association A recognized accrediting agency in the United States, usually voluntary and non-governmental, it administers accrediting procedures for a given geographical location.

National Issues Forums A civic education movement, started in 1981, sponsored by the US Office of Education under the leadership of John Studebaker. These are *study circles* or *town meetings* that study three national issues each year and report their findings to policy-makers. See *Des Moines Forum, Washington Week.*

National Literacy Day A United Nations day – 8 September each year.

National Network for Curriculum Co-ordination in Vocational and Technical Education Established in 1972 by the US State Department of Education in order to reduce duplication in curriculum innovation by introducing co-ordination centres and liaison personnel.

National Open College Network A national UK network of colleges concerned with educational opportunities for adults, wider access, innovation and wider accreditation.

National Programme for Tele-Education (PRONTEL) Brazilian *distance education* organization.

National Programme on Adult Education The *literacy* programme of India.

national qualifications framework A framework instituted by government in a number of countries within which to standardize the wide variety of educational qualifications. See *National Vocational Qualifications*.

National School Volunteer Program US programme for *volunteers*. They are used extensively in American society.

National Self-Help Resource Center American *clearinghouse* concerned with *self-help*.

National Society for Performance and Instruction International organization founded in 1962 in the United States, committed to increasing productivity in the workplace through the application of performance and instructional technologies. Previously called the *National Society for Programmed Instruction*.

National Society for Programmed Instruction See *National Society for Performance and Instruction*.

National Society for the Promotion of Industrial Education Established in the United States in 1906 to act as a lobby for *vocational education*.

National Society of Quality Circles Formed in 1982 in UK by some 20 organizations operating *quality circles* with the aim of encouraging their development.

National Swedish Federation of Adult Education Associations The federation of ten education associations sponsoring *study circles* in Sweden.

National Technological University (NTU) American consortium of universities and businesses that have combined to provide graduate degree courses in the United States.

National Training Act (1982) Canadian federal government act that located more responsibility for the funding of *vocational education* with central government.

national training awards Launched in the United Kingdom in 1987, to enable employing organizations to demonstrate that they are offering efficient training programmes for employees.

National Training Institute of Social Education Japanese institute for training in *adult education*.

National University Continuing Education Association (NUCEA) Formerly the *National University Extension Association*. US association of adult educators concerned with university continuing education.

National University Extension Association Established in 1915 by 22 universities in the USA to provide an official and authorized organization through which universities involved in continuing education might co-operate. Rapidly became a national organization with a wide membership and changed its name to *National University Continuing Education Association*.

National University Teleconference Network (NUTN) Established in 1982 as an international organization, based in America, to provide a live, interactive, teleconferencing service to universities, colleges, businesses, industry and the professions.

National Vocational Education Act   US act of 1963 that allowed federal money to be granted to individual states to enable them to develop *vocational education*.

National Vocational Qualifications (NVQ)   Qualifications framework introduced in England and Wales for accrediting occupational competencies. There are five levels from basic skills to the ability to use fundamental principles across a wide range of occupational contexts. See also *General National Vocational Qualifications, Scottish Vocational Qualifications*.

National Women's Education Centre   The Japanese government established this in 1977 as a national centre for the education of women.

naturalism   General philosophical belief that what is studied in the natural world is all that there is, ie that there is no supernatural intervention in the world.

naturalistic research   A qualitative approach to research, making no positivistic claims, but employing rigorous methods to study the social world. See *humanistic psychology*.

need   1. Term used in *adult education* implying that there is a deficit in a person's knowledge, skill or attitude that can be rectified by education. See *comparative need, educational need, expressed need, felt need, hierarchy of needs, normative need, primary need, secondary need, want*, demaind. 2. The term reflects a rationale for the provision of educational programmes and regards them as part of the social welfare policy of a government.

need gratification   The satisfaction of need.

need to achieve   The motivation to achieve success.

needs analysis   See *needs assessment*.

needs assessment   The process whereby the teacher assesses the learning needs of the students. See also *diagnosis of needs, program planning*.

needs meeting   A philosophy in *adult education* that argued that it exists to meet the needs of potential learners, it reflects the policy of social welfare.

needs meeting programme   The theory that curricula or programmes in *adult education* should be based upon a *needs meeting* philosophy.

negative correlation   A statistical term to describe an inverse relationship between two variables.

negative reinforcement   Punishment for unacceptable behaviour in order to deter it in future.

negative transfer   A situation to which new learning has not been transferred.

negotiated curriculum   An approach to teaching in which the teacher plans the curriculum in conjunction with the students, taking their needs into consideration. It more frequently applies to negotiated content than to teaching methods, so that it is in actuality a form of negotiated syllabus, within specified limits.

negotiated learning   A style of teaching and learning in which the teacher and learners negotiate contents or methods of their learning.

Nehru Literacy Award   An award made by the Indian Adult Education Association for services to *adult literacy*.

Neighborhood Guild   The first *university settlement* established in New York in 1886 by Stanton Coit.

network   1. The webs of social relationships which pervade all social activity.

2. Loose association of independent persons or institutions, to exchange information and/or to co-operate in other ways on an issue of common interest. 3. A web of relationships maintained through electronic means.

networking   The development and use of contacts, the linking process of individual and collective skills, information, and advice.

New Opportunities for Women (NOW) Programmes of *adult education* courses established in the United Kingdom to provide opportunities for women to return to education and to study for a new career.

Newbattle Abbey Adult College Scotland's only residential *adult education* college.

night school   1. Term for adult education. 2. School for adults in the evening, after the working day.

1919 Report   See *Final Report of the Adult Education Committee of the Ministry of Reconstruction, 1919.*

nodal agency   The University Grants Commission in India established a number of the leading university departments of adult education as nodal agencies to facilitate the flow of information about adult education throughout their regions (both from and to universities and colleges) on its behalf.

Noma Prize   A *literacy* award of $5,000 established by Shoichi Noma of Japan in 1980, and administered by *UNESCO.*

nominal group technique   A variation of *snowballing* in which individuals respond to a question in writing. All the responses can be read and discussed by the group, with the group leader classifying, ordering, and synthesizing the group's final conclusions.

nomothetic approach   This refers to the process of explanation, proposing or

prescribing patterns or laws; educational research sometimes assumes laws or patterns of human behaviour and seeks to test them. See *logical positivism.*

non-advanced further education   This covers basic craft or technician level training and is available to anybody who has left initial schooling in the United Kingdom.

non-award bearing courses   Courses that are organized and run without an award for successful completion. See also *non-credit, non-competence.*

non-competence giving   A *non-award bearing* educational programme.

non-credit   A course or programme is not intended to be, or not accepted as, part of the study requirements leading to a degree, diploma, certificate, or other educational qualification. This term is more commonly used in the United States.

non-directive counselling   The process of counselling in which the counsellor acts as a listener, helping the client decide for themself about the decision that should be taken.

non-directive interview   An interview in which there is a free exchange of views between the interviewer and the interviewee, rather than one in which the former directs the process.

non-formal education   The educational process organized outside of the formal educational system, often to respond to the *learning needs* of specific groups of people. Used a great deal in Third World countries.

non-governmental organization (NGO) An organization that is not a statutory body and not completely financed by the state, which exists to undertake a social or community task. Many adult education organizations fall into this category.

non-judgmental An approach that seeks to examine situations without making moral judgements.

non-linear A relationship between two variables that is too complex to be depicted by a straight line in a graph.

non-participation Non-enrolment in adult education.

non-resident 1. One who does not live on the premises provided for a course of study. 2. In the United States, non-residents are those who live outside the boundaries of a State and may be required to pay different tuition fees.

non-respondent An individual who fails to reply to a questionnaire, or complete a test, etc.

non-schooler One who does not attend school, usually from remote areas in Third World countries.

non-structured interview See *unstructured interview*.

non-teaching staff See *support staff*.

non-traditional education An American term that refers to *external degree, experiential learning* and other forms of flexible and innovative education.

non-vocational education A form of education that is not orientated to work and employment. See also *general education, liberal education*.

Norborg Conference An international adult education conference organized by the Danish Ministry of Education in 1972 to examine comparative methodology in *adult education*.

Nordic Association of Adult Education The association for *adult education* which seeks to co-ordinate the work of the national adult education institutes in Scandinavia.

Nordic Folk Academy Established in 1968 and funded by the Nordic countries, this academy is a resource for leaders and teachers in the *folk high schools* throughout the Nordic countries.

Nordic Folk High School Council The association seeking to co-ordinate the work of the *folk high schools* in the Scandinavian countries.

norm That which is normal, or which occurs most frequently as the socially accepted or expected form of behaviour in a social group. It is a non-moral term in the social sciences.

norm-referenced testing An approach to assessment that seeks to compare one person's performance against the average for the group rather than against specific criteria. See *criterion-referenced testing*.

normal curve of distribution A bell-shaped curve depicting the normal frequency distribution of a phenomenon around the arithmetic mean.

normative 1. Prescribing to a standard. 2. Behaviour that responds to social pressure, ie conformist.

normative need Needs are assessed against norms or other standards. See *need*.

North of England Council for Promoting Higher Education for Women Formed in 1867 to co-ordinate women's groups concerned with higher education; James Stuart, founder of the *university extension* movement in Britain responded to an invitation to give a series of lectures organized by this Council.

Northern College An adult education residential college founded in Barnsley, UK, in 1978.

Nottingham University The university in which the first *adult education* department in the world was established and the first professor of adult education appointed in 1920.

novice   A beginner.

null hypothesis   The reverse of the research question in order to avoid bias in the research, eg the research question asks if there is a relationship between A and B; the null hypothesis is that there is no relationship between A and B.

numeracy   Competence in basic mathematics.

numerate   One who is both competent in mathematics and is able to understand information presented in mathematical terms, eg charts, tables and graphs.

nurse teacher   An educator of nurses, formerly called *sister tutors*.

Nyerere, Julius (b. 1922)   Former President of Tanzania, and a powerful advocate for adult education.

Oo

objective 1. The immediate aim or goal of a lesson or an educational course. Aims are generally regarded as more philosophical. 2. Descriptive term for a research procedure that seeks to eliminate the subjective biases of the researcher.

objective assessment An attempt to evaluate the performance of learners through elimination of the subjective biases of the assessor.

objective test Test which may be marked objectively by any marker, such as a multiple choice test, where the answers are allegedly right or wrong independent of the marker's or test-setter's perception. See *multiple choice question*.

observation A method of research that involves careful viewing of a situation, phenomenon or process. Some forms are more structured than others but in some of the more structured the observer is looking for specific topics or issues. See also *participatory research*.

observation checklist A prepared list of characteristics that an observer should look for during the process of observation.

observation entry 1. A trainer interruption in a group process in order to focus upon the nature of the group process. 2. An entry into a journal, etc recording an observation.

observational learning Learning through watching someone else. See *Sitting by Nellie*.

observed score A term sometimes used to refer to raw data in research.

obsession Any idea that constantly invades a person's consciousness.

obsolescence The condition arising from use of knowledge, theories, concepts, techniques, etc that are less effective in solving problems than others that are currently available. As the knowledge explosion continues this has become a significant concept in continuing professional education.

obstruction method A research technique used in psychology whereby subjects are obstructed from the goal in order to test their motivation.

occupation A person's paid employment.

occupational analysis The process of analysing all the tasks demanded by a specific occupation and specifying them as competencies for which education and training might be given. See *competency-based education*.

occupational education See *vocational education*.

occupational guidance A service providing guidance to people about occupations for which they might be suitable.

occupational therapy A form of learning and doing provided for those who are elderly or handicapped.

off-campus programme   The programme of courses established by an educational institution away from its own campus, often to accommodate part-time adult students. See also *university extension*.

off-quota   Students on a specified course who are paying the full fee and who are not subsidized in any way by grants to the educational institution, from government or other agency, to provide that specific course.

off-the-job training   Training that takes place away from the normal place of work. See *on-the-job training*.

Office of Adult Learning Services   Adult education office of the *College Level Examination Board*. Its aim is to improve access to education for adults.

Office of Educational Credit   A *clearinghouse* in the United States concerned with educational *credit*.

older adult   One who is 65 years of age or older, according to the Congress of the United States.

Older and Bolder   The initiative of the *National Institute of Adult Continuing Education* in the United Kingdom to create an awareness of third age education.

older worker   A working person over the age of 55 years.

olfactory learner   One who learns best through the senses of smell and taste.

Olsson, Oscar (1877–1950)   Founder of the Swedish *study circle* movement in 1902 at the Lund branch of the International Order of Good Templars.

on-course experiential learning   *Experiential learning* as part of a taught course. See also *sandwich course*.

On-line   Newsletter of the *American Association for Adult and Continuing Education*.

on-the-job learning   A form of work-based learning.

on-the-job-training   Training given in the normal work situation.

On The Move   The title of a BBC series of television broadcasts that constituted an early *adult literacy* scheme in 1974–75. See also *Your Move*.

One for All   The monthly magazine of the *adult school* movement, started by the Midlands Association of Adult Schools in 1891.

One Hour a Day   An attempt was made to get the Fifth UNESCO World Conference in Hamburg to support the movement of one hour a day for learning.

One Hundred and Fifty Hours   The 150 refers to the amount of time that workers could get free to study each year in the Italian *paid educational leave* scheme.

one-parent family   A family that consists of a single parent and a child or children.

ontology   1. The philosophical study of existence. 2. The assumptions about existence underlying any conceptual scheme or and theory or system of ideas.

open access   The policy of waiving entry qualifications as a prerequisite of enrolment for a course of study. See also *open admission, open enrolment*.

open admission   See *open access*.

open book examination   An examination where the candidates are allowed to consult books during the examination.

Open College   1. The Open College commenced broadcasting on 21 September

1987 in conjunction with Channel 4 on commercial television in the United Kingdom. It is a *further education* media institution offering a wide range of learning opportunities, mostly of a vocational nature. 2. The term given to a network of colleges operating in south London, linked to institutions of higher education, providing *access* opportunities for mature students.

Open College Network   In the United Kingdom open college groups have been established which have a number of foci: education for adults, adult access to educational opportunities, innovation in education, and wider accreditation for experience and learning.

open continuing education   Term used in Germany to refer to the continuation or the resumption of organized learning after the completion of initial education.

open day   Scheduled periods during which educational institutions invite visitors to see the work of students, but increasingly to see the facilities of the institution in order to try to attract future students. See *open house*.

open education   Term used in American education in a manner similar to progressive education, eg open to new ideas and change. In this form of education there is minimal teaching as students pursue their own interests. This is close to what adult educators might regard as good practice in the classroom with adult students.

open-ended question   A question that allows the respondent to develop an answer, since the question is so phrased not to demand a specific answer.

open enrolment   See *open access*.

open entry-open exit   See '*roll-on/roll-off*' *curriculum*.

open further education   Term used in Germany for those forms of further education which are open to all students.

open house   Commonly used in the United States to refer to an *open day*.

open learning   The title given to more flexible methods of study, and teaching in which there is openness in access, content, delivery systems, and assessment. There are college- or provider-based systems in which learners attend centres; local-based systems with *flexi-study* and support but at which the learning is undertaken in the learner's homes; and *distance learning* systems.

Open Learning   Journal of *distance education*. Replaced the *Open University* journal *Teaching at a Distance*.

Open Learning Federation   A UK association of colleges involved in *open learning* schemes.

Open Learning Institute   Hong Kong *distance education* institution. Renamed *Open University*.

open plan   Having no, or few, dividing walls between areas. Some schools were planned in this manner in the 1960s and 1970s, but few occurred in adult education.

open question   The type of examination or essay question that does not restrict the respondent's response too greatly in terms of content. See also *closed question*, *open-ended question*.

Open School   During the period 1977–80, a number of schools were established in the Netherlands for *adult basic education*.

Open Tech Programme   Started in the United Kingdom in 1982 by government in order to produce open learning materials for vocational education – a partnership between government and further education institutions.

Open University   1. Established in the United Kingdom in 1970, a distance teaching university which admits students without initial qualifications. 2. There are now open universities in many countries of the world. 3 Term used in parts of the continent of Europe for *university extension* type classes.

operant conditioning   Any behaviour which is brought under stimulus control; it can be strengthened by reinforcement. Associated with the work of B F Skinner.

operant learning   An approach to learning in which learners are cautious in using evidence but concerned with logical problems and rationality.

operational definition   A working definition.

operational hypothesis   A hypothesis that can be tested.

operationalize   1. To put into practice. 2. In statistics, it refers to making a construct measurable, eg intelligence tests to measure intelligence.

opinionaire   Questionnaire designed to elicit course participants' opinions and attitudes about the course. It is an evaluation instrument.

option units   Some modular courses are constructed of a core, which all learners study, and options, from which students make a selection based upon interest or occupation.

options   1. Journal of the Michigan Association of Adult Education, started in 1986. 2. The name given to the *Restart* programme in the United Kingdom in September 1986, when it changed to a short course programme.

oracy   Verbal skills.

oral examination   See *viva voce.*

oral history   Historical data gathered by word of mouth, a technique frequently used in research with non-literate people. It is also used in literacy crusades.

ordinary degree   A pass degree, as opposed to an *honours degree.*

organic literacy   A form of literacy that links words to 'reality'.

organismic learning   A concept of learning that views the person as an active, growing and developing whole.

Organizations of Popular Learning   The twenty organizations in Denmark that sponsor most of the *study circles.*

organized learning   A term used in Germany to typify adult education. It has three main features: a topic, an aim, and a continuing dialogue between teacher and learners.

orientation period   Often a one to two week period at the start of a course of study devoted to helping the new students familiarize themselves with the requirements of the course, geography of the institution, and assist those who are returning to learning with study skills.

orthopedagogy   A European term for the study of special education.

Our Right to Learn   A campaign conducted in Scotland in October 1981 seeking positive legislation and local government provision for *adult education.* See *Save Adult Education Campaign.*

out-centre   A subsidiary centre of an adult education institution, situated at a distance from the main centre.

outcome-based education   Education that places emphasis on the outcomes of the learning, which is generally accredited some way. See *competency-based education.*

outcome evaluation A process of evaluating a curriculum/course etc by its end-product. See *summative evaluation, impact evaluation*. There is a major conceptual problem with this approach: it is difficult to determine what precisely is the outcome and at what time does one measure it – immediately after a course, six months after etc – from any course of learning

outdoor education Education that occurs where the subject matter exists. Education about the natural world, often conducted in the natural setting.

outdoor education centre An educational centre dedicated to teaching the skills of all forms of countryside pursuits, such as hill climbing, water sports, etc.

outdoor study The idea underlying outdoor education is that the education should occur where the subject matter exists. Thus it utilizes visits, field trips, demonstrations, etc. The emphasis is upon primary experience in learning.

outline A framework or summary.

outreach The process of seeking to reach people who do not attend normal educational provision.

outreach education An educational programme located some distance from the premises of the educational institution, which is organizing it, aimed at reaching people who do not normally enrol in its programme. A form of *community education*.

outreach teaching Teaching conducted off campus in non-formal educational situations.

outreach worker A community educator, employed by an adult education institution, who seeks to reach people in the community who do not normally enrol in the educational programme.

outsourcing The process whereby employing organizations place certain of their activities with organizations other than their own so that, for instance, the responsibility for the *education* and *training* of some organization's workforce is given to an educational organization.

Outward Bound Trust A UK educational organization which seeks the self-development of young adults through adventurous pursuits.

over-educate To provide more education than the situation demands. This phenomenon might have been promoted in the West by professionalization, in which many more educational qualifications are being demanded by high-status occupations than are necessary for the pursuit of a particular employment. See *over-qualify*.

overhead projector A projector that projects an image on a screen from an acetate transparency.

over-learn The practice of learning to such an extent that the learner does not think about the learning, so that actions are performed automatically.

over-permissive Allowing, even encouraging, a lack of discipline. It might be claimed that adult education practices are over-permissive since adult learners should be autonomous and self-directed learners.

over-protective The practice of not exposing students to the actual situation because the teachers are anxious about their students.

over-qualify To have more academic qualifications than is necessary for the role being performed.

overtime To work longer hours than the worker is expected according to the contract.

over-train The practice of preparing people to a greater extent than is necessary for the satisfactory performance of their role.

overt response An open and observable response to a stimulus.

overt stimulus An observable stimulus.

Pp

pacing The speed with which learners progress through educational or learning activities. See *group-pacing, self-pacing*.

package See *learning package*.

paid educational leave (PEL) The opportunity for workers to continue their education during their work life by being granted leave of absence with pay. See *learning accounts, vouchers*.

panel 1. Two, or more, speakers who make presentations to a class or an audience. 2. Two, or more, experts who respond to questions from a class or audience.

panel interview An interview conducted by more than one interviewer.

paper 1. An academic treatise, or publication. 2. A research report. 3. A written discussion document. See *term paper*.

paper and pen test Any academic test requiring a written response. Sometimes called a *paper and pencil test*.

paper and pencil test See *paper and pen test*.

paradigm 1. It usually refers to a taken-for-granted perspective on a phenomenon. 2. A pattern, or a model.

parameter The boundary of a phenomenon.

para-professional See *sub-professional*.

parent education Systematic development of knowledge, attitudes and skills, required for the upbringing of children, family relationships and the performance of the parental role in the family and society.

parent outreach program Organized by US schools to reach parents with parent education.

parenthood education Providing the necessary knowledge for, and preparing young people generally in the art of, parenthood. See *parent education*.

part learning The process of breaking down information to be learned into smaller sections and learning them individually.

participant A course or group member, a member of a teaching and learning session.

participant observation A research technique in which the researcher plays a role in the phenomenon under investigation.

participant observer One who is utilizing the research technique of *participant observation*, that is playing a full role in a social process but also acting in a research capacity at the same time.

participant satisfaction As education is becoming a market commodity, so it has become more important to assess the satisfaction of *participants* at the end of a course or conference. It is a form of customer satisfaction.

participation training The process of preparing individuals to use group processes.

participatory research A form of research in which the researcher is a part of the process under investigation, solving their own problems and creating their own knowledge. It is sometimes regarded as a more democratic form of research than the more traditional research methods. See *action research*.

partnership schemes Schemes whereby two, or more, educational institutions collaborate.

part-time adult educator One who is employed to teach adults for a limited number of hours each week. See *full-time part-time adult educator*.

part-time student One who is a registered student, but who has other obligations, such as work or domestic commitments, and so is unable to pursue studies full time.

part-time tutor A teacher who is employed to teach for a specified number of hours, or courses, in an educational institution.

pass degree 1. A general degree, the standard of which is not considered high enough to achieve an honours award. 2. A degree with a restricted syllabus, in which no honours award are made.

pass mark The arbitrary grade that a course team decides should be considered as having achieved a satisfactory standard. In the United States, this is sometimes referred to as a passing grade.

pass rate The proportion of candidates sitting an examination, or taking a course of study, achieving a pass mark.

passive learning The process of acquiring information, which is presented to the learner by a teacher, who directs the whole learning process.

paternalism 1. In feminist literature, this refers to male dominance. 2. To act as a father figure, eg 'teacher knows best'. See *authoritarianism*.

pathway A route through a modular curriculum.

peace corps US programme that trains young volunteers who work on aid programmes in developing countries.

peace education See *peace studies*.

peace studies The objectives of peace studies courses encompass the following: understanding the growth and strategy of nuclear planning; assisting peace movements engaging in the public debate; redressing the balance in educational resources made available to knowledge of military studies; and encouraging a greater understanding of the peace movement.

peak experience A term used to characterize a profound moment in life, or self-actualization.

peasant schools Started in Spain in 1970–71, as cultural centres for regional development.

peasant university A *popular university*, started in Zagreb, Yugoslavia, between the two World Wars and modelled on the Danish *folk high school*.

pedagogics The study of *pedagogy*. This is a term employed much more frequently in continental Europe.

pedagogy An activity involving the purposeful creation of learning experiences. Generally assumed to refer to teaching children although, in recent years, *adult pedagogy* and *social pedagogy* have also assumed significance in adult education in some societies which prefer it to the use of the term.

peer assessment   A form of *assessment* in which peers (students, practitioners or professionals) assess each other's performance or work without reference to other authorities or experts.

peer counselling   Providing counselling support to one's peers, often under supervision.

peer culture   The sub-culture that emerges within a group.

peer group   A group of individuals who act as reference for each other.

peer learning   Learning from one's fellows. Often practised in adult education when peers teach and learn together without the presence of a teacher or an expert, using the experience of all the members of the group. See *collaborative learning*.

peer learning community   See *peer learning*.

peer rating   See *peer assessment*.

peer review   A review of one's work by peers.

peer teaching   The process of teaching one's peers. If this is a student activity, it is frequently conducted under supervision, eg *micro-teaching*. See also *peer learning*.

peer tutoring   Usually refers to a group of students teaching and learning from each other, although it can refer to any other group of people in the same position. See *peer teaching*.

Peers, Robert (1888–1972)   The first professor of *adult education*. He was appointed the Director of Department of Adult Education at the University of Nottingham at its inception in 1920.

pegboard test   A test for manual dexterity in which pegs must be placed in holes as rapidly as possible.

penal andragogy   The term used in Yugoslavia for *prison education*.

pencil and paper test   Any form of written test.

people   The term 'people' is used throughout the *adult education* world in the same way as folk or popular or adult, so that there are People's Colleges, People's Educational Associations, People's Institutes, People's Universities, and so on.

People's Library   In 1939–40 Lyman Bryson tried to establish a people's library in the United States, and eleven books were published in the series.

per capita allowance   Money made available to an educational institution by local or national government, or to a department by a college or university, according to the number of registered students within it.

perception   Those processes that give coherence and unity to experience. It includes physical, physiological, neurological, sensory, cognitive and affective domains.

perceptual field   The range of stimuli of which an individual is aware.

perceptual style   The preferred manner by which individuals perceive situations. See also *cognitive style, learning style*.

perceptual skills   The ability to process perceptions accurately.

performance analysis   The systematic analysis of the way a task is performed. Often undertaken by a human resource specialist. See *performance appraisal*.

performance appraisal   Systematic assessment of the way that a worker carries out their occupation in order to determine the training needs. See *needs assessment*.

performance audit   A technique employed in human resource development in which organizational behaviour is assessed against the cost to the organization of its performance.

performance-based education   The form of teaching and learning that stresses the actual performance outcomes, as evidence of *learning*. See also *competency-based education*.

performance objectives   The *behavioural objectives* that are the intended outcomes of teaching or learning.

performance-oriented methods   Teaching methods that relate learning closely to the practical situation, such as *on-the-job training, learning from experience*, etc.

performance test   The assessment of skill.

period   A unit of time into which school or college timetables are sub-divided.

peripatetic school   A school that moves from place to place to be where the students are located.

peripatetic teacher   A teacher who teaches in a number of different educational institutions.

permanent education   See *education permanente, lifelong education*.

person   A philosophical concept of the nature of the individual.

personal chair   An academic appointment of professor in a UK university, awarded as a result of the individual contribution that the individual has made to research, scholarship or the life of the university.

personal construct   An umbrella term for each of the ways in which individuals try to

perceive, predict and control the world. Each person's constructs function like hypotheses, since George Kelly regarded human beings rather like scientists whose lives are experiments.

personal development   1. This is the development of the individual's own abilities and interests, often through liberal adult education. It can be seen as distinct from professional development, although some scholars have argued that the two should be regarded as synonymous. 2. Sometimes used to refer to adult developmental psychology.

personal identity   A psychological concept about a person's essential, continuous self.

personal teaching   Individual tuition.

personalism   A psychological approach that maintains that the individual person is the central construct against which all else should be considered. It is a form of reductionism.

personality   Many different definitions depending upon the school of thought of the writer. Broadly, it refers to the sum total of aspects that constitute the individual.

personality problem   Individual psychological problem.

personality test   Scales and tests that seek to measure specific aspects of *personality*.

personality trait   Personality characteristic.

personality type   Division of people into categories according to certain *personality traits*.

personalized system of instruction   A system of teaching through the use of short modules in a sequence, usually having behavioural objectives which must be met before proceeding to the next one. See *mastery learning, Keller Plan*.

personhood The concept of the person is less frequently used in *adult education* than is the self. However, it is a broader concept involving the whole person, body, mind and self.

personnel officer Member of staff whose responsibility is for the employees. Often involved in *human resource development*.

personnel selection The process of selecting employees for specific employment.

perspective A mental view of, or a cognitive orientation towards, a situation. See *cognitive style, paradigm*.

perspective transformation 1. A change in cognitive orientation towards a phenomenon. 2. Mezirow introduced this concept to *adult education* and he regarded it as an emancipatory process in which adults develop even more inclusive meaning schemes to interpret experience.

persuasion The process of trying to get people to adopt certain sets of values, attitudes, etc. See *indoctrination*.

Peuple et Culture A French *community education* movement established in Grenoble towards the end of the Second World War in 1944; it moved its headquarters to Paris in 1946.

phenomenology A philosophical approach to understanding, developed by Husserl, who believed that any analysis of a phenomenon should begin with a scrupulous introspection of one's own intellectual processes, so that one is conscious of what is experienced, rather that its objectivity.

Phillip Frandson Scholarship Fund Fund established in memory of Phillip Frandson to support extension students at the University of California.

philosophy The study of knowledge, ideas, values and the logical structure of language and speech. Prior to the twentieth century, it was sometimes regarded as the supreme form of study.

philosophy of education Philosophical study of education. There are few philosophical studies of *adult, continuing,* or *lifelong education*.

PICKUP Acronym for Professional, Industrial and Commercial Updating – a national programme started in the United Kingdom in 1982 to help colleges and universities meet the updating needs of people at work.

pictogram One or more pictures used to represent objects or concepts in a display of basic data.

picture storage A memory technique whereby facts to be remembered are related in the mind to a familiar picture or object.

pie chart A method of recording data in which the total population is depicted as a circle and the subgroups are recorded as appropriate segments of the circle.

Pilgrim College An adult education college in Boston, Lincolnshire, UK; an extension college of Nottingham University.

Pilkington Report A UK report in 1962, into educational broadcasting. It suggested that more television channels should be created so that the education of adults could be extended.

pilot course An initial trial course, which is usually thoroughly evaluated to ensure that the course responds to the perceived needs of the learners.

pilot study An exploratory study, which is often used to pre-test a research instrument or to refine the research question.

pilot survey The implementation of a small survey, prior to a major piece of research, to test the research instrument and the planning for the research as a whole.

pilot test   The pre-testing of a research instrument.

Pitman Examination Institute   An institution involved in examining secretarial training in further education.

placement   A practical work placement whilst undergoing training for an occupation or profession.

planned learning experience   The provision of an opportunity to learn a specific skill or piece of knowledge.

planning   See *program planning*.

Plater College   An adult education resident college for men and women who are concerned to develop a Christian perspective on politics, trades union studies and the social services. The college is primarily Roman Catholic and is located in Oxford.

Pleasant Sunday Afternoon (PSA)   A movement run by the churches in England in the late nineteenth and early twentieth century in order to provide culture and education to a wider group of people than just churchgoers.

Plebs League   In 1909 a secession from *Ruskin College* resulted in the formation of the *Labour College* – supporters and former students were known as the Plebs League.

Plebs, The   The monthly magazine of the *Plebs League*.

pluralism   A philosophical theory that reality consists of more than one basic substance or principle. It can refer to the alternative explanations of reality that exist or, in political theory, to the possibility of there being more than one seat of power in society.

Point Four Program   Established by President Truman in 1948 as an agency for technological and educational development in the Third World. It was succeeded in 1961 by the *United States Agency for International Development (USAID)*.

Pole, Thomas (1753–1829)   Author of *The History of the Origin and Progress of Adult Schools*, published in 1816. Probably the earliest published book about *adult education*.

political education   A term for *civic education*.

political science   The study of government.

polytechnic   1. An institution of higher education, offering a wide range of courses. In some countries, it is regarded as not having as high a status as a university. 2. In the United States, it refers to the nineteenth-century land grant agricultural, mining and mechanical engineering colleges, and also to the *mechanics institutes*.

Polytechnics Association of Continuing Education (PACE)   Established in 1981 in the United Kingdom to provide opportunity for the polytechnics involved in *continuing education* to co-operate with each other.

pool of ability   A reservoir of ability.

pooling   A discontinued method of financing certain advanced courses of education in the United Kingdom, where each local government body paid funds into a central pool, which then paid the providers of the approved courses.

popular culture   The culture of the people. Often used pejoratively in relation to the culture of the dominant groups in society.

popular drama   The use of drama to portray everyday events, or to depict everyday experiences in a different manner for people to consider. Used in adult education, especially in the Third World. It is a technique that liberates the imagination and enables people to conceptualize reality in a different manner. See *popular theatre*.

popular education 1. In Europe, the term is used almost synonymously with *adult education*. It is non-formal education, which a variety of groups can organize. In some countries, such as Denmark, some groups can claim state subsidy for the purpose. 2. The term is widely used in Latin America. It has the following connotations – education is a right of all people; designed for the people by the people; an instrument in the ideological class struggle, radical and often revolutionary; is a form of praxis inasmuch as what is learned is then put into practice in the class struggle.

popular school Established in Spain in the 1970s, they are to be found in working-class urban areas and are staffed mainly by volunteers.

Popular Schools Act 1929 law passed in Yugoslavia, establishing *adult schools* in agriculture, home economics, co-operative economics and *adult literacy*.

popular theatre The use of drama in the community to inform and assist people in considering and understanding social, cultural, and political problems. It can be used as a form of community education or development education, depending upon its context. See *popular drama*.

popular university Independent adult education institutions in Europe. They have usually been attached to universities and are similar in some ways to university extension, although they tend to be a little more autonomous.

Popular University Movement Began in France after the Dreyfus affair but only lasted for a short period of time.

population 1. The total number of people in a society. 2. The total number of people in a sub-section of the population from which a sample is drawn.

portfolio A collection of documents, certificates, or publications that verify the professional and academic standing of an individual. Sometimes used in the *Assessment of Prior Learning*.

positive correlation A statistical measure that indicates that there is an association between two variables.

positive reinforcement Reward for acceptable or desired behaviour, so that the behaviour will be repeated subsequently.

positive transfer The successful transfer of learning from one situation or task to another one of a similar nature.

positivism The philosophical theory that claims that all genuine human knowledge is produced scientifically, using *experimental research*. This theory has been open to considerable questioning in recent years, since it reflects an Enlightenment tradition.

post-basic education Education and training after the initial preparation for an occupation. See also *continuing education*.

post-compulsory education All education that is provided after the legal minimum school-leaving age.

post-doctoral study A planned study programme that follows the successful completion of a doctorate. In the United States, this is often associated with public or private funding.

postgraduate education Studies beyond the first degree. See *graduate education*.

postmodern The theory that suggests society has moved beyond *modernity* and has entered a new phase that questions the

Enlightenment philosophies, such as rationalism and science. It is often criticized for being relativist. See also *late modernity*.

post-registration training   Term used in nursing, to refer to *continuing education* after having been listed on the nursing register.

post-secondary education   1. All learning activities undertaken after completing secondary education, with the exception of adult basic education and education in the secondary curriculum. 2. It is a generic term for *higher education* or *tertiary education*.

post-secondary educational institution An educational institution offering education to those who are beyond the legal age of compulsory schooling.

post-test   A form of *assessment* that occurs at the end of a course.

postal enrolment   Enrolment for a course through the mail rather than by attending the educational institution in person.

postal tuition   See *correspondence education*.

poster   A form of wall chart containing the summary of the main points to be made.

poster session   Usually short and informal presentations around one or more posters displayed for the purpose at a conference.

potential   The promise of successful performance at a later time.

potted version   Summary.

poverty   A low standard of living; the conditions in which much radical adult education has found a great deal of response.

poverty level   Denotes the level of income designated by government as necessary to live without poverty in a society. However, this is an inaccurate means of assessment.

power   1. The exercise of control or force, as opposed to authority. Teachers frequently exercise this in the process of teaching. 2. Capacity to act granted by virtue of the position an individual fulfils in a social organization.

power-load-margin model   A model for living espoused by McClusky, an American adult educator, who regarded power as the resources a person can command, load as the demands made upon a person, and margin the relationship between them.

power test   1. Any test that measures ability by determining the degree of difficulty of material that can be mastered with no time pressures. 2. Statistical procedure for measuring the strength of correlation.

practical ability   *Skills* as measured through performance.

practical assessment   The *assessment* of the practical *competencies* in occupational performance. Often used during a *practical placement* during occupational training.

practical knowledge   1. Knowledge how to perform a skill, as distinct from being able to perform it. Practical knowledge is interdisciplinary and subjective, always learned as result of experience and practice and legitimated pragmatically. 2. In Aristotle's writing, it referred to the ability to act correctly in morally ambiguous circumstances.

practical placement   A work experience during professional preparation.

practical work teacher   A teacher of *practice*.

practice   1. The actual performance – performance is an art form. 2. Repetition of a skill until it has been thoroughly learned. 3. The reordering of experiences in order to make them more meaningful. 4. A professional occupation, or business, eg a legal practice.

practice audit   1. An inspection and analysis of practice before and after a learning exercise designed to improve that practice. 2. The process of observing professional practice to determine what knowledge and competencies are needed to perform effectively.

practice effect   The influence of previous practice upon subsequent performance.

practicum   A period in which students are taught in a situation as close to the reality of practice as is possible. See also *sandwich course*.

practitioner-researcher   One who undertakes research into practice whilst still being employed as a practitioner.

pragmatics   The study of the purposes, effects, and implications of meaningful language.

pragmatism   A philosophical perspective introduced by Charles Peirce in which phenomena are tested by the empirical differences that they cause, so that *knowledge*, for instance, is legitimated by its performability.

praxiology   In some countries this constitutes a subject in the *adult education* curriculum; it is the study of the practical aspects of the occupation.

praxis   A term used in Marxist thought to relate to the synthesis of being and thought; it has also been associated with the relationship between theory and practice, and *Paulo Freire* adapted it to refer to the congruence between individual reflection and the action that results from it.

preach   To expound. Often used in a derogatory manner in education to imply that teachers are expounding their own views.

pre-adult   US term for young adult.

preceptor   A teacher. In nursing education in both the United Kingdom and the United States the term refers to an experienced nurse who teaches newly qualified nurses when they enter clinical practice.

pre-clinical course   A theoretical course undertaken before entering practice – term used in medicine.

pre-coded questionnaire   A closed questionnaire in which the responses to the questions are coded ready for analysis.

precognition   The hypostasized ability to have *knowledge* about future events.

preconscious   A psychoanalytical term that refers to *knowledge* or *emotions* that are not within the consciousness but are easily accessible to it.

pre-conscious learning   A form of learning whereby the learner acquires knowledge or skill without being consciously aware of it.

predictable   The capability of being foretold.

predictive validity   The extent to which a test is able to achieve what it claims to test, eg that those passing a test will meet successfully certain other criteria demands at a later date and that those failing it will fail to meet those criteria demands at a later date.

prejudice   A preconceived bias.

pre-modern   Traditional society; a form of society unaffected by the Enlightenment in Western Europe.

Preparation for Retirement   A Council of Europe report published in 1977.

pre-preparation skills training   A basic skills training course for unemployed people.

prerequisite course   A course that has to be studied before another can be undertaken within an educational programme or course of studies.

Pre-Retirement Association of Great Britain and Northern Ireland   An association formed to offer education and training about preparation for retirement.

pre-retirement education   Educational courses organized to help individuals to prepare for their retirement from work and to use their leisure beneficially.

presentation   1. The mode, or method, by which a teacher introduces students to the content to be learned. 2. The actual performance of giving a paper.

pre-service training   Preparation for an occupation prior to employment.

pressure group   A group that seeks to influence power without assuming it. Adult education has frequently acted as a pressure group or lobby. See *interest group*.

pre-test   A diagnostic test that is conducted before, or at the start of, a course to assess the learning needs of the learner(s). It is an approach to formative assessment.

Pre-University Certificate   A school-leaving certificate in the Netherlands.

primary experience   Direct or first-hand experience through the senses. See *immediate experience*.

primary need   Bodily *need*. See also *hierarchy of needs, secondary needs*.

primer   An introductory text-book.

principal   The senior executive officer of an educational institution in the United Kingdom. In the United States, it can refer to a number of senior administrative positions in the educational institution.

principal lecturer   An academic post in some colleges and universities of further and higher education in the United Kingdom.

prior experiential learning   Relevant learning specifically from informal or uncertified sources such as work, hobbies, or life experiences in general that has occurred before the start of a formal course of study on a subject.

prior learning   Relevant learning that has occurred, either formally or informally, before one starts a formal course on a subject.

prison education   The adult education service in prisons in the United Kingdom. It has four main functions: educational, personal growth, amusement, and personal behaviour. See *correctional education*.

private education   Education that is financed by sources other than the government.

private instruction   An early method of *adult education*. Private instructors advertised their services from as early as 1745 in London and 1766 in the United States.

private vocational school   A non-public school in the United States that offers vocational education.

proactive   Describes an activity in which the actor has assumed the initiative rather than responded to events.

probability   The likelihood of an event occurring. See *probability theory*.

probability theory   A statistical approach to predicting the likelihood of events occurring.

probation   A trial period, often prior to a permanent appointment.

problem   An educational problem is a condition or a test that learners have to surmount during a learning exercise.

problem-based learning   Problem-based learning starts with a problem, or a query, which the learners wish to solve. It has been introduced into profession preparation, helping learners problem-solve actual practical cases in an attempt to overcome the theory-practice divide.

problem-posing education   A form of *learning* that encourages the learners to pose their own problems and then seek to solve them. Used by *Paulo Freire* as an antithesis to *banking education*.

problem-solving education   See *problem-based learning*.

process   Term frequently used in education to refer to the sequence of events in *teaching* and *learning*.

process education   A form of preparation in which skills form the basis of the curriculum.

process evaluation   The evaluation of the *teaching* and *learning* process.

process model   A curriculum model that places emphasis upon the process rather than the product. It tends to assume the humanistic perspective, and in adult education relates to the theories that stem from John Dewey, involving the learner in the planning of and dialogic approaches to teaching. See *product model*.

Pro-Chancellor   A senior post in a UK university.

proctor   1. In the United Kingdom, a disciplinary officer of the university. 2. In the United States, a person responsible for supervising examinations. See *invigilator*.

product   An outcome.

product model   A curriculum approach that emphasizes the end-product of the education rather than the process. This tends to be behaviourist and non-progressive. See *process model*.

production school   In Denmark, these are similar to *folk high schools* although the young adults are taught to make products that are then marketed.

profession   A term for a high status occupation – there are no agreed definitions although many offered.

professional association   An association organized by and on behalf of members of a high status occupation.

professional code   A code of ethics issued by the professional association by which members are expected to abide.

professional degree   A degree awarded in a professional subject, or in the study and practice of an occupation.

professional development   Staff development, or *human resource development*.

professional education   *Vocational education* for high status occupations.

professional placement   Practical experience provided in a place of work, during the process of *professional training*.

professional training   Initial preparation for work in a high status occupation.

professionalization   The process of structural change that occurs in an occupation as it develops its objectives of obtaining public recognition of its status as a *profession*.

professor   1. In UK universities a professor is a title awarded to an academic either for academic or administrative ability. 2. In the United States, a professor is a member of the teaching and research staff of an academic institution.

professor emeritus   A honorary title awarded to outstanding professors in their retirement.

proficiency   The capability to perform effectively.

proficiency-based education   See *competency-based education*.

profile   A set of measures of different characteristics of a learner that have been standardized to allow comparison.

profile analysis   The analysis of a *profile*.

profiling   A description of students' achievements and characteristics on multiple dimensions, eg academic or personal characteristics, which is used for assessment purposes; it was a reaction to the traditional methods of examining and introduced into the United Kingdom in the 1970s.

program planning   US term – the study and practice of designing, implementing and evaluation of adult education courses. It is being employed more frequently in the United Kingdom. See *curriculum design, tutor organizer*.

programme   1. Units of learning which comprise part of a training initiative. 2. The courses offered by an institution of education or training. See *curriculum*.

programme evaluation   The evaluation of the educational curriculum of an educational institution.

programmed instruction   A form of instruction that is provided sequentially and determined by an individual learner's needs.

programmed learning   The use of specially prepared texts or programmes that guide the learner through a learning process.

This sometimes occurs in conjunction with teaching machines.

programmed learning text   A prepared learning manual, book, or computer programme that represents material in a step-by-step manner for learning.

programming   The process of individual and collaborative effort in adult education institutions by adult educators and adult students in planning, designing, implementing, evaluating, and accounting for adult educational provision.

progressivism   An educational philosophy introduced by John Dewey that emphasized democracy and creativity in the classroom; it also encouraged good relationships between teachers and pupils and the school and the wider community. It was influential in adult education philosophy, and its fundamental tenets include *learner-centred education* and *learning from experience*.

project   A learning exercise, or research undertaking, requiring a period of time and requiring *self-directed* and *problem-solving* abilities.

Project Literacy USA (PLUS)   A multi-media programme to combat adult literacy in the United States, which commenced in 1986.

project method   A teaching and learning technique in which the learners undertake a task, or a research exercise, that has usually been initiated by the teacher.

Project Share   A US *clearinghouse* for improving the management of human resources.

Project 2000   The introduction of new approaches to the preparation of nurses and midwives in the United Kingdom, determined in the light of the projected health care requirements at the end of the 1990s.

projective test   A variety of devices used in personality assessment and clinical psychology in which the subject is presented with standardized unstructured stimuli and expected to respond to them in an unrestricted manner.

propaganda   Organized dissemination of information selected to support or oppose the programme of a movement, a political party, etc. In the United States, it is associated with the attempt to indoctrinate the people.

proposal   Something planned. Students are required to submit their dissertation proposal, authors write a book proposal for the publishers, etc. It is also called a *prospectus*.

proprietary school   A private school.

Prospect Union Educational Exchange The first educational brokering agency, established in Boston, USA, in 1923.

Prospects   An educational journal published by *UNESCO*.

prospectus   1. A publication by an educational institution containing the list of courses that it is offering over a specified period. See also *brochure, catalogue*. 2. See also *proposal*.

protocol   1. A code of behaviour. 2. A proposal or procedural statement. See *interview schedule*.

Pro-Vice Chancellor   Senior administrative office, usually filled by academics, of a UK university.

provider   An organization, or individual, that organizes and runs educational programmes for adults.

proxemics   The study of people's use of space.

psychoanalysis   A therapy using techniques and theories pioneered by Sigmund Freud.

psychodrama   A form of group therapy in which patients or clients act out, before an audience, situations from their past lives. Sometimes used as a teaching technique. See *socio-drama*.

psycholinguistics   The psychological study of language.

psychometrics   Measurement and testing in psychology.

psychomotor skills   Manual dexterity as opposed to any form of cognitive process. See *cognitive skills*.

public examination   An open examination, often administered by an examination body.

public forum   The forum is usually a lecture followed by open discussion on a variety of topics. See *National Issues Forum*.

public health   The health of a community or society.

public language   A term used in linguistic analysis to refer to non-formal language.

public lecture   Lectures open to the general public. One of the oldest forms of adult education, with the first being advertised (with admission fees) in 1584 in London, and 1726 in the United States.

Public Libraries Act   Act of Parliament in the United Kingdom in 1850, establishing a *public library* service in Britain.

public library   A collection of books, or other learning materials, which is open to the general public. The first public library in the United States was opened in Boston in 1673, although the first free public library was opened in Peterborough, New Hampshire on 9 April 1833.

public school   1. In the United Kingdom, public schools are private institutions of initial education open to fee-paying families. 2. In the United States public schools are open to the general public, supported by revenue from taxation, and are used as *adult education* institutions. The first *evening schools* were conducted in Boston and Louisville in 1834.

public service   University academic staff in the United States are expected to play a role in providing service to a wider public than just enrolled students of the university. See *co-operative education*.

public television   The term used in the United States for a non-commercial television broadcast station devoted to educational and cultural programming.

pupilage   The period of *apprenticeship* that a qualified barrister must undertake with a senior barrister before being allowed to practise independently.

purpose   A declaration of intent for a specific teaching and learning session – similar to *objective*.

pyramid of leadership   Cyril Houle suggested that in *adult education*, in the United States, there is a pyramid of leadership. It consists of volunteers at the base; those who have a responsibility for adult education, although they are not primarily adult educators; those whose primary concern and responsibility is adult education.

Qq

qualification   A formal award that records the successful completion of a course of study.

qualification inflation   The tendency to award more academic qualifications as higher education expands means that they lose their value (see *massification*) and, consequently, there is a continual search to gain more advanced qualifications, which then only have the same value as the previous ones did in a previous generation. See also *diploma disease*.

qualifying association   A professional association that prepares and tests new recruits for entry to a profession.

qualitative research   An approach to social research in which data are recognized as being normative and evaluative rather than empirical, and include the researcher's own subjective responses to the research situation. This approach frequently assumes a phenomenological perspective. See also *quantitative research*.

quality assurance   Procedures to ensure that the production of a commodity, eg an academic course, meet the standards demanded by the *validation board* or the accrediting agency.

quality circle   A group of people, often between four and twelve, in the work place, who meet together voluntarily to teach and learn from each other about aspects of mutual concern in their work, such as quality. Popularized in industry by Japanese practices. See *study circle*.

quality control   Techniques employed to ensure that the standards of production and performance are satisfactory. Increasingly being used in the production of educational courses.

quantitative research   An approach to research that assumes a positivist paradigm assuming that all phenomena are describable empirically and that data can be collected numerically and analysed. This approach endeavours to be objective, but it is not applicable to many aspects of education of adults.

quarter   The division of the academic year into four parts, each called a quarter. Used in US universities, where teaching occurs in three quarters, and the fourth quarter is often devoted to summer schools. See *semester*.

quarter credit hour   A US term for the number of class enrolments that a student has in a single *quarter*. Unit used to measure participation rather than achievement.

question   A form of words seeking a response from another person.

question bank   The store of questions that can be used in examinations.

question entry   The type of interruption made by a trainer when raising a question about the group process.

question period   A specified period of time, often after a formal lecture, devoted to questions.

questioning　A teaching method in which the teacher poses questions rather than providing answers. See *Socratic teaching*.

questionnaire　A research instrument consisting of a bank of questions, specifically designed to elicit responses about the phenomenon under investigation.

quiet period　The use of silence as a teaching technique, devoted to encouraging class members to reflect on a subject.

quota sampling　A non-random *sampling* technique in which a specified number or proportion of categories are selected from a *population*.

quota system　A selection system, employed more frequently in the United States, in which specific proportions of each category in the *population* are selected.

Rr

race   A human group having a common genetic inheritance. It is very unlikely that such a phenomenon as a pure race exists today.

racism   An ideology which claims that groups of people have different characteristics determined by hereditary factors and which endows some races with superiority over others; the social and political practices to maintain superiority.

racism awareness training   Originated in the United States, it was introduced into the United Kingdom in the 1980s. It is a form of training that seeks to make individuals aware of any racist attitudes that they might have through self-expression and group interaction.

radical adult education   An approach to adult education that regards it as a movement having a social mission to change society and to empower learners to be aware, active and seek to change the oppressive conditions in which they live.

radicalism   An ideology that seeks to change the nature of society and its institutions.

radio-assisted practice   This is a teaching practice situation where the student teacher, whilst teaching a lesson, is observed by a supervisor and guided on what to do by radio communication. In this way the supervisor does not have to interfere with the lesson, or even be in the room if it is equipped accordingly.

radio college   A system of *distance education* using the radio, started in West Germany in 1969.

Radio ECCA   The cultural radio station of the Canary Islands and run by the Ministry of Education, providing *literacy* and other *adult education* courses.

radio listening group   Group established to listen to educational radio broadcasts and to discuss their content.

Radio Popular University   Established in Holland in 1930, the *popular university* of the air.

radio school   Radio broadcasts used in the Third World to help local communities, who have study booklets provided for them.

radio study group   See *radio listening group*.

Radosavljevic, P R (1879–1958)   The first Yugoslav scholar known to have engaged in the study of *adult learning*.

Raikes, Robert   The founder of the first Sunday School in England, in Gloucester in 1789.

Ramsay, Allan   Started the first *circulating library* in Edinburgh in 1726.

Rand School of Social Science   Opened in New York in 1906, to provide workers with an education so that they could play their part in the labor unions, socialist party and the co-operative movement. Financial difficulties forced its closure.

random learning   See *incidental learning*.

random sample   A sample in which every member of the population has an equal chance of being selected every time a selection is made. It is the only pure manner of sampling.

rank order marking   A technique of *assessing* students' work through placing them in order of merit, according to specified criteria.

rapid reading   Techniques that enable readers to read faster than normal.

rate-of-return studies   Studies that have examined the incomes of adults in relation to the cost of their education, showing the rate of return on the original educational investment.

rate of return to education   A method that seeks to analyse the cost-benefit of education, by comparing the earning of adults with extended education to those whose education has been more restricted.

rationality   The use of reason or logic to think out a problem. The fact that a solution is rational does not mean that it is either correct or the only possible solution to a problem. See also *instrumentalism, technical rationality*.

raw data   Unanalysed data in research.

raw score   Statistical data that have not been analysed by statistical techniques.

re-accreditation   The process in which members of a profession have to undergo specified continuing professional education and be examined for professional competence in order to retain the right to continue to practise. In the United States, this is sometimes called re-certifying or re-licensing.

reaction time   The period of time between the presentation of a stimulus and a response to it.

reactive   Responsive to stimuli. See *proactive*.

readability   1. The ease of understanding written material. 2. The total of all the elements in a piece of written work that affect the success a reader will have in understanding its intended meaning. 3. Formula purporting to measure reading difficulty as indicated by grade level.

reader   1. A position in a UK university which is usually awarded for high academic achievement. 2. A person employed by a publisher to assess the suitability of book manuscripts and proposals for publication. 3. A symposium of articles collected to form the basic reading for a course of study.

Readers' Advisory Service   The first specified *adult education* role within the American library service – it started in 1926.

reading age   A score on a standardized reading test given in terms of age equivalent reading scores.

Reading Camps Association   The forerunner of the *Frontier College* in Canada – started in 1899.

reading circle   Used in the Roman Catholic Church in the United States from the 1880s as a means of adult Christian education, and to improve the educational opportunities of adults through prescribed courses of prepared reading. See *study circle*.

reading disability   A general term signifying an inability to read to the normally expected level for a person of that age.

reading level   The level of achievement in reading attained by individuals. It is usually defined by age/grade levels.

reading list   A list of recommended books for a specific course or topic.

reading scheme   A plan prepared to assist a learner to master the art of reading, or to study a specific topic.

reading test   Technique used to assess the level of reading ability.

Reading with a Purpose   A series of reading lists and introductory essays on 67 different topics published by the American Library Association between 1925 and 1933.

realism   The belief that universals have an actual existence, independent of thought.

reason   The faculty for rational argument and judgement. There are generally considered to be three categories of reason: evidencing (showing why something is true); motivating (providing the reason why somebody did something); and causally necessitating (demonstrating the causes of an event or phenomenon).

recall   The process of retrieving information from memory.

receiver role   The role of the learner who merely receives information.

re-certify   See *re-accreditation*.

reciprocal questioning   A teaching and learning technique whereby the teachers and learners question each other.

recognition   The awareness that an event or a phenomenon is one that has been previously, seen, experienced or learned.

recollection   A memory.

record of achievement   In the United Kingdom it was planned that, by 1990, all children leaving school would have such a record. See *portfolio*.

recorder   A member of a group who has been allocated, or volunteered for, the task of recording the group dynamic and/or discussion.

recruitment   The process of attracting new people or students to an occupation or educational institution.

recurrent education   Organization of *lifelong education* into periods of systematic study alternating with extended periods of other activity, eg work or leisure. Exponents of recurrent education argued that people have a right to keep returning to education throughout their lives. See *entitlement, continuing education*.

red brick university   The civic universities in the United Kingdom have become known as the red brick universities.

reductionism   1. Any doctrine that seeks to explain and reduce a complex proposition to a simpler one. 2. The belief that understanding human behaviour can be reduced to, or interpreted by, the behaviour of lower animals.

redundancy   The extent to which *information* provided is unnecessary.

re-education   1. To re-learn something that has been lost or forgotten. 2. Learning new *knowledge* or *skill* in order to replace that which has become redundant.

re-enact   To re-experience a phenomenon, in as far as that is possible.

refer   The process of giving a student an opportunity to improve upon a grade or an academic performance in an assignment before the final decision is made.

referee   1. An assessor of a paper or book who judges whether it is suitable for publication. See *reader*. 2. One who writes a reference, recommendation, or testimonial on behalf of another person.

reference group   A group with whom an individual identifies, or to which an individual is compared for testing and assessment purposes.

referral   1. Directing a student to improve upon an academic performance prior to the final decision being made. 2. Re-directing an enquiry, request, or a person with a problem to a more suitable person.

reflection   The process of thinking about a previous experience or event.

reflective learning   Learning by thoughtful review and analysis of experience.

reflective practitioner   A practitioner who reflects in practice. See the work of Donald Schön.

reflectivity   A dimension of *cognitive style*. See also *impulsive learning*.

reflex   A mechanical, bodily response to a stimulus.

reflexivity   The process whereby society is forced to reflect upon itself as a result of the outcomes of the implication of previous policies.

reformism   An ideology of change, often found among adult educators. Reformist change is gradual, initiated by those in power and certainly not radical.

refresher course   A course of study designed to assist learners in relearning or revising knowledge or skills that have already been learned.

regent   A member of the governing body of a US university. See *State Board of Regents*.

Regional Advisory Council (RAC)   For a period there were ten such councils co-ordinating further and vocational education in the United Kingdom. They were financed by local government. Subsequently replaced by *Training and Enterprise Councils*.

regional institutional accrediting association   A recognized voluntary agency, which administers the procedures for *accreditation* in the United States.

register   1. List of students attending a class. 2. A list of professionals who are accredited and licensed to practise their profession.

registrar   A senior member of the staff of a college or university, responsible for the academic administration of the organization.

Regius professor   A professorial appointment in an established university in the United Kingdom that is in the gift of the Crown.

regression   1. A psychological state of reverting to a more primitive or more child-like state of behaviour. 2. A statistical term used to indicate an association between one variable and other variables in the analysis.

regular education   Term used by UNESCO to refer to the normal and continuous sequence of full-time education from school through to higher education.

regulations   Rules of procedure or behaviour.

rehabilitation   The process of restoring an individual who has been physically or mentally disabled, or who has been imprisoned, to readapt to the demands of society.

reification   The process by which an abstract concept is treated as if it had concrete existence.

reinforcement   Reward for acceptable behaviour in order to reinforce it or punishment for unacceptable behaviour.

reinforcer   The stimulus that reinforces acceptable behaviour.

relativist   1. One who regards all *knowledge* as relative. 2. A *learning style* in which the learner seeks to assess all knowledge within its context.

relativity   A scientific theory discovered by Albert Einstein that the definition of motion depends on the position of the observer, and that space and time depend upon each other. This has had repercussions for epistemology; some philosophers now regard a great deal of *knowledge* as relative.

relaxation technique   Techniques designed to assist individuals to relax the mind, their muscles; used to manage anger, stress, etc.

released time   Time that an employee is given to attend educational activities.

relevance   An activity planned in response to needs.

reliability   The extent to which something is dependable, so that it is used in psychology in personality assessment and in statistics to record the consistency in the relationship between variables.

re-licensing   See *re-accreditation*.

religion   Basically a system of beliefs about the meaning of the universe and life within it. See *adult religious education*.

remedial adult education   Adult education provided for low achievers, slow learners, non-achievers and the mentally handicapped. See also *adult basic education*.

remedial loop   Term used in programmed learning to refer to the additional learning process which is incorporated into the learning sequence, for those who gave an incorrect response to a question at the end stage of a programme.

remember   To recall, recollect, retrieve, or reproduce knowledge, skill, attitude, or other experience.

reminiscence   A form of recall of past experiences. This is an important element in some forms of educational gerontology and in preparing people to face death.

repeated reading   A technique in literacy education. A learner reads a piece to the teacher, who notes the time taken, and then subsequently re-times it on additional readings, until the necessary reading speed is reached.

repertory grid   A technique to measure the relationship of personal constructs, devised by George Kelly.

REPLAN   Commenced in 1984 and run until 1989 by the UK government. Its objectives were to create more and better learning opportunities for unemployed people.

Report on the Special Programme Committee on Education of the Canadian Association of Adult Education (1943)   This was a report advocating a radical programme of reconstruction after the Second World War. It led to the formation of *Citizens' Forums*.

representationalism   A generic term that broadly refers to theories of perception in which the mind, it is argued, does not have direct experience of phenomena but only through the medium of ideas transmitted to it, usually through language. This is a significance concept in understanding *experiential learning*.

representative sample   A sample in which the proportion of each category is the same as the proportion in the total population.

repression   In Freudian analysis – a process, which operates at the unconscious level, preventing previously learned experiences that could produce anxiety, guilt, and so on, from reaching the conscious level.

reproducing orientation An approach to learning in which the learner relates to syllabus, and seeks to memorize facts rather than meaning. Education is, consequently, also regarded as an agent of social reproduction.

required course In the United States, this is the compulsory element in an educational programme. See *core curriculum*.

research A systematic investigation into a phenomenon to collect facts, information, or principles about it, so that it can be better understood. There are a variety of types of research, such as quantitative, qualitative, empirical, naturalistic.

research assistant A person who assists a researcher on a project.

research methods A course on the techniques of research.

research seminar A seminar conducted on a research theme.

research student A person undertaking a higher degree by research.

reserve of ability That adult ability which is lost to a society because of elitist selection mechanisms to higher education. These mechanisms initially deny entrance and consequently inhibit unsuccessful adults at that stage from developing their talents later in life.

residential college A college, in which the students live and undertake their own education. There are short-term and long-term residential colleges and the *folk high school* movement is founded on the same principle.

reskilling 1. Retraining. 2. Continuing vocational education in which new skills, or even skills for a new occupation are gained. See also *deskilling*.

resource A supply of materials, aids, ability that can assist the performance of any process.

resource allocation The equipment grant made by the centre to a college, department or course for a specific activity.

resource-based learning A form of teaching and learning in which learners are given direct access to knowledge that is stored, while teachers act as facilitators. The growth of this approach to learning is related to the growth of *resource centres*.

Resource Center for Planned Change US *clearinghouse*.

resource centre A centre in which resources for learning, eg books, journals, records, audio-tales, compact discs, etc are stored and made available to learners.

resource person An expert who is willing to be consulted during a learning project. In some styles of teaching the teacher might be viewed as a resource person.

response The direct effect of a stimulus.

response rate The proportion of a sample that responds to a sample request to complete a test, questionnaire, or other form of enquiry.

responsibility The notion that people are autonomous and answerable for their actions.

Responsible Body In the United Kingdom from 1924 until the 1980s, certain educational organizations (universities and the Workers' Educational Association) were so designated and were responsible for the provision of non-accredited *adult education* at university level for the general population in their areas.

Restart UK educational programme for the unemployed; originally intended for long-term unemployed and to run for one year, it was reduced to six months in 1987 and became *Options* in 1988 when it was reduced to a short course programme.

restricted code   The speech form that Basil Bernstein discovered that related mostly to the working classes. It is a code of speech that does not use elaborated constructions, uses a lot of pronouns and non-verbal gestures. While his work was undertaken with children, this form of speech probably relates to adults as well.

résumé   See *curriculum vitae*.

retention   The process of holding on to a thing – most commonly used in respect of information and the memory.

retirement education   Education for retirement from work. See *pre-retirement education*.

retraining   The process of learning new *skills* in order to keep abreast with changes in the patterns of employment.

return to study courses   Courses that are organized to assist adults in returning to academic study. They usually consist of such topics as study skills, time management, educational guidance, and counselling.

review   To look back or re-examine. Formal reviews are conducted in certain forms of assessment and evaluation.

review of the literature   The practice of examining all published work on a subject under investigation. It is used in developing research proposals and general academic surveys of a topic.

reward   A prize. It is a reinforcer in conditioning theory.

Rewley House   The adult education centre at the University of Oxford.

Right to Learn   The declaration of the 4th UNESCO Conference on adult education at Paris in 1985.

Right to Read   The first phase of the adult literacy campaign in the United Kingdom.

rights   Legal entitlement.

rigidity   1. A state of muscular tension. 2. A personality trait characterized by inflexibility in behaviour or perception.

risk   An action that jeopardizes something valuable.

risk society   Society in a period of rapid change, unable to test the outcomes of solutions to problems before implementing them and so jeopardizing the society, its environment, etc.

rite   A culturally designated ceremony.

ritual   A sequence of patterned behaviours, often socially or culturally designated. Many such rituals exist in the education system.

ritualism   To go through the motions of a behaviour pattern without being committed to its outcomes.

Robbins Principle   Derived from the Robbins Report on Higher Education in the United Kingdom in 1966, that higher education should be available to all who are qualified by ability or attainment to pursue it.

role   1. The rights and duties of a social position. 2. The manner people fashion their own social behaviour within designated social positions.

role conflict   Situation in which an individual is expected to perform different roles simultaneously, either as a result of self-perception or as perceived by different members of the role set.

role education   To prepare individuals to perform specified roles.

role model   The person whose behaviour is copied by a learner.

role modelling   Learning by observing and then imitating the behaviour of another. See *role model*.

role play   A participative method of *teaching* and *learning* in which learners play roles in order to experience affectively as well as cognitively. A useful method in *professional education*; it is similar to but different from *simulation*. See also *educational drama*.

role reversal   The reversing of roles in a relationship – can be used in *role play* in *professional education*.

role set   That group of people in specified social positions with whom a role player has to interact in order to perform their role. Hence an adult educator has a specific role set and there may be similarities in that role set wherever an individual performs a similar role within the same socio-cultural environment.

'Roll-on/roll-off' curriculum   A form of curriculum that allows students to commence a course whenever they wish to and to complete it whenever they desire; it is not controlled by the academic term or year. Courses are usually modular and contain a number of different routes through them. In the United States, this is sometimes called *open entry-open exit*.

Romanticism   A broad movement in thought in philosophy that was a reaction to the technical rationality and empiricism of the Enlightenment. It has had its effects in education with its concerns for *qualitative research* and in the *curriculum*. See *romantic curriculum*.

romantic curriculum   A curriculum that reflects the multi-culturalism of contemporary society but which also indicates that there is no dominant knowledge or truth so that there are a variety of 'truths' to be learned.

rote learning   Learning by memorizing uncritically a text or a sequence of events.

rote memory   The process of learning mechanically and uncritically and recalling the information in precisely the form in which it was presented.

round table   An educational technique for creating discussion groups in which people from different positions in society sit down together to solve problems and to learn from each other.

rubric   A set of instructions. In education, it usually refers to instruction given to a candidate and printed on an examination paper.

rule learning   One of the higher forms of learning postulated by R M Gagné – it is the ability to respond to a stimulus by a series of learned responses.

Ruskin, John (1818–1900)   He was the Slade Professor of Fine Art at Oxford University, a well-known writer and a committed adult educator who taught at the *Working Men's College* with F D Maurice.

Ruskin College   1. An adult residential college in Oxford, formerly known as *Ruskin Hall* which was founded in 1890. Assumed its present name in 1907. Students have been able to sit an Oxford University diploma since 1910, although it is independent of the university. Its initial aim was to prepare people for the Labour movement. 2. In Trenton, Missouri USA, Avalon College which was opened in 1895 was renamed Ruskin College in 1900.

Ruskin Hall   Original name of *Ruskin College*, founded in 1890. Ruskin College still uses the Hall.

Russell Report   Entitled *Adult Education: A Plan for Development*, this report was published in the United Kingdom in 1973. The report produced a list of 118 recommendations about non-vocational adult education.

Russell, Sir Lionel (1904–1983)   Chairman of the committee that prepared the *Russell Report*; he was chief education officer for Birmingham from 1946 to 1968.

Ss

sabbatical   A period of time that academic staff are released from administration and teaching in order to pursue their own reading and research.

sample   Proportion of a total *population* selected to be tested, interviewed, etc.

sampling frame   Information about the total *population* from which the *sample* is to be selected.

sandwich course   A course of professional preparation in which a period of work practice is situated between two periods of theory based in the educational institution. See *practicum*.

Save Adult Education Campaign   A movement started in UK in 1980 to save *adult education* at a time when it looked as if the government was going to terminate local provision. The campaign had lost impetus by 1982.

Savicevic, Dusan (b. 1926)   Professor of adult education at the University of Belgrade and the scholar from whom *Malcolm Knowles* learned the term *andragogy*.

scale   Any procedure or device used for the purpose of arranging *data* in a progressive sequence.

scan   1. To read rapidly in order to get a general meaning. 2. To feed data into a computer by using a scanner.

scapegoat   To cast blame upon someone for another's action.

scepticism   1. A Greek school of thought that maintained that reality is unknowable, so that all *knowledge* should be treated accordingly. 2. Broadly, that certain knowledge might be sought but it cannot be found.

schedule   1. A *timetable*; schedule is the term more frequently used in the United States. 2. A list or sequence of questions for an interview.

Schedule 2   Schedule 2 courses are those that lead to an academic qualification and can receive funding from the Further Education Funding Council. They are usually vocationally orientated.

scholarship   1. A high standard of academic work. 2. A financial grant or award for scholastic achievement or in order to support it.

scholasticism   An early philosophical form that concentrated upon abstract subject matter, careful logic, authority and esoteric debate.

Schön, Donald   Originator of the concept of the *reflective practitioner*, emphasizing the place of *reflective learning* in professional practice.

school   1. An institution which provides education. 2. A group of scholars who adhere to similar approaches to study.

school education   See *initial education*.

School for Adult Educators   Established in Croatia by the Association of People's and Worker's Universities in Yugoslavia. Its aim was to prepare recruits for their role as *adult educators.*

School for Living   A radical *adult education* project in Spain, in which small groups of people explore social alternatives to contemporary society.

School of Social Sciences   The first institution in Finland to establish a lectureship in adult education in 1929; by 1949 this had become a professorship at the University of Tampere.

schooling for social promotion   The term used in Belgium for *adult schooling.*

Schouten, George Hendrik Leonardus (1906–1981)   'Bob' Schouten was a Dutch adult educator and one of the initiators of the *European Bureau of Adult Education* in 1953.

Schouten Memorial Fund   Fund established in honour of Bob Schouten to acquaint young *adult educators* with adult education in a country other than their own.

science   1. Systematic study of the way in which the physical universe behaves. 2. Any body of knowledge organized in a systematic manner. 3. A method of research. See *scientific method.*

Science and Art Department   Established in 1853 in England to increase the means of industrial education and to extend the influence of both science and art on productive industry. The first British government department to have responsibility for the education of adults.

Scientific Educational Association   Established in Hungary in 1841; it is still the only organization in the country which deals exclusively with the education for adults.

Scientific, Literary and Artistic Atteneo of Madrid   Founded in 1820, this association has continued to organize adult education courses and conferences under a variety of names. It also houses one of Spain's most important libraries.

scientific method   An investigative method which follows a number of precise stages: identification of the problem; hypotheses about its solution related to existing knowledge; hypotheses tested; conclusions drawn. See *empiricism, technical rationality.*

score   Quantitative data about a phenomenon under investigation.

Scottish Vocational Qualifications (SVQ)   The qualifications framework introduced in Scotland to accredit work-based competencies. See *General National Vocational Qualifications, National Vocational Qualifications.*

screen   1. An instrument used in an audio-visual display upon which an image is projected. 2. In psychological theory, to screen something out is unconsciously to prevent it coming to the conscious mind; or to prevent the meaning of a phenomenon from being recognized or understood.

screen hypothesis   An alternative to the *human capital theory*, which maintains that employers treat educational qualifications as indicators of personality traits rather than of cognitive ability. Hence as education expands, so do the educational requirements for entry increase.

search committee   Committee convened to administer the process of seeking people for senior or academic appointments in the UnitedStates and the United Kingdom.

second chance adult education   Education offered to those in their adulthood who were not successful in their initial education.

second degree   A higher degree.

second language teaching   As more countries are receiving immigrants, so they are having to teach the immigrants the language of the host country, so that this is quite a large part of *adult education* provision in some countries, eg Israel.

second level course   The second year of a three-year/level undergraduate degree course.

second route education   See *second chance adult education*.

secondary education   A form of initial education organized by day schools for children of about 12 years and older, some with a vocational strand and others with a more general education approach. Often, second chance education is directed towards providing opportunities for adults to undertake or repeat this period of their education.

secondary experience   The process of experiencing a phenomenon through another medium than direct sense experience, eg in conversation, through a book or the mass media. See *mediated experience*.

secondary group: A social group in which social interaction occurs, but of a less intensive nature than that which occurs within primary groups.

secondary memory   See *long-term memory*.

secondary need   A learned *need*. See *hierarchy of needs, primary need*.

secondary school leaving certificate   US certificate, awarded after six years of secondary education.

secondary socialization   The process of socialization that occurs after children have undergone primary socialization within the confines of the family or group of origin.

secondment   1. A period of time spent away from work for additional staff development or training. 2. A loan of personnel from one post to another.

Secretary's Initiative on Adult Literacy On 7 September 1983, Secretary of State Bell and President Ronald Reagan convened a meeting at the White House to promote *adult literacy*. The outcomes were the *National Adult Literacy Project* and the *College Work-Study Program*.

selection   The process of choosing among candidates for a course or position. It is a process of discrimination in which those who are considered to be the most appropriate are chosen, but the methods of selection are far from scientific.

selective attention   In a situation where individuals are exposed to multiple stimuli, some are selected and attention focused upon them.

selector   A person whose designated role is to make a choice on behalf of others. See *gatekeeper*.

self   A concept frequently used by humanistic adult educators to refer to the subject person; often used synonymously with the person. It tends to relate to the conception that the person has of himself or herself as a social human being. Sometimes used synonymously with *self-concept*. See *mutable self*.

self-acceptance   Accepting oneself with one's uniqueness.

self-actualization   The highest level of personality development and the realization of one's own potentialities. See *hierarchy of needs*.

self-administered questionnaire   A *questionnaire* that is completed by the person from whom the information is being elicited, rather than by the researcher.

self-advocacy   The opportunity for people to speak out for themselves. This has been applied especially to those with a mental handicap.

self-appraisal   Individuals undertaking an appraisal of their own activities; part of many appraisal processes.

self-assessment   The process of students assessing their own work.

self-awareness   Being conscious of oneself, in a relatively objective manner. See *self-acceptance*.

self-concept   1. One's concept of oneself, in as complete and as thorough a description as possible. 2. See *self*. This concept appears to have at least three elements: self-image, ideal self, and self-esteem.

self-consciousness   Self-awareness, in a manner that sometimes results in embarrassment in behaviour.

self-consistency   The internal consistent pattern of behaviour displayed by most people.

self-control   The ability to control one's emotions and behaviour.

self-criticism   Criticism of oneself by oneself.

self-deception   Deceiving oneself about one's own abilities and limitations so that one is no longer able to be objectively self-aware.

self-denial   Foregoing of pleasure and satisfaction.

self-determination   The ability to control one's own behaviour and to act upon one's own beliefs. See *self-directed learning*.

self development   The development of the individual person.

self-directed learner   One who seeks to control and manage his or her own learning. See *autodidact*.

self-directed learning   1. Learning that is controlled and managed by the learner. 2. A personality trait. 3. Sometimes, it is regarded as a teaching technique, but in other instances it is learning outside of the educational institution undertaken by learners out of their own interests, needs and concerns. See *autodidaxy*.

self-directed learning readiness scale   A scale devised by Gugliemino to test people's attitudes towards self-directed learning; it is a 58-item self-administered questionnaire. Not all scholars accept the scale as reliable.

self-direction   See *self-determination*.

self-discipline   See *self-control*.

self-disclosure   The willingness to reveal aspects of one's own personality, thoughts, etc.

self-effacement   Modesty.

self-enrichment   The motivation to improve oneself; it has formed a basis of a great deal of non-accredited adult education.

self-esteem   The value that people place upon themselves, frequently relating to the value other people appear to place in them. It is also the desire to see oneself as having certain qualities such as strength, competence, or independence.

self-evaluation   Personality testing in which the subject provides information about himself or herself.

self-expression   An action that helps to develop one's personality through feeling free to express one's own feelings.

self-financing   1. A policy that ensures that a course pays for itself through fee income, rather than being supported by the educational institution, government, etc. 2. Students who pay their own fees.

self-fulfilling prophecy   A term that is used to refer to those situations where the outcome of a situation turns out to be precisely what was expected, since the one who expected the outcome behaved in such a manner as to contribute to its occurring.

self-help   A nineteenth-century movement in which people sought to improve themselves intellectually, through setting their own goals and pursuing them in their own time at their own expense. Samuel Smiles' book *Self Help*, published in 1859 in Britain was at the heart of this movement. See *self-improvement*.

self-help groups   Groups of learners convened to help themselves, without the presence of a teacher.

self-identification   The process whereby individuals develop identification with another people who possesses similar characteristics to themselves.

self-identity   The characteristics individuals attribute to themselves.

self-image   The impression people have about themselves, largely a reflection of the way that other people view them.

self-improvement   A US movement in which individuals engaged in reading, public lectures, attended lyceums and mechanics institutes, etc in order to improve their knowledge and their social and cultural standing.

self-instruction   See *self-directed learning*.

self-instructional device   A teaching tool that can be used by a learner without the assistance of a teacher.

self-learning   Learning by comparing

personal and ideal characteristics as perceived by the learner with those characteristics identified by others. This is a process of self-discovery.

self-pacing   The pace of learning set by the learner rather than by any external agency. See *group pacing*.

self-perception theory   A theory that suggests that people's attitudes and beliefs are determined in part by observation of their own behaviour patterns.

self-presentation   The manner by which one puts oneself forward in order to convey the public image that the actor wishes to present.

self-preservation   A pattern of behaviour that ensures the survival of the self.

self-realization   The achievement of potential.

self-report technique   Used in the study of personality to show how descriptions of behaviour relate to one's *self-concept*.

self-starter   One who can initiate behaviour without the need for external stimulus. See *self-stimulation*.

self-stimulation   One who can initiate behaviour without external stimulus.

self-study   A course of study organized for individuals to study by themselves.

self-study materials   Materials designed for *self-directed learning*.

self-teaching   The process whereby individuals assume primary responsibility for planning their own learning, and then for implementing it.

semantic memory   The general knowledge remembered, removed from the context within which it was learned.

semantics   The study of the meaning of words.

semester   The division of the academic year into two parts, each being approximately fifteen weeks. See *quarter*.

semester credit hour   American term used to refer to the number of hours of instruction per week for a one semester course. Used to measure participation rather than achievement.

semi-illiterate   This was defined in the United Kingdom as a reading ability above that of a 7-year-old but below that of a 10-year-old.

semi-literate   The state of not being completely literate and able to use literacy skills independently.

seminar   1. A discussion focused upon an expert presentation, project report, research paper, etc. 2. Used more generically to refer to nearly any format of education in the business and professional markets.

seminary   A theological college.

semiotics   The study of signs and symbols, especially language.

semi-profession   An occupation that has lower status than the established professions, often because it has a shorter period of initial training.

senate   The ruling body of an academic institution. In some educational institutions, senates are run on the principles of democratic representation – this is especially true in the USA where the institutions are run like corporations so that the Senate does not have a great deal of governing power.

senile   Aged person whose patterns of thought and behaviour have deteriorated.

senior   A term used for *third agers*.

senior college   A *four-year college* in America.

senior lecturer   An academic grade above a lecturer in UK universities and colleges of further education.

senior studies   A term used to refer to programmes of learning activities for older learners.

sensation   The apprehension of a stimulus.

sensationalism   The philosophy that *sensations* are the real and ultimate components of the world.

sentence   A self-contained, grammatical, linguistic unit of words relating to each other in a meaningful manner.

sentence completion   A psychological test, in which subjects are given incomplete sentences to complete.

sequencing   The ordering of material in a lesson to obtain the most effective learning.

serial learning   Learning to make a series of responses in an exact order. See *rote learning*.

serialist   An approach to learning in which the learner learns one aspect at a time in a linear progression. It is a *cognitive style*, the opposite of *holism*.

sermon   A period of exposition or instruction in a service of religious worship – it has also become a derogatory description of some forms of didactic teaching.

Service-Learning Resource Center   A US *clearinghouse*.

Service Members' Opportunity College Established in 1972 for *two-year colleges* and 1974 for *four-year colleges* under the sponsorship of the Carnegie Foundation and the US Department of Defense to enable military service personnel to enrol in colleges without having the necessary entrance qualification.

Servicemen's Readjustment Act
Known as the *G.I. Bill of Rights*, this was passed in 1944, enabling veterans to continue their education after the Second World War. Possibly the most significant adult education act, since it made US educational institutions more flexible and forced them to meet the demands of adult learners.

Sesame　The UK Open University students' newspaper.

session　1. A period of teaching. 2. An academic period, such as a term, semester, or year.

sessional tutor　A tutor who is employed part-time to teach a specific course, or courses.

set　A classification sharing a common property, so that a group of students embarking on a course of study at the same time might be referred to as a set.

set book　A text-book for a course, which the students are expected to study.

settlement　See *university settlement*.

settlement house　1. A dwelling, general purpose building, or administrative centre within a *university settlement*. 2. In the USA, it was a privately-funded, community-based social service centre.

sex education　Education about the impulses and processes of reproduction.

shadowing　The process whereby a person being inducted to a new role, spends time (maybe several days) with the person currently undertaking the role in order to understand what it entails.

shaping theory　A theory of *teaching* in which learners are shaped and moulded into a predetermined pattern. See *behaviourism*.

shared facilities　The joint use of facilities, such as rooms, between different institutions.

short-term goal　An educational objective.

short-term memory　Memory of information that has received little processing. It is regarded as the first of two information processing systems and information stored for immediate needs is stored here. It is not necessarily processed to the *long-term memory*.

shut-in personality　A person who is extremely withdrawn.

sign　An indicator, hint, or clue. More specifically, it is used as a symbol of communication.

sign language　A form of language, using signs, for the purpose of communication with, and between, deaf people.

sign learning　A form of learning that relates to the relationship between signs.

signal learning　Term used by Gagné for one of his lowest forms of learning; a form of conditioning.

simulation　A teaching method in which an actual situation is recreated in the *teaching* and *learning* process so that learners can have opportunity to experience the situation and practise their understanding of the way that they should act in that situation before being expected to perform it in reality. This is a useful technique in *professional education*, especially to help learners understand the affective domain. See also *role-play, educational drama*.

simulator　The person or machine through which real-life situations are created in *simulation* learning.

single honours degree   A first degree in a single subject, at honours level.

single loop learning   A concept introduced by C Argyris and D Schön which suggests that people learn to design their actions so that they do not disturb the social context within which they learn; the opposite of double loop learning.

sister tutor   Original name for a *nurse teacher*.

Sitting by Nellie   A slang term for *apprenticeship* or even mentoring. See also *buddy system*.

situated learning   Learning in the situation. Knowing that resides in the doing rather than being derived from, or applied to, other sources. See *experiential learning*.

situated pedagogy   A form of teaching that locates the subject in the culture of the learners, so that they can become critically aware of their own reality. It is almost essential to dialogical education.

skill   The ability to perform correctly and effectively in action-based situations – a psycho-motor action.

skill centre   A centre offering training for workers, often for the unemployed.

skills analysis   The process of breaking down complex skills into the component parts, so that they can be learned more easily.

Skinner box   An experimental apparatus named after B F Skinner. It is a small chamber having two components – a device for providing food and an instrument to activate the device. See *operant conditioning*.

skip programme   A programmed learning text in which a student making a correct response to a problem omits some of the questions in the sequence.

slide   Also called a transparency – a positive photograph mounted on a transparent surface that can be projected on to a screen. In the USA, an overhead projection transparency is sometimes called a slide.

slow learner   Someone unable to learn at the normal speed. See *adult basic education*.

small group   A group, usually no larger than eight persons, used for teaching and sometimes serves as a focus in affective education. See also *T-group*.

small group teaching   Teaching method by dividing a class into small groups, and devising exercises whereby the group work together.

Smiles, Samuel (1812–1904)   Author of the book *Self Help* in 1859. See *self-directed learning*.

Smith, Arthur Lionel (1850–1924)   Master of Balliol College and Chairman of the committee that produced the *1919 Report*.

Smith-Hughes Vocational Education Act (1917)   US Act that made federal funds available for education in agriculture, home economics, industry and commerce; it also created the Federal Board for Vocational Education.

Smith-Lever Act (1914)   This US Act established the *Co-operative Extension Service* by funding each State annually upon the presentation of a satisfactory plan. The Act also required each *land grant college* to create a separate Division of Extension. The Act was amended in 1983.

snowballing   A teaching technique in which a question or problem is initially addressed individually and then in pairs. The pairs then group into fours, and so on as the snowball grows. People always remain with their initial partners throughout the process. This is a useful *ice-breaking* technique and also a good problem-solving teaching method.

social action   1. Action designed to influence the behaviour of others. 2. Action in the community designed to influence policy and social conditions of existence.

social administration   The study of organization and social policy.

social advancement   Term used in France for *continuing vocational education*.

social agogy   The term was used by Ten Have in the Netherlands to refer to the process of educating, forming, guiding, or supporting a social event, social behaviour, human relations, or group living. See *social pedagogics*.

social anthropology   The study of social behaviour, especially culture and beliefs.

social change   The structural change in society.

social class   Social class is defined by one's position in relation to the means of production of a country. It is a Marxist concept, whereas socio-economic class is more Weberian and includes social status; the latter is more likely to be employed in most stratification studies.

social climate   The atmosphere and ethos of a society or an organization.

social control   The process of ensuring social conformity. Education is often regarded as one of the most powerful forces creating social and cultural reproduction.

social correspondence education   Term used in Japan to refer to *correspondence education, distance learning*.

social disadvantage   People who are handicapped mentally, physically or socially. See *underclass*.

social distance   The degree of separation between different social groups.

social drive   Social pressures that cause individuals to seek social interaction. It has been argued that interaction is important to the formation of the person and quite central to understanding learning.

social ecology   The study of the relationships between human beings and their environment. See also *classroom ecology, ecology*.

social education   1. The term is occasional used in a similar manner to *community education*. 2. In Japan, the term for *liberal adult education* is translated as social education.

Social Education Law   Passed in Japan in 1949, this law gives Japanese people the right to receive *social education* and makes it mandatory for the government to provide it.

social exchange theory   A model of social behaviour based upon the idea that social behaviour is predicated on the expectation that an individual's behaviour is based on the expectation that another's will result in some form of commensurate return.

social exclusion   Social disadvantage that occurs because of gender, ethnic origin or social position. It is sometimes felt that some forms of social exclusion can be overcome through educational programmes. See *underclass*.

social gospel   A movement in the Christian churches, which used the social teaching of Christ to influence public life. It had a great influence on *adult education*.

social intelligence   The ability to engage in effective, mutually beneficial *problem-solving*.

social interaction   The process of interdependent behaviour when people communicate with each other.

social learning theory   A theory of learning that starts from the assumption that individuals are social selves and their learning is influenced by the social environment in which they are situated.

social mobility   Individual movement through the social structures.

social movement   A popular movement for social change.

social need   Any *need* having a social basis.

social network   The web of social relations that provides individuals with security and support.

social norm   The general pattern of behaviour that occurs within a group of people. Frequently, *need* is measured against the norm. See *normative need*.

social order   1. The totality of institutions and social practices comprising the social structure. 2. The stability of the social institutions.

social pedagogics   The term used in parts of Europe for adult teaching skills.

social pedagogy   Term used in continental Europe to refer to the study of *adult education, community education* and youth work.

social policy   The analysis of the intentions and effects of government plans and legislation.

social pressure   The collective influences of others to induce certain forms of behaviour.

social reality   Reality as constructed and defined by the social group.

social reproduction   The process of recreating similar social structures across generations. Education is regarded as one of the most powerful forces of social reproduction. See also *cultural reproduction*.

social role   The role performed by an individual within a social context.

social self   The characteristics of a person's self, either seen by others or deliberately displayed by an actor for others to see.

social skills   Skills necessary to undertake normal living within society. Many courses in adult education are designed to improve people's social skills.

social stratification   The hierarchical manner in which a society or organization is structured.

social welfare   Programmes devised to assist the disadvantaged. *Adult education* has been conceptualized as a welfare provision but this is rapidly changing in Western society.

social work   Welfare activities designed to meet the needs of the *socially disadvantaged*, in which adult basic education might play a part.

socialization   The process whereby children learn informally the sub-cultures into which they are born. However, it has been recognized more generally as a lifelong process in which adults are also having their *knowledge, attitudes, behaviours* and *beliefs* shaped by their social experiences.

socialism   Political ideology that relates to communal ownership of property and state welfare for individuals.

socialist halls of science   Established in the 1830s by Robert Owen, these were organized by the working classes for their own education. They were a short-lived phenomenon since they ran into financial difficulties and were also opposed by the middle classes.

Society for Arts and Sciences   Established in 1784 in the Netherlands to provide adult education type activities.

Society for Common Benefit
Established in 1784 in the Netherlands as a

voluntary organization committed to disseminating new educational and philanthropic ideas.

Society for Mutual Education The original name of the *lyceum* movement in America. See *Society for the Improvement of Schools and Diffusion of Useful Knowledge.*

Society for Participatory Research in Asia This is an *International Council for Adult Education* project seeking to incorporate research into adult learning from a number of countries in Asia.

Society for Popular Culture Founded in Finland in 1874, the oldest *adult education* organization in that country.

Society for Promoting Christian Knowledge (SPCK) Founded in Britain in 1699, this organization was established to provide adult religious education, as well as children's religious education. It is also a publisher.

Society for Research into Higher Education (SRHE) Independent UK academic research society, concerned with *higher education.*

Society for the Advancement of Games and Simulation in Education and Training (SAGSET) A UK academic society concerned with participative methods of education and training.

Society for the Diffusion of Useful Knowledge Established in England in 1826, as a society to promote cheap literature for the working classes. Disbanded in 1846, since much of what it published seemed far removed from the concerns of working people.

Society for the Diffusion of Useful Knowledge among the Peasants and Working Classes Established in Sweden in 1833 to present the people with useful knowledge.

Society for the Encouragement of Arts, Manufacture and Commerce Established in 1754 in England; this was to become the Royal Society of Arts.

Society for the Improvement of Schools and Diffusion of Useful Knowledge The name the *lyceum* movement adopted after *Society for Mutual Education.*

Society for the Improvement of the Working Class Established in 1854 in the Netherlands, it was dominated by employers and ran evening classes without a great deal of success.

Society of Industrial Tutors Established in the UK to provide opportunity to assist those who teach industrial studies, and to develop it as a field of study.

Society to Encourage Studies at Home Formed in the USA in 1873 as a very early attempt at *correspondence education.*

socio-cultural adult education The translation of the term used in Belgium to refer to liberal adult education.

socio-cultural animation 1. The term used in parts of continental Europe to refer to the manner in which people can be helped to play their part in society as responsible citizens to help make it a more democratic place. 2. Elsewhere, it seems to carry the connotations of leisure-time adult education, mostly the pursuit of hobbies and other practical activities.

socio-drama The simulation of social situations to help people solve problems. Sometimes used as a teaching technique. See *psychodrama.*

socio-economic class A system of social stratification based upon both the occupation and its status.

socio-linguistics Study of the sociology of language.

sociology of knowledge   The study of knowledge, relating its creation to the social structures. This form of study emerged from earlier studies of *ideology*.

sociometry   A social psychological technique that studies social inter-relationships; it uses networks and graphical illustrations to record results.

Socratic teaching   After the Greek philosopher, Socrates, who was noted for his method of teaching through asking questions. This is a teacher-led method.

software   Computer programs.

somatic learning   Those forms of learning founded on the biological rather than the psychological.

sophist   A school of educational thought and practice that emerged around the middle of the fifth century BC in Greece; it emphasized human interest and concentrated on the skills of rhetoric.

spare-time adult educator   Term occasionally used for *part-time adult educator*.

spare-time university   Established in China to serve a part-time student population that has not been relieved of their occupational duties in order to study.

Spearman's rank order co-efficient of correlation   A statistical technique in which two sets of scores are arranged in rank order and the relationship between them calculated.

special education   Educational provision for those having special needs, eg physical, mental and emotional.

special needs   A term used to refer to the needs of the disabled.

specialist   Person who concentrates on specific areas of work.

specialist teacher   One who is employed to teach a particular topic or students needing specialist teaching.

speech   Verbal communication.

speech act   Acts performed when words are spoken. Habermas' theory of communication action is perhaps the most well known use in *adult education* theory at present.

speech discrimination test   A standardized test to measure the ability to discriminate between speech sounds.

speech therapy   Treatment for speech disorder.

spiral curriculum   An approach to *curriculum* that entails a broadening and deepening study of the subject as the course progresses, by continual return to the original subject matter.

split-session   Condition of employment for a *tutor* who is expected to teach for the first and third sessions of the day (morning and evening) but be free during the second (afternoon).

sponsor   An organization or person who provides financial and other support of (learning) opportunities.

sponsored experiential learning   *Experiential learning*, in the form of *work experience*, during the process of a course of training.

sponsorship schemes   Schemes of various forms which provide financial support to educational institutions to mount specific courses or to students so that they can pursue their education.

staff development   The education and training of employees. See *human resource development, job development*.

staff-student association   An association comprising both academic staff and students within an educational institution to assist in the smooth running of the organization and its courses.

staff-student ratio   The ratio of the number of academic staff to the number of students in an academic institution.

staff tutor   1. One who is employed to perform an academic function in an educational institution, but who is not employed as a full-time academic. 2. In the British Open University staff tutors are employed in regional offices running the academic services, but their primary function is not to take academic responsibility for preparing teaching material.

stage concept   Refers to theories of development, in which people are claimed to pass through different levels of development – physical, cognitive and social.

Stages I, II, III   These are three stages in the courses for the preparation of *adult educators* in the United Kingdom – Introductory (I), intermediate (II) and final stage of certification (III). Together, the three stages are regarded as equivalent to a full-time year course and successful completion results in the award of a Certificate of Education.

standard deviation   A statistical measure indicating the average amount which all values deviate from the mean.

standard industrial classification   A manual listing the main types of industrial activities in which organizations are involved.

standard occupational classification   A manual listing and classifying the main types of work performed by the population.

standard performance   A work-study term relating the output that a worker is expected to achieve under normal working conditions.

standardized test   A test that has been established and validated, so that it can achieve a relatively objective measure.

standards   The generally accepted levels of performance in academic and other work and behaviour.

Standing Conference on University Teaching and Research in the Education of Adults (SCUTREA)   A UK organization established to provide a forum for universities THAT have an interest in the academic study of the education of adults.

Stanford-Binet Intelligence Test   An intelligence test, based upon a scale prepared by Binet in 1911. The first test by this name was a revision of the original scale and published by Stanford University in 1916.

Start Helping Adults to Read Education (SHARE)   A campaign in the UK, organized by the National Co-operative Education Association, to protest against the cut-back of liberal adult education in the early 1980s.

State Board of Regents   The management committee of a state university in the United States. See *regent*.

state centre for political education   In Germany, federal states have their own *adult education* centres for political education.

state college   Public college in USA, offering a four-year degree programme. See *state university*.

state education agency   US term to refer to an organization responsible in law for any specific educational function.

state plan   The written plan that each US State has to submit to the Federal government in order to get appropriate funding.

state university   A public four-year degree awarding university in America.

status The well-defined prestige ascribed to a person or position within a social grouping.

status deprivation The loss of desired prestige.

status discrepancy The difference between degrees of status that individuals experience in different groups.

status group 1. A group of people, classified together and sharing the same status. 2. A group of people who share the same status in a society.

status need The psychological need to achieve high status, ie ambition.

status symbol Symbols demonstrating, or suggesting, that individuals occupy high status positions in society.

statutory school leaving age The legal age in any country before which a child may not leave school. Hence, *adult education* might be referred to as *post-compulsory education*.

stereotype A set of relatively fixed, often simplistic generalizations about a category of persons.

stigma A mark or blemish, typically culturally or economically defined, that causes some people to be treated as different by others.

stimulation Any event that causes a receptor to become active.

stimulus Any event that causes an organism to respond.

stimulus-response (S-R) Behaviourist approach to learning in which the response to the initial stimulus is regarded as the indicator that learning has occurred.

storefront schools Originated in USA. They are attempts to take education to the people through using shops on the thoroughfare as schools in order to try to attract more people to education – this is usually an *adult basic education* enterprise. See also *street academy*.

strategy The art and science of planning.

street academy See *storefront school*.

stress A state of psychological tension that often results in breakdown or *burnout*.

structural unemployment A form of unemployment caused by major changes in the structures of society, eg the decline of manufacturing occupations in the West.

structuralism A method of analysis, based on the idea that the key to understanding a phenomenon lies in the underlying patterns of relationships of its components.

structuration The structuring of social relations across time and space, as a result of the reproduction of practices.

structure An organized pattern of relatively stable components.

structured interview An *interview* that follows a carefully prepared schedule of questions.

Stuart, James (1843–1913) Fellow of Trinity College, Cambridge. Generally regarded as the first university extension lecturer. He delivered a series of lectures on behalf of the *North of England Council for Promoting Higher Education for Women* in 1867. He organized the first *adult education* conference in Sheffield in 1875.

Studebaker, John W Initiator of the *public forums* movement for discussing public affairs in the USA, whilst he was a member of the US Department of Education. See *Des Moines Forum*.

student   One who studies a subject or discipline.

student body   The total number of students enrolled in an educational organization.

student-centred education   Education which concentrates on the learners' needs and learning processes rather than on teaching and the teacher's intentions for the session. This has been a traditional approach in adult education. See *learner-centred education*.

student-centred learning   See *student-centred education*.

student loan   A system whereby students are assisted financially by granting them loans whilst they are studying, to be repaid at a later date. A number of countries have introduced this approach to assist in funding *higher education*.

student participation   Enlisting student involvement in the preparation of education programmes.

Student Potential Program   A US project in which potential students are assessed by a variety of means to see whether they should be able to complete a college programme.

student record   The file of academic achievement, and other aspects of the students' achievements, held by an educational institution.

studentship   A award, often financial, to enable a person to study an academic course.

Studies in Continuing Education Australian *adult education* journal.

Studies in the Education of Adults Formerly *Studies in Adult Education*, a UK academic journal established in 1969.

Studies in the Social Significance of Adult Education in the United States
A series of 27 books prepared in the 1930s and published by the *American Association for Adult Education* under the sponsorship of the Carnegie Foundation.

studio   A room in which artists work or study.

study centre   A local centre for academic study, not usually at the academic institution that is organizing the course being studied.

study circle   An informal group meeting for a common study purpose. First established in Sweden by Oscar Olsson in 1902. The groups are democratic in their constitution and often determine their own discussion topics.

study circle association   There are eleven associations that organize study circles throughout Sweden. They are recognized by the government and receive a government grant to undertake this work. See *study organization*.

study guide   A prepared guide to assist learners in mastering the content of a specified piece of learning. It may consist of guidelines to reading a book or to observing the performance of a procedure, etc. Study guides should contain an explanation of the reasons for learning, the anticipated outcomes, the process and procedure of the learning exercise.

Study Handbook   The title of the annual study notes of the adult school movement after 1919. See *Lesson Handbook*.

study method   Strategies used by individuals for studying.

study organization   The eleven organizations in Sweden that sponsor *study circles*. They are also called educational organizations. These are educational organization working within non-formal adult education, based on the voluntary participation of adult learners; their main character, image and priorities are affected by the different member organizations that might be affiliated with them (political parties, trade unions, religious movements, and other non-governmental organizations).

study pack   A prepared learning programme on a specific topic for study. In the United States this might also refer to selected additional readings for a course. See *course pack*.

study skills   The skills required to study successfully, such as different reading techniques, note-taking ability, managing one's own learning, writing skills, etc. Many educational institutions run courses to help students, and especially *adult returners*, improve these skills.

study week   A unit of measurement for an academic course in Finland, equal to approximately 40 hours of study time.

styles of learning   See *cognitive style, learning style*.

subculture   Refers to the culture of a group or a category of people. Hence an adult class can develop its own subculture, which in some ways is comparable to its ethos, a term used in educational circles.

sub-degree course   A course of study that is not considered to be at first degree level.

subject   1. The knowledge content of a course. 2. An area of study or research.

subject co-ordinator   Academic member of staff of an educational institution responsible for the teaching of a specified subject.

subjective   1. Relating to the mind of a thinking person. 2. A personal perception/interpretation of reality.

subjectivism   A moral philosophical approach emanating from the person. In its simplest form, all moral values are regarded as a matter of personal preference.

sub-library   An outpost of a main library – usually located a distance from it. A branch library.

subliminal learning   Learning of which one is not conscious. See *preconscious learning, incidental learning*.

subliminal perception   The perception of a stimulus without being consciously aware of its cause.

subliminal stimulus   Any stimulus that occurs below the threshold of consciousness.

submission   A proposal for which approval is sought; the process of presenting a course of a validating agency, a proposal to a funding agency, etc.

sub-normal   With a mental handicap.

sub-professional   US term for an assistant or a support person for a professional. Often called a *para-professional*.

subscription library   A voluntary association of people contributing towards a fund for the purchase of books, which can then be borrowed. The first one was organized in 1731 in Philadelphia, USA, by Benjamin Franklin.

success case method   A method of evaluation used in human resource development in which those apparently successful products of the process are interviewed to assess how they utilized the teaching and learning process through which they had gone.

success ratio   Proportion of students completing a course successfully.

successive approximations   A term used by *behaviourists* to refer to the *shaping* of behaviour by rewarding the subject as the behaviour approximates to the desired behaviour pattern.

suggestibility   The willingness to accept suggestions.

summative assessment   The assessment that occurs at the end of a course of study, eg end of course examinations. See *formative assessment*.

summative evaluation   The process of evaluating the outcome of a course or a programme of courses. See *summative assessment, formative evaluation*.

summative profile   The *profile* prepared by a student at the end of a course of study.

summer school   An educational event held during the summer, often residential in nature.

summer session   A *summer school* at a university, often having a continuing education theme. The earliest were held at Harvard University in 1869.

summer university   The use of the university campus to teach academic subjects to a wider public, during the summer period.

Sunday school   1. Early adult education institutions, established to help people become literate. The earliest one was founded by Robert Raikes in England in 1760. 2. Religious schools, organized by the churches.

sunrise semester   Established in 1963 in the USA, early morning educational television.

superego   A Freudian concept; the third element of the self that might be equated with the internalization of the cultural values that a child does during its development and this is associated with the *conscience*.

supervision   The process of advising and guiding a student in a learning situation. The US term is *advisement*.

support staff   The non-academic staff employed in an educational organization to support the academic work.

surface processor   A learning style that refers to the process of acquiring knowledge at the surface level, eg the acquisition of facts. See *deep processor*.

survey   An approach to research by collecting data by questionnaire or interview methods from a number of people. See *sample*.

suspension   An interruption, or a temporary debarment, from a course of study or membership of an organization.

sustainability   1. The term used to convey the idea that once a movement, or a programme, has been implemented it can be paid for within the budget of an organization or country. 2. A programme or movement should function without waste.

swot   To study.

syllabus   An outline of the content of a curriculum.

symbol   An object or a diagram representing something else, eg language can be defined as an arbitrary symbol. See *semiotics*.

symbolic analysts   The term used by some writers for *knowledge workers*.

symbolic interactionism   The study of the self-society relationship as a process of symbolic communication between social actors. See *interactionism*.

symbolism   The practice of using symbols.

symposium   1. A meeting to hear and discuss a variety of approaches to a subject or theme. 2. A collection of academic papers on a subject.

synapse   The region in the brain in which impulses pass from neuron to neuron.

syndicate   See *group work*.

syndicate room   Usually small rooms appropriate for small *group work*.

syndrome   Any combination of characteristics that indicate a disorder.

synectics   A method of identifying and solving problems that depends on creative thinking, use of analogy, and discussion.

synergogy   A learner-centred teaching method which offers the learner meaningful direction in the form of learning designs and learning instruments; a teamwork situation through the design of learning teams having explicit learning goals; and a sharing of all learning opportunities and outcomes.

syntax   Rules of grammar in language.

synthesis   The drawing together of diverse sources and aspects of knowledge to create a new knowledge. A high form of understanding, according to Bloom's Taxonomy of Educational Objectives.

synthetic trainer   Any training instrument that simulates the actual conditions of practice, used for acquiring that skill.

Syracuse University Publications in Continuing Education (SUPCE)   The largest university-based publications organization in the United States.

Syracuse University Resources for Educators of Adults (SUREA)   A large archive and resource centre for adult education based at Syracuse University.

system   A set of variables that are interrelated such that a change in one will have an effect on all the remainder.

systematic reflection   Term used to refer to the process of reflecting on life's experiences regularly in order to identify what has been learned from them.

systems learning   Learning by achieving a specific goal through a specific system or plan.

systems theory   A theoretical perspective seeking to understand social reality by treating it as an interconnected system.

Tt

taboo (tabu)   Any banned or prohibited object, stemming from religious observances. The object may be regarded as sacred or as unclean.

tabula rasa (*Latin:* blank sheet)   The theory that at birth the mind is completely empty and unencumbered by innate desires, drives, etc. Consequently, all knowledge is based upon *experience*.

tabulation   A means of recording quantitative date in table form.

tacit knowledge   A dimension of practical knowledge. The type of knowledge that people have who have immersed themselves in a subject so deeply that they appear to understand aspects of it implicitly as well as explicitly. The concept has been expounded most fully in the work of M Polanyi.

Tagore Memorial Award   Instituted by the Indian Adult Education Association in 1987, to commemorate Rabindranath Togore (1861–1941) who founded a number of educational institutions all having a humanistic basis and non-formal in their approach to education.

TALIS (Third Age Learning International Studies)   1. An international network of scholars who are studying learning in the third age, organized from the University of Toulouse. 2. The occasional journal of the network.

talking book   1. A book that has been recorded on to an audio-cassette, used with blind people. 2. *Paulo Freire* introduced the term to refer to books that contain records of dialogues.

Tampere University   Formerly the Civic College and the *School of Social Sciences*, but it was the first school in Finland to establish a lectureship in adult education in 1929. In 1949, the position became the first professorship of adult education in Finland.

tape library   *Library* with a collection of audio- and video-cassettes. Many book libraries have separate sections. See *resource centre*.

target group   The group at which a commodity is aimed. As education becomes a market commodity, so this term refers to that group of people who might respond to a certain course and to whom the advertising should be directed.

target population   The source of felt needs, from which an educational programme can be planned. See *target group*.

task allocation   The distribution of jobs by one who has the authority to designate work.

task analysis   An assessment of the behaviours or skill required to complete a task effectively.

task-based curriculum   The *curriculum* which is constructed, based on an analysis of the actual job.

task card   Sheet containing directions, sometimes in pictorial form.

task-centred group   A group that sets out to achieve its aims.

task-oriented leader   One who seeks always to achieve the specified purpose of the group, irrespective of group dynamics. See *expressive leader*.

'taster' activities   A term sometimes employed to refer to *adult education* institutions which provide opportunities for potential students to get to know something about a course of study by offering free introductory sessions.

taxonomy of educational objectives   A list of objectives, initially in the cognitive domain and structured hierarchically, initially proposed by Benjamin Bloom. Later taxonomies were prepared in the *affective* and the *psycho-motor* domains.

teach   1. The process of presenting knowledge, skills, attitudes, or values, which can be transmitted to and learned by others. This is commonly called *didactic teaching*. 2. A process of *questioning*, so that the students can learn through the sequence of questions and answers. This is called *Socratic teaching*. 3. The creation of situations and experience, through which students have the opportunity to learn. This is called *facilitative* teaching. 4. In a Skinnerian sense, teaching is about arranging the contingencies of reinforcement.

teacher   One who teaches, or facilitates learning.

teacher education   The professional preparation of teachers.

teacher fellowship   Some universities and institutions of higher education award fellowships to practising teachers, so that they can spend a period of time studying education.

teacher mobility   The amount of movement between jobs in the teaching profession.

teacher practitioner   A professional practitioner who has educational preparation and teaches students in the professional work setting whilst remaining a practitioner. See *field work teacher, practical work teacher, lecturer practitioner, labourer teacher*.

teacher preparation   See *teacher education*.

teacher training college   Also called college of education, or teacher's college. 1. A school-teacher training college in the United Kingdom prior to the mid-1970s, when mono-technical educational institutions were discouraged and thus many diversified or amalgamated with other types of higher education. 2. A college in an American university devoted to the preparation of school-teachers and to the study of education. Many departments of adult education are located in these colleges.

teachers' centre   An *in-service* centre for teachers in UK.

teachers' certificate   A professional licence to teach.

teaching assistant   One who is employed to assist a teacher in the classroom. See *para-professional*.

Teaching at a Distance   The journal of the UK *Open University*. Replaced by *Open Learning*.

teaching hospital   A hospital in which medical students are taught, usually attached to a university.

teaching load   The workload of a teacher in terms of the number of classroom hours of teaching, preparation, advising, marking, etc.

teaching machine   A device or computer that allows a learner to use a programmed text for the purposes of learning without the help or presence of a teacher.

teaching methods   The variety of different approaches to teaching, eg *lecturing, group discussion*.

teaching observation   A period during which trainee teachers observe experienced teachers working in the classroom.

teaching practice   The provision of opportunity for trainee teachers to have some teaching experience, usually under the guidance of a mentor or supervisor, in the educational institution. See *internship, professional placement*.

teaching staff   The complement of academic teachers in an educational institution.

teaching style   Teachers' characteristics of teaching, which can be classified by attitude, authority, expectation, manner, etc.

teaching techniques   See *teaching methods*.

team teaching   An approach to teaching in which either (1) more than one teacher teaches the same lesson together, each using his/ her own knowledge and skills to enrich the lesson; or (2) more than one teacher teaches a course, so that one teacher will conduct one session.

Technical and Further Education (TAFE)   Australian system of technical and further education, distinct from schools and universities.

Technical and Vocational Education Initiative (TVEI)   Started in the UK in 1983, a curriculum project for 14–18 year olds still attending initial education, intending to equip them for the world of work.

technical college   1. In the United Kingdom, it is a college of further education. 2. In the United States, it is a community college offering occupational and vocational education at post-school level.

technical education   See *vocational education*.

Technical Instruction Act   In 1899 legislation in England enabled local government to spend a penny rate, local household tax, on technical education.

technical rationality   Term adopted by D Schön in the book, *The Reflective Practitioner*, to refer to instrumental rationality – this is the rationality of means and ends – that it is rational to do something to produce something else as efficiently as possible through the application of scientific theory and technique. It reflects the rationality of *modernity* but it is now open to question.

technical unit   A vocational education unit attached to a normal school.

technological university   A university specializing in *technical* and *vocational* subjects.

technology   The application of practical sciences within industry and commerce.

technology transfer   The transfer of knowledge from one institution to another.

teleconferencing   Two-way interactive audio-visual link-up. See *compressed video*.

tele-course   The use of open-circuit television for educational courses. See *distance education*.

teleological ethics   A form of ethical argument that suggests that the goodness of an action lies in its outcomes. The most well known form of this is utilitarianism. See *deontological ethics*.

teleology   Philosophical theory of striving to achieve ends.

tele-teaching   Teaching through audio-visual electronic systems. See *teleconferencing*.

tele-university   A university using television as its main medium of communication to its students.

telemathic teaching   Teaching at a distance.

telemathy   Learning at a distance.

temperament   A term to describe how people react to situations, a personality characteristic.

tenure   The right to permanent employment within an organization.

Ten Have, T T   Leading Dutch adult educator who popularized *andragology* in Holland.

term paper   An essay, or other form of academic assignment, submitted at the end of a course, or after a specified period of time. See *course paper*.

terminal assessment   See *summative assessment*.

tertiary college   An educational institution providing *tertiary education*.

tertiary education   Used mainly to refer to *post-secondary* education. While it does not refer specifically to *adult education*, adult students are regarded as part of the potential clientele of most tertiary colleges. It includes higher education and further education.

tertiary socialization   Some sociologists use this term to refer to occupational socialization, and in this sense it relates to *vocational education*.

test   1. An *examination*. 2. In the sciences, it is a procedure to detect the presence or the absence of a substance.

test item   The individual items on a schedule of questions to be employed in educational or other research.

Test of English as a Foreign Language (TOEFL)   An examination to test the proficiency of a candidate in the English language.

test of significance   A statistical test to determine whether a research finding is likely to occur by chance.

test-study method   An approach to teaching in which the students are pre-tested to establish the level of knowledge or skill upon which the educator or course has to build. See *needs assessment*.

testimonial   A reference or recommendation.

text   The actual written script is sometimes called the text.

textbook   A set book for a specific course of study.

T-group   An educational or *therapy group*, focusing upon the affective domain.

thanatology   The study of death and dying. This is an area of educational concern for those working with the health professions and with counselling.

thanatos   Freudian concept of the death instinct.

theatre workshop   1. Use of drama in *community education* to understand community problems. 2. Theatre company running its own acting workshop, either for the purpose of teaching acting or to teach others to understand the meaning of the piece being played.

thematic approach   An approach to teaching and to curriculum design that organizes knowledge around themes. It is sometimes referred to as a *topic approach*.

theme   A topic or idea expanded in a discourse, lesson, or series of lessons.

theory 1. A set of ideas that organize, or order. 2. A body of generally accepted knowledge about some phenomenon or process; this is seen as distinct from *practice*. Recently, it has been argued that the status of theory in contemporary society is that of *information*. 3. In philosophy, it refers to a logically deduced construct. 4. An idea, or a hypothesis.

theory in use C Argyris and D Schön use this term to refer to a theory of action which underlies an action, but which the actor may not necessarily regard as their own, as opposed to their espoused theory which they are able to articulate.

Theory X One aspect of MacGregor's management theory that people are basically lazy, dislike work, will avoid it if they can and have little or no ambition, so that they have to be coerced into working. In contrast, see *Theory Y* – a theory that has been adapted to teaching.

Theory Y The other aspect of MacGregor's management theory, that people are interested in work, want to do so, and are willing to assume responsibility for it. In contrast see *Theory X* – it has been adapted to teaching.

therapy A treatment for a disorder; in many cases it is a learning process, and some aspects of its approach have been adapted in *adult education*.

therapy group See also *T-group*.

thesis 1. A case or theory maintained in *discussion* or *debate*. 2. A written dissertation, or piece of original research, usually presented for a *higher degree*. In the USA, this term is usually reserved for a masters degree whereas in the UK it is more frequently used in relation to a doctorate.

think A covert cognitive or mental manipulation of ideas, images, symbols, propositions, memories, concepts, etc. There

are different kinds of thinking, which can be described as *cognitive styles*.

think tank 1. A group of people called together to solve problems, assist make policy decisions by thinking through problems and giving advice. 2. A term used to describe some policy institutions, whether government sponsored or independent.

third age The period of active life after retirement.

third age learning A general term used to cover and embrace all those learning and educational activities in which *third agers* are involved.

Third Age News The newspaper of the Universities of the Third Age in the United Kingdom.

third ager A person involved in a variety of activities after retirement.

Thomism A school of philosophy derived from St Thomas Aquinas.

thought 1. A general term covering the cognitive processes. 2. A specific term that refers to the body of ideas that one thinker has produced.

Tie Lines Established in 1966 by the Canadian Association of Adult Education, subsequently renamed *Learning Resources Kit*.

time and motion study The study of work that relates job performance to the time taken to perform each task. It is associated with the scientific management movement.

time management The ability to plan and control the use of time effectively.

time sampling A process by which a phenomenon is investigated over a period of time. Instead of taking continuous measurement, investigations are made at periodic intervals.

timed test   A test that has to be completed within a specified time period.

timetable   The formal arrangement and timing of classes in an educational institution, or activities in another organization. See *schedule*.

To Educate the People Consortium   An innovative five-year first-degree programme initiated by Wayne State University. See *weekend college*.

Tolley Medal for Distinguished Leadership in Adult Education   The William Pearson Tolley award is made from Syracuse University, USA, for contributions in adult education leadership.

Tompkins, Father James   Roman catholic priest and the founder of the *Antigonish Movement* in Nova Scotia. Perhaps the most famous advocate of the movement was Tompkins' cousin, Father Moses Coady.

topic approach   See *thematic approach*.

top-up   Obtaining additional credits or passes in examinations.

total immersion method   A method of teaching or learning a language in which the learner is exposed only to the language and culture being learned for 24 hours a day.

Total Literacy Method (TLM)   This is an approach to literacy based upon the idea of an enabling movement which motivates targeted people to participate in literacy programmes – used in Bangladesh.

town hall   A method of training used by the League of Political Education in the United States in the 1920s to provide citizenship training for adults.

town meeting   1. Community problem-solving, decision-making instruments in a town, initially used in New England. The idea underlying it is for local democracy. 2.

The idea has been used in a number of democratic adult education movements, such as *The International League for Social Commitment in Adult Education*.

Toynbee Hall   The first *university settlement* in London.

track record   A record of past achievement.

trade test   An occupational examination.

trades union studies   The study of the movement and activities of trades unions. In the USA, the term used is Labor union.

Trades Union Training Authority (TUTA)   Established in Australia, and funded by the State, as a result of the *Trades Union Training Authority Act*, in order to provide training for members in relation to the powers and functions of the movement.

Trades Union Training Authority Act   Passed in 1975, in order to establish a national body, the *Trades Union Training Authority* and an Australian trade union college.

Trades Union Congress Education Department   Established in 1964 in the UK, to offer a programme of training for Trades Union members and officials. It also has its own Educational Centre and runs an Open School.

Trades Union Congress Educational Trust   An educational trust, which offers financial support to trades union members wishing to pursue a course of study.

traditionalist   One whose *attitudes, ideas* and *behaviour* are grounded in an earlier culture.

train   To instruct, teach.

train and visit system (T&V)   A system widely used in agricultural extension, it involves continuous training and frequent visits by staff. See *co-operative extension*.

trainability   The ability to be trained or prepared for an occupation or profession.

trainee   One who is being trained.

trainer   1. One who *trains* learners, especially in an industrial context. 2. One who coaches sports people. 3. One who trains educators or trainers. See *training the trainers*.

training   1. A planned and systematic sequence of instruction under supervision, designed to impart skills, knowledge, information and attitudes. Frequently contrasted to education and used with reference to *vocational education*. Usually refers to shaping the learners' behaviour and habits. 2. A planned and systematic effort to modify or develop knowledge, skill or attitude through learning experiences. 3. Sometimes it refers to teaching techniques, such as *demonstration*.

Training and Enterprise Council (TEC)   Local councils are independent companies, established by government in the UK, to initiate training, education and enterprise opportunities for adults.

training bay   An area set aside within a organization for training purposes.

training centre   A department of a commercial or industrial organization devoted to human resource development within the company.

training college   A college devoted to preparing individuals for an occupation. In the UK, it was the term frequently used for institutions in which school-teachers were trained.

training cycle   A sequence of four events often depicted as a cycle for training: identify, plan, implement and evaluate.

training function   An activity of training within a work organization.

training needs   The term often used by trainers to refer to the *knowledge, skill* or *attitudes* that workers need to acquire to be proficient in their occupational role.

training objective   A statement of what the *trainee* should be able to do at the end of a course of training. This is usually stated in terms of a demonstrable or measurable skill or changed behaviour.

training officer   One who is employed to organize the training needed by employees in a company. See *human resource developer*.

training the trainers   The professional preparation of those who will become *trainers, training officers*, or *adult educators*.

transaction   The interaction between two people in which there is an exchange process. The teacher-learner interaction is likely to be a transaction when it is conducted in a mature manner.

transactional analysis   A neo-Freudian theory of personality which suggests that there are three elements to personality and that behaviour is controlled by whichever aspect of personality is in charge at the time that the behaviour occurs. It is practised in a group acting in which the major objective is to have the client achieve an adaptive, mature, and realistic approach to living. Often used in *affective education*.

transactional encounter   Underlying transactionalism is the idea that knowledge is gained from interactive experiences with the environment.

transactional mode   In adult education there are, it is claimed, three modes of transaction: individual, group, and community.

transcript   The official copy of the course

studied and the grades obtained by a student in a college career. This term is much more common in North America and where courses of study are modular in structure. See *profile*.

transdisciplinary   Knowledge that emerges from a particular context, but cannot be located within a prevailing disciplinary framework.

transduction   The process whereby something is transformed, eg in psychology, sensory processes are transformed into patterns of neural impulses that give rise to sensory perception.

transductive reasoning   Thought processes that appear to be neither *deductive* nor *inductive*, where the thinker appears to move from one thought to the next.

transfer of training   The idea that new knowledge or skills learned in training can be utilized in practice.

transferable skills   Skills learned in one situation that can then be used in others.

transformative education   A concept that refers to the expansion of consciousness and the working towards a meaningfully integrated life. It is a relatively new concept within the field of lifelong education but there are a number of activities within the field of educational gerontology that might be conceptualized within this framework.

transformative learning   *Mezirow's* theory of learning in which he suggests that individuals' meaning perspectives are transformed through a process of construing and appropriating new or revised interpretations of the meaning of an experience as a guide to awareness, feeling and action. See *perspective transformation*.

transformative research   Research relating to transformative education – there is a

research network in this area sponsored by the *International Council for Adult Education*.

translation   The process of expressing what is communicated in one language in another.

transmission model of teaching   *teaching*, where the teacher seeks to transmit knowledge, or skill to the learners.

Travelling Folk High School   A *folk high school* in which experience and travel form a major part of the *curriculum*.

travelling theory   A theory of teaching which regards the subject under review as a terrain to be explored, with the teacher as the learners' guide and support.

trial and error method   A learning process in which the learner selects a direction towards a specific objective and modifies the process as they move in that direction, rejecting those elements that are irrelevant to the objective concerned.

triangulation   An approach to research in which two or more different methods are employed to study the same phenomenon in order to understand it more fully. It is a useful approach in studying the education of adults. Used to account for reliability in *qualitative/phenomenological research*.

trimester   The division of the academic year into three blocks.

true/false question   A method of testing students by asking questions that require only a response specifying the statement contained in the question is either 'true' or 'false'.

trustee   The legally appointed governors or managers of an organization, fund or trust.

tuition   Teaching, often on a personal basis.

tuition assistance   Educational programmes in which the employing organizations pay all, or part, of an employee's course fees – often at approved educational organizations only.

tuition fees   Course fees. In the USA, the term is used almost exclusively to refer to the cost of attending an educational institution.

tuition reimbursement program   A US programme of study in which the employer is expected to pay all, or part, of the fees for the course of study undertaken.

tutee   The student of a specific tutor.

tutor   1. To teach. 2. A teacher.

tutor-marked assignment   Course work assignments, graded by the course *tutor*. In some instances this is in opposition to *computer-marked assignments*.

tutor notes   Guidelines prepared for *tutors* either to guide their teaching or their marking of academic assignments.

tutor organizer   An adult educator who has responsibility for planning the provision of a curriculum or a programme in an adult education institution in the UK. See *program planning*.

tutorial   A discussion between a *tutor* and one or more students, usually with special reference to academic work.

tutorial class   Albert Mansbridge recognized that the large numbers of people in individual lectures that were initially provided by the *Workers' Educational Association* would not necessarily result in a high standard of teaching and learning. He launched the tutorial class in 1907 with the intention of providing university standard teaching. The first formal regulations for the tutorial class followed in 1913.

tutorial group   A group of students that meets regularly with a *tutor*.

tutorial system   A teaching method in which students are allocated to a tutor for regular teaching and guidance during a course of study.

tutoring   A form of teaching on a one-to-one basis, usually conducted by a tutor or private teacher.

Tutor's Bulletin   A magazine that was started in 1978 by the University of Leicester for *extra-mural* tutors. It did not survive many years.

twenty-one hour rule   A regulation in the UK that allowed unemployed adults to take part in twenty-one hours of part-time education, whilst still being considered to be unemployed, and eligible for unemployment benefit.

twilight class   An *evening class*, but used with specific reference to those who are full-time day students and are expected to attend a third session.

two cultures   Used with reference to the difference between the cultures of the arts and the sciences.

'Two-thirds rule'   In studies of speech in the classroom in initial education, this 'rule' has been shown to be generally applicable: two-thirds of the time spent in class is speech; two-thirds of the speech is the teacher's; two-thirds of the teacher's speech consists of directing the teaching either through lecturing or asking questions. Research into adult classrooms still needs to test this out.

two-year college   US *community college*.

typescript   Typed copy of a document, such as an essay.

typology   1. The study of types or classifications. 2. A specific classificatory scheme, eg adult education institutions.

Uu

ujamaa   A form of socialism, associated with Tanzania, which is based on self-reliance in doing, thinking and planning for action – associated with *adult education*.

ulpan   Residential schools for immigrants in Israel in which Hebrew language and culture are taught in a *folk high school* spirit for a period of five months.

ulpanit   A non-residential language school in Israel for immigrants.

Ulster People's College   Established in 1983, an *adult education* college in Belfast.

unclassified degree   A pass degree.

unconditioned response   The normal response to a *stimulus*.

unconscious   1. A lack of awareness. 2. Processes in the mind occurring in a manner of which the person is unaware. 3. The primordial repressed desires that Freud characterized in his psychology, such as id.

unconscious memory   The memorization of events, feelings and actions that have been repressed.

underachiever   One who has not attained the level that they would be expected to attain in an educational process; one whose performances are far less than would be expected as a result of an intelligence test. There are many underachievers who return to adult education and who might be classified as a *late developer* if successful at a later time.

under-class   That category of people in society who are so disadvantaged that they appear beyond class and beyond the normal social hierarchy – they are the 'social drop-outs' of society.

under-educated   Those who have not been educated within the system to a sufficiently high standard to that required for their occupation or place in adult life.

under-employed   Form of employment demanding from workers less than they are capable of achieving, or less training or education than they have undertaken.

undergraduate   Student in *higher education* studying for a *first*, or *baccalaureate*, degree.

understanding   To learn, know, and have the ability to provide an explanation of a phenomenon; a form of deep learning.

Unemployed Workers' Association   Established by the Workers' Educational Association in Toronto, Canada, at the time of the 1931 Depression.

unemployed workers' centre   A centre established to assist the unemployed, often running *adult education* courses for them.

UNESCO (United Nations Educational, Scientific and Cultural Organisation)

Founded in 1946 to further all its objectives throughout the world. It is based in Paris.

UNESCO Adult Education Information Notes   Published quarterly in a variety of languages.

UNESCO Institute for Education
Established in Hamburg in 1951 for the study of education. It has been responsible for many projects in *adult* and *lifelong education*. It publishes its own newsletter and also the *International Review of Education*.

Union for Rural Education   Established in Finland in 1952 to co-ordinate the educational work of rural organizations; it organizes its own *study centre, study circles* and courses and lectures.

unit   1. A module in a curriculum. 2. A branch or division of a larger organization.

Unit for the Development of Adult Continuing Education (UDACE)
Established by UK government, following the closure of the Advisory Council for Adult and Continuing Education, under the *National Institute of Adult Continuing Education*. It was to be funded for three years, but eventually it received funding for six years.

United Nations Declaration of Human Rights   Accepted, in part, by all member nations. It includes the right of everybody to work and education.

United Nations International Research and Training Institute for the Advancement of Women   Established to stimulate and assist women to participate more fully in developmental activities at all levels through research, training and the sharing of information.

United Nations University   Established in Japan.

United States Agency for International Development (USAID)   United States agency for educational and technological development in the Third World, since its establishment in 1961. See also *Point Four Program*.

United States Armed Forces Institute
Established in 1942 in Madison, Wisconsin to provide a variety of services to civilian and military personnel, including *distance education*.

United States College Examination Board   The board responsible for overseeing the nation-wide college level examination programme.

universalism   1. An approach that assumes ethical standards are universal. 2. The belief that education should be available to everybody.

Universities Association for Continuing Education (UACE)   Title adopted by UCACE in 1993 when *higher education* in the UK was re-organized with the creation of the new universities from the polytechnics.

Universities Council for Adult Education (UCAE)   Established in 1947 to provide a forum of university *extra-mural departments*. Changed its name in 1982 to incorporate the idea of continuing education.

Universities Council for Adult and Continuing Education (UCACE)   The title adopted in 1982 by the *Universities Council for Adult Education* in the United Kingdom, reflecting the changing emphasis in the education of adults. The title changed again in 1993 to the *Universities Association for Continuing Education*.

university extension   University's *adult education* outreach. First suggested at Exeter College, Oxford University, by William Sewell in 1850. James Stuart, University of Cambridge, gave the first extension lectures in 1873. The movement spread widely throughout the world thereafter. The first experiments with it in the United States were at Columbia University in 1889.

University Extension Outreach The official newsletter of *university extension* in Australia.

University for Industry This is part of an initiative by the Labour government in the United Kingdom to create a learning society by establishing a commercial-like business in the supply of learning opportunities, through *kite marking* and *franchising* of learning materials. It is to be fully operating by 2000 as an independent public-private partnership linking people and businesses with learning opportunities through information technology.

University of Mid-America Established in 1974, a consortium of universities in the mid-West interested in forming a *distance education* university.

University of the Air 1. The name by which the UK *Open University* was popularly known before its inception. 2. There are a number of *open universities*, such as that in Japan, known by this name.

University of the Third Age (U3A) Voluntary educational organization for the education of older adults. Founded in Toulouse in 1972, and established in the United Kingdom in 1981. There are two different forms: the first, which is connected directly to a local university (the French model) and those that are independent voluntary organizations (the British model). There are now both national and international networks of U3A – see *Association internationale de universités de troisième âge*. It is wrongly claimed that the Toulouse University for the Third Age was the first institution for seniors' learning – see *Institute for Retired Professionals*.

university settlement movement Established in 1885 so that the universities could reach and work with people from the working classes, especially in the East End of London. The first settlement was Toynbee Hall, but others soon followed. All had an educational element in their work, which varied from one settlement to another. In 1886 a similar movement began in the United States, with the founding of the Neighborhood Guild in New York by Stanton Cost.

university without walls 1. Concept of a university that takes the whole world as its classroom or area of study. 2. An open learning movement in America that gives academic *credit* for career and life experiences and organizes teaching and learning courses. See also *free university*.

unlearn A process of shedding one piece of learning and to acquiring a new one in its place is said to be unlearning.

unlearned Descriptive term for behaviours and acts that occur without having been specifically learned.

unpack A term borrowed from computer studies to refer to the recovering of original data, used in social sciences and education to refer to the process of recovering the original, or intended, meaning of a statement.

unstructured interview A planned interview technique, as opposed to an informal discussion. The interviewer guides the interview in the planned direction and covers the requisite aspects of investigation, but not covering the questions in a predetermined order. This is a skilled technique; sometimes called non-structured interview. See *structured interview*.

untenured post An academic post for which there is no security of employment.

update To keep abreast with new developments in a field of study or practice.

upward mobility Social movement upwards, eg from working to middle class. See *downward mobility*.

Urania A society for the dissemination of scientific *knowledge* to adults, first founded in Berlin 1888. There are similar societies in other central and eastern European societies. They have influenced the development of *popular universities.*

urban education Education provided in inner-city areas.

Utopia The ideal society.

Vv

vacation   Holiday.

vacation school   Holiday school – often a summer school.

vade mecum   A handbook or other aid carried by a person for immediate usage when needed. Such handbooks are sometimes prepared by educational institutions for professional groups, or in association with them.

validation   An examination of the proposed *curriculum* or *programme* to see whether it meets the standards expected of it by the organization offering the course or making an award to successful learners.

validation board   A committee that acts on behalf of an *accreditation* agency, or a statutory body, to assess an educational curriculum submitted by an educational institution.

validation visit   A formal visit to an educational institution to assess the extent to which the institution is able to undertake in a satisfactory manner the courses that are validated by the awarding body.

validity   The extent to which a *test* or other *instrument* measures what it is intended to measure.

value   The worth of an object, phenomenon or experience. It is either subjective or dependent on the market.

value judgment   A term used in philosophy to imply that an assessment of worth is being made rather than an objective judgment.

value system   The interlocking constellation of beliefs and values that a group, social class, or society normally holds. It forms part of the culture of that social grouping.

variable   1. A characteristic that is assumed to affect a subject under investigation. 2. Subject to change.

variance   A statistical measure of the extent to which scores are scattered.

verbal intelligence   1. Ability with words. 2. *Intelligence* tested through verbal tests.

verbalism   Speech that has little substance.

verbal skills   The ability to speak fluently.

verbatim   Precisely as spoken.

vernacular   The common language.

vertical thinking   Thought processes that are modelled on the scientific method, logical deduction and systematic enquiry. See *lateral thinking, deductive thought*.

veterans' education   US education of military veterans as a result of federal funding. See *G.I. Bill*.

videocassette   A cassette that stores video images. They have become a recent and valuable addition to the audio-video aids for the teacher of adults. They are also prepared as a part of a study pack in *distance education*.

videotape   See *videocassette*.

village college   A term used in the United Kingdom to designate a community college in a rural area. Henry Morris (1899–1961) proposed in 1924 the creation of village colleges in which the college was to become the centre of the cultural life of the village in which children and adults were to be educated together. He was also concerned with their architecture and wrote about their design.

Village Education Resource Centre (VERC)   Established in Bangladesh in 1977 as a result of co-operation between Save the Children Fund (USA) and UNICEF. A non-governmental organization seeking to empower the people through education, in order that they might be involved in the development of their country.

village extension worker   In the *train and visit* system, village workers are trained to go into the villages in order to introduce new skills and knowledge to farmers.

virtual learning environment   The use of electronic means to create a situation in which teaching and learning can occur when teachers and learners are separated from each other in space and time.

virtual university   A university that functions only through electronic communication.

visiting fellow   A fixed-term, sometimes honorary, appointment, in an educational institution.

visiting professor   A fixed-term, sometimes honorary, appointment at professorial level, in an educational institution.

visiting student   A student enrolled in one institution, but studying for a limited period in another one.

VISTA   This is 'volunteers, in-service to America'. It is a national anti-poverty agency, heavily involved in *literacy* work.

visual ability test   A *test* designed to test an individual's ability in such areas as *perception* and contrast.

visual aid   A visual phenomenon, an object or picture etc used to enhance teaching.

visual handicapped   With limited vision.

visual learner   One who learns best through seeing.

visual literacy   The ability to recognize and understand at a conscious level the indigenous written languages used within a culture and to produce visual messages in those languages.

viva voce   An oral examination, common in higher-degree assessment. Since they are person-to-person examinations, they are expensive and time-consuming.

vocabulary   1. A list of words. 2. The aggregate of words in use.

vocabulary test   A *test* of a person's knowledge about a specified number of words.

vocation   1. Formerly it meant a calling. 2. An occupation.

vocational choice   Choice of occupation.

vocational education   Education that is orientated to work and employment – usually a form of initial preparation for work. See *professional education*.

vocational education and training (VET)   This term is beginning to be used for *competency-based education* in order to broaden the perspectives on occupational preparation.

vocational guidance   The process of making *assessment* of individuals' abilities in order to match them with occupational requirements and guiding them about their career prospects.

vocational school   A school that has a specific purpose of preparing people for an occupation. In the United States its functions are defined by the Higher Education Act of 1965.

vocational training   The preparation of people for an occupational role.

Voluntary Adult Education Forum   An association of voluntary associations launched in 1985 in the United Kingdom.

Voluntary Service Overseas (VSO)   An organization which recruits trained personnel to go and work in the Third World, often in an educational capacity.

volunteer   One who gives a service without reimbursement.

Volunteer Centre   The UK advisory agency on *volunteer* and *community* involvement.

voucher   A document that provides evidence that the fee, or part of the fee, for an educational course will be paid for by some other person or organization. See *educational voucher, individual rights.*

Vygotsky, L S (1856–1934)   Russian psychologist famous for his studies with children, some of his theories of learning have relevance to *adult learning.*

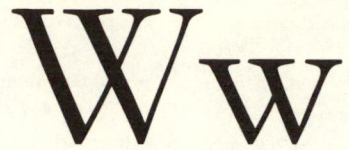

Ww

want   Sometimes confused with the term *need*, although this term reflects the way in which education is becoming market led and *demands* are replacing the welfare concept of need.

warden   Often refers to one who has the administrative responsibility for the educational institution.

Washington Week   A week when the results of the *National Issues Forums* are debated in Washington with Congressional representatives and other relevant policy makers.

weekend college   See the *To Educate the People Consortium*.

Welsh circulating schools   Started in 1731–1732, these schools were founded by *Griffith Jones* to provide free education for children and adults; the language of instruction was Welsh and the curriculum was limited to reading and the catechism. At its height there were in excess of 3,000 schools but the movement came to an end before the end of the eighteenth century.

Western Co-operative College
Established in 1959 to serve the ideals of the co-operative movement. The college changed its name to the *Co-operative College of Canada*.

Western Governor's University
Established in 1997 in the United States, as a totally electronic university.

whiteboard   The modern equivalent to the *blackboard*. A prepared surface, usually affixed to a wall (or on an easel) upon which a teacher or students can write – usually with a coloured marker pen.

white-collar worker   A person occupied in a non-manual occupation. See *blue-collar worker*.

White House Conference on Aging
There have been at least three conferences (1961, 1971, 1981) designed to increase the visibility of older people in the United States.

whole learning   A term used occasionally to refer to the technique of teaching from the whole topic to its constituent elements.

whole man   A term used to refer to an all-round, broad education. It is also used sometimes by affective educators in contrast to the emphasis placed on cognitive knowledge in much education.

Why Stop Learning?   The first book in the United States, published in 1927, to try to popularize *adult education*. Written by Dorothy Canfield Fisher and sponsored by the Carnegie Corporation.

Wider Opportunities for Women (WOW)
The provision of *adult training* courses for women, a UK government initiative.

Wider Opportunities Training Scheme (WOTS)   A programme of *training* for the unemployed in the United Kingdom through working in community development programmes.

Window, The The magazine of the *Workers' Educational Association* of Sweden.

Wireless Discussion Group The adult school movement in Britain arranged a number of discussion groups to follow early BBC broadcasts; the movement lasted from 1929 to 1946.

wisdom 1. The ability to use knowledge, experience, and understanding to act in a wise and common sense manner. 2. Accumulated knowledge over the years, eg the wisdom of the elderly. 3. Wise sayings or teachings. This concept clearly relates to knowledge and belief.

Women and Development Unit (WAND) Established in the Caribbean in 1978 to act as a clearinghouse for the work of women in the region.

woman returner Women who return to education after having reared a family.

woman school Opened in New York in 1975 to provide more educational opportunities for women.

Women Returners' Network A network of tutors and organizers involved with working with women returners.

Women's Institute (WI) Founded in 1897 in Stoney Creek, Ontario, Canada, the WI rapidly became one of the largest providers of *adult education* for women – its concern is wider than education since it focuses on home legislation, economics, health, agriculture, amongst other things. It was established in the United Kingdom in 1915.

Women's Museum Established in 1984 in Germany, this museum sets out to document the place women have played, and are currently playing, in society.

Women's Network A Brazilian *non-formal education* network for women.

women's studies The academic study of the place women occupy in society.

women's vocational school These were established in several towns in the Netherlands as a result of an initiative by the Women's Union of the Federation of Dutch Trades Unions. The schools offer a wide variety of vocational courses for women.

Woodbrooke College Established in Birmingham by the Quaker movement in 1903 as an *adult education* residential college.

Woodbrookers Term used in the Netherlands to refer to the adult education residential colleges patterned on the Quaker schools in the United Kingdom. See *Woodbrooke College*.

word recognition The ability to recognize words and to read them.

work-based learning Recognition is now given to the fact that a great deal of vocational learning occurs on the job. Increasingly, educational programmes are prepared that plan for many of the learning activities to be undertaken in the work setting, and credit is given for them. See also *factory college, corporate university*.

work-book 1. An exercise book or textbook having questions and a space for answers. 2. A book containing instructions for work or study, eg *study guide*. 3. A book in which reflective thoughts about the job are recorded, eg *learning log*.

work card A card on which is written a problem or a task for a student, or group of students, to undertake.

work experience A period of practical placement during the preparation for an occupation.

work load The workload of a teacher in terms of preparation, teaching, advising and marking time, etc.

work sample test   A job analysis, carried out on-the-job, to enable a *human resource developer* to assess the demands of the job and the *training* required.

work study   1. Undertaking a study of a particular occupation. 2. A management technique based upon the theories of Frederick Taylor, who believed that people would do more work if it were scientifically organized. Used to analyse an occupation. See *time and motion study*. 3. In the United States, it refers to undergraduate students taking work for their university while they are studying.

work therapy   A form of therapy through learning and doing – it is also called occupational therapy.

worker-teacher   In Canada's *Frontier College*, teachers also did their normal job of work and taught in their leisure time. See *labourer-teacher, teacher practitioner*.

Workers' Educational Association (WEA)
Founded in England, in 1903, by *Albert Mansbridge* as the *Association to Promote the Higher Education of Working Men*, it became the WEA in 1905. It is a *non-governmental organization*, which became one of the main providers of *adult education* in a number of countries.

Workers' Educational Trades Union Committee (WETUC)   Founded in England in 1919 to promote co-operation between the Trades Unions and the WEA. It was subsumed within *Trades Union Congress Education Department* in 1964.

Workers' Statute   The Italian law that entitles workers to paid educational leave. In 1973, they were entitled to 50 hours per annum provided they attended a further 25 hours of study in their own time. It could be deferred for three years and so it became known as the *One Hundred and Fifty Hours* programme.

workers' theatre   The use of drama to educate people about social situations. Established in Canada in the early 1930s and won a number of awards for drama.

workers' universities   They were established in some Eastern European countries.

working class   Usually refers to those who are employed in manual occupations.

working hypothesis   An unproven hypothesis upon which decisions and policies are made until such time as more evidence emerges to change it.

working men's club   Established in England in mid-1800s by the Reverend Henry Solly with the intention of providing *adult education* and combating the problem of alcohol.

Working Men's College   The first was founded in Sheffield in 1842, but the most famous was the one established in London in 1854, by F D Maurice and the Christian Socialists.

Workingmen's Institute   Established by Johns Hopkins University in 1879, as the first US university involved in workingmen's education.

working men's reading room movement
A *self-help* activity, often associated with *adult schools* intended to be run by working people.

World Campaign for Universal Literacy
In 1962, UNESCO spelt out a ten-year campaign for universal literacy.

World Conference on Adult Education
The first world conference on adult education was held in Cambridge, UK, in 1929.

World Conference on Continuing Education for Engineers   One of the first occupational world conferences on *continuing education*. It was held in Mexico City in April 1979, for engineers and scientists.

World Conference on Higher Education The first *UNESCO higher education* world conference was held in Paris in October, 1998.

World Literacy A non-profit-making organization funded by the Canadian government for educational research.

World University Service Established in 1920 for the overall benefit of university education.

worldview English translation of the German noun 'Weltanschauung'. It means an individual or group system of knowledge and beliefs about the world. There are two elements to this: the religious, in its broadest sense, which is about the meaning of the world and life, and the non-religious, which is concerned about ideological issues of daily existence.

writing school Established in America to teach writing.

Yy

Yeaxlee, Basil (1883–1967) British scholar and adult educator. He was awarded the first ever PhD in adult education by the University of London in 1925 for his thesis on 'Adult Education and Spiritual Values'. He was also the first author to write about *lifelong education*, with a book by this title in 1929. He was also a member of the committee that produced the famous *1919 Report*. See *Hallenbeck* who was awarded the first PhD in the United States in this subject.

young adult Current term for young person between the ages of about 16 and 25 years.

Young Men's Christian Association (YMCA) Founded in London in 1844 by George Williams, and started in the United States in 1851. Initially it had evangelical objectives but it has gradually become more involved in education.

Young Men's Christian Association College A professional education centre training youth workers.

Young Women's Christian Association This organization was originally two separate organizations which were founded simultaneously by Miss Roberts in the South of England and Lady Kinnaird in London in 1855. They united in 1877. Their objective is to provide opportunity for young adult women to develop themselves and fulfil their own potential.

Your Move UK adult literacy scheme in 1970s. A follow-up to *On The Move*.

youth club A leisure time association for young people.

youth culture A subculture that revolves around the values and attitudes of young adults. As the period between biological and social maturity has lengthened, this subculture has emerged.

Youth Opportunities Programme Programme devised to provide *education* and *training* to unemployed young adults.

youth service Statutory and voluntary service for young people.

youth tutor A teacher concerned with the social development of *young adults*.

Zz

Znanie   The All-Union Society for the Spread of Scientific Knowledge: the Russian umbrella organization which co-ordinates a great deal of the *adult education* work in Russia.

Zweiter Bildungsweg   This is the German *second chance* educational system. It consists of a part-time period of study followed by one and a half year full-time study in order to prepare students for the Abitur which allows university entrance. See *evening high school*.